DEATH IN HOLLYWOOD

PETER UNDERWOOD

**This book is for
my grand-daughter
Laura Charlotte Elizabeth Derby
with love**

First published in 1992 by Judy Piatkus Ltd

A CIP catalogue for this book
is available from the British Library

Contents

-

Contents

Acknowledgements

In the compilation and writing of this book my grateful thanks are due to: my wife for her encouragement, understanding and help; my daughter Pamela Derby for many unusual and little-known volumes and collectors' editions pertaining to actors, actresses and Hollywood; my son Chris for adding to my library on films and filming over the years and for professional advice and help; John Austin of Los Angeles for his kindness and co-operation in allowing me to reproduce pictures from his personal collection; Honor Cobb for memories of her father Sir C. Aubrey Smith; Shaun Considine of New York for his kind co-operation and help; Peter Cushing for his courtesy and help; Roy Fox for his memories of Jean Harlow; Andrew Hewson, my literary agent, for help in many ways including supplying little-known American books – and not forgetting the cartoon reminding me that there are such things as deadlines!; John A. Hogan, Organiser of the Edgar Wallace Society for his kind interest and help in the loan of a rare book; Arthur Marx, son of Groucho, for his interest and help; Sheila Merritt of Boulder, Colorado, for maps, cuttings and American biographies; Peter Noble for his kind words and for permission to quote from his biography of Ivor Novello; Penelope Wallace, daughter of Edgar Wallace, for her interest and help in supplying a photograph of her father; Leatrice Gilbert Fountain and her publishers for brief extracts from *Dark Star;* Lenore Coffee and her publishers for a quote from *Storyline;* the Los Angeles Convention and Visitors Bureau for their invaluable and generous help in several ways; the Hospital Council of Southern California for information and obituary notices; the Public Libraries and their staff at Alton, Hampshire; Farnham, Surrey; Westminster Reference Library; British Film Institute and the Reference Centre, US Embassy.

Every effort has been made to trace copyright and the author and publishers apologize in advance for any inadvertent infringement, they will be happy to include appropriate acknowledgement in future editions.

Introduction

Death in Hollywood may sound a rather gruesome subject for a book but I recommend the words of James Mason: 'Why is it that Hollywood deaths seem so special? Because all of us think that we have known those people so well ...' There really is something special about Hollywood and the people who lived and worked and died there. And 'it's not a bad place to die' is the verdict of most visitors – 'Almost worth going there for' added a friend of mine recently. I think most of the people I write about would have chosen to die there.

Hollywood has been described as seven suburbs in search of a city; 'a neurosis in concrete', but there has never been anywhere quite like it and there never will be again. It is still entirely movie-orientated. On Hollywood Boulevard there is a movie theatre every few hundred yards, many of them opening at noon and closing at five the following morning; and the pink and grey pavements are studded with the names of motion picture stars and movie directors. Although today there are only two major film studios actually in Hollywood itself, Paramount and Columbia, I have used the term 'Hollywood' in its widest sense, but I would not go as far as some writers and call it 'the world's largest parking lot'. The biggest film studio in the world is Universal (where a fire in 1990 destroyed a small portion of the gigantic area but there are still public tours), situated north of Hollywood in an area known as 'The Valley'. At Universal windows in the building are black, so that they can see out but you can't see in. Hollywood has everything and it has nothing. There is an expectant atmosphere of hustle and the place is almost exactly as any movie fan would expect it to be – with the addition of smog.

I have tried to keep my stories of Hollywood's famous departed reasonably unsensational but it has to be admitted that Hollywood has quite a lot of skeletons that repay a little gentle stirring. In doing so I have endeavoured not to offend anyone or overstep the mark of reasonable and decent reportage.

So many stories have had to remain untold: how the significant star of silent films, Madge Bellamy, once hailed as

Introduction

'Someone Really Extraordinary', lived for years in obscurity selling farm tools and finally dying after a fall in her ninetieth year and how bit-player Peg Entwistle, disillusioned by Hollywood, climbed the steep slopes of Mount Lee towards the giant 'Hollywood' sign and there clambered to the top of the letter 'D' and jumped to her death; over the years other disappointed starlets have followed her lead and the famous Hollywood sign became a notorious and appropriate place finally to sign off.

I consider myself very fortunate in having met and talked with a number of show-business personalities over the years, people like Lilli Palmer, James Mason, Sammy Davis Jr, Peter Cushing, Boris Karloff, Conrad Veidt, Douglas Fairbanks Jr and Charles Chaplin, to name a few personal favourites. This has enabled me to present for the first time a lot of previously unpublished material pertaining to those who were unfortunate enough, or fortunate enough, to meet death in Hollywood.

I have sought to limit those eligible for inclusion in this volume to those who actually died in or around Hollywood and inevitably one is led to wonder whether the area itself, its potential happiness and success but all too often its sadness and disappointment, may affect some of the people who choose to live there.

It has been said that there are two Hollywoods: the Hollywood where people live and work and the Hollywood which lives in the minds of the public, more legend than fact. I have worked hard to ensure that this book is more fact than legend but it cannot be denied that in Hollywood the two often mingle in a curious way that sometimes makes it difficult to distinguish between what is and what is not factual.

Sammy Davis once said to me, 'Tinseltown consists of the studios, the film industry, the financiers, all the actors and actresses, the rigmarole of show business, the pimps, the con men, the lawyers, the psychiatrists and last but not least, the audiences – mix them all together and you have Hollywood.'

Almost any story of any Hollywood star is what might have been. One example out of a dozen I came across while researching this book: the German film director, Friedrich Wilhelm Murnau (*Nosferatu*, 1922) went to Hollywood where he made *Sunrise* (1927), *Four Devils* (1928) and *Our Daily Bread* (1929), released as *City Girl*, before he collaborated

Introduction

with Robert J. Flaherty on *Tabu* (1931), a silent film with a synchronized score, haunting exoticism and remarkable visual beauty. In 1931, a week before *Tabu* was premiered, Murnau was travelling in a powerful new Packard, driven by a young Filipino who was showing off. There was a tremendous collision between the car and a lorry and Murnau was killed outright. With him Hollywood lost one of its most interesting European film-makers. *Tabu* was to achieve worldwide success.

I hope that *Death in Hollywood* is not a morbid book nor a sad book. It attempts to present a rounded picture of some of the people who died in Hollywood, looking at their success and their happiness as well as their disappointments and eventual death. Life in Hollywood is rarely what those who live and work there think it is going to be, nor is it often as they would like it to be. Towards the end of his life Alan Ladd probably spoke for a lot of stars when he was asked what he would have liked to have changed about his life, and he replied, 'Everything.' Now *that* I do think is sad.

Of course Hollywood affects different people in different ways. It has made some cynical. Sir Cedric Hardwicke once said to me: 'I believe that God felt sorry for actors so He created Hollywood to give them a place in the sun and a swimming pool. The price they had to pay was to surrender their talent.' That may have been true in some cases but certainly not for every Hollywood actor, not even I think for Cedric Hardwicke or for most of the actors and actresses whose stories I have tried to recount objectively and who finally found death in Hollywood.

Peter Underwood
Savage Club
1, Whitehall Place
London SW1A 2HD

1

The Pills that Cure All Ills

-

DEATH FROM DRUGS

Either by accident or design, drugs – usually in the form of pills – have accounted for more premature deaths in Hollywood than any other single cause.

It may be that something becomes too hard to bear – such as a lost love, an abortion, the sudden death of someone close, ill health, alcoholism, depression or debts – but for whatever reason the enormous number of drug-related deaths in Hollywood must reflect unfavourably on the ease with which it was possible in the past, if not today, to obtain lethal drugs in Hollywood.

Often these unhappy people were seeing several physicians at the same time, all of whom seem only too ready to have sought to placate their clients with drugs and sleeping pills without sufficient safeguards. It is to be hoped that such a situation no longer exists.

Among the countless number of film actors and actresses who took their own lives in this way we will look at just a few, from those seemingly at the pinnacle of success to some lesser stars of the Hollywood firmament, who lived out their all too short lives and sad deaths in Hollywood: Carole Landis, Marilyn Monroe, Barbara La Marr and Lupe Velez.

2

Marilyn Monroe

Marilyn Monroe in her
last and unfinished film
*Something's Got
to Give*

Carole Landis

-

A Senseless Death at 29

Carole Landis has been described as a 'blonde and bouncy sexpot'. She was 'discovered' by Busby Berkeley, the undisputed king of the Hollywood musical. She enjoyed a brief heyday as a popular Hollywood actress but four unsuccessful marriages, a much-publicized but unrewarding affair with Rex Harrison and growing financial problems seemed to convince her that suicide was the only way out.

Berkeley met Carole Landis when he chose her for one of the chorus girls in *Variety Show*. It was her first break into pictures. He and Carole became friendly and he helped her to get a film contract.

Hollywood producer Milton Sperling has suggested that it was not difficult to become very friendly with Landis who, at Fox Studios, became known as 'the studio hooker' and he says she was a regular visitor to notorious Darryl Zanuck's office where the film mogul regularly had young female employees 'entertain' him at four o'clock every working day.

Landis is perhaps best remembered for exhibiting her shapely form in Hal Roach's *One Million B.C.* (1940) with Victor Mature and in such lavish musicals as *Moon Over Miami* with Betty Grable and Don Ameche and *My Gal Sal* with Rita Hayworth. She was very popular during the war years and after America's entry into the war she made a tour of North Africa, entertaining the troops and afterwards wrote a book, *Four Jills in a Jeep* (the other actresses accompanying her being Martha Raye, Kay Francis and Mitzi Mayfair). The book was later filmed by Twentieth Century-Fox.

Landis took part in several amateur beauty contests while she was still at school and married for the first time when she was only fifteen, a marriage that effectively ended after 25 *days*. By the time she was legally divorced she was already worldly-wise and working as a singer and hula dancer at the Royal Hawaiian Night Club; then she set her sights on Hollywood and films.

In 1940 she married for the second time, but again the marriage foundered after a couple of months and divorce followed three months later. While in London in 1942, she married a captain in the US Air Force but soon they were living apart and divorce followed in 1945. Carole then married a Broadway stage producer, W. Horace Schmidlapp, and it was while she was still Mrs Schmidlapp, although not living with her husband, that she met Rex Harrison at Palm Springs — Carole wearing all four wedding rings, almost like the trophies of a huntress!

Rex, according to his biographer, 'quickly succumbed to the undeniable charms of Miss Landis, embarking on another little extra-marital adventure'. He was of course married to Lilli Palmer at the time and apparently intended to have a quick romance and then return to his understanding wife but, particularly on Carole's part, the affair became intense and serious.

Rex had to return to England to make *Escape* (1948) for Twentieth Century-Fox; but the couple had no intention of allowing the Atlantic to separate them and, as luck would have it, Carole had been signed to work on two films in England, so they planned to continue to meet, more or less clandestinely.

With Rex working on location on Dartmoor and Carole in London, the couple used to meet at Plymouth, but very discreetly and they never seem to have actually been seen together while they were in England. Rex completed his film and returned to Hollywood, together with Lilli and their young son Carey. Carole had to remain in England a few more weeks but they kept in contact with frequent telephone calls and Rex wrote regularly.

Rex went into the production of *Unfaithfully Yours* (1948); while the film was in production Carole returned to Hollywood and the affair continued, increasingly becoming public knowledge. Towards the end of the film Rex found himself being repeatedly questioned about his relationship with Carole Landis. He continued to shrug off any suggestion of an affair and loyal

Lilli, when she was approached for her comments on the growing rumours, replied characteristically, *'Carole is our friend.'*

The time had come however for Rex to face his responsibilities and he finally confessed all to his wife. She said that once she had completed her current film in Hollywood she would return to New York and she hoped, while she was away, that Rex would sort out his life and let her know his decision.

Although Carole was finding it increasingly difficult to obtain work and to meet her financial commitments, she was so besotted with Rex that when she did have the opportunity of work, she allowed her dreams and desires to influence her judgement. Director Ross Hunter had planned to have Carole play the lead in *Dream Girl* but, as he put it,

> *She was much more interested in her gigantic love affair with Rex Harrison than she was in anything else. She was absolutely insane about him – and he was wonderful to her. They seemed to think that nobody knew about their great romance, which was ridiculous because Carole was really smitten by this man; she was head-over-heels in love with him.*

With Lilli out of the way Rex would visit Carole at her home on Capri Drive, only a few minutes from his own house on Manderville Canyon. The visits were still discreet and only Carole's maid, Fannie Mae Bolden, positively knew and she had no doubt about Carole's genuine love for Rex. 'She would make me so mad because he would be eating his food and she would just sit there watching him ...' Whatever she intended Lilli's absence in New York brought Rex and Carole even closer together and her departure from Hollywood made her position in the matter all too clear. The next move must come from Rex.

It seems indisputable that Carole was obsessed with Rex and, a keen amateur photographer, she took numerous photographs of him, developed them herself and displayed them all over the house; with photographs of Rex on every wall the place looked like a shrine but still things were very diffi-cult for Carole financially and she began to run up debts that were soon vast; she even put her house up for sale. She hoped against hope that she would soon find lucrative work; her only other hope seemed to be a a future life with Rex.

Although Rex continued to keep in touch with his wife Lilli by telephone, calling her most mornings, he no longer had any excuse to leave Carole and return to his own home. He realized that he was boxed in. Carole obviously expected him to divorce Lilli and marry her; her film career seemed to be all but over and to settle down with the man she loved for the rest of their lives seemed the ideal solution.

Rex was in a quandary. He had entered into the affair lightly and without any serious intentions. Now it was all going wrong. With Lilli in New York, he began to see what life would be like without her and Carey. At the same time he was undeniably infatuated with Carole and felt he had to pick the right moment to sort things out with her. Unfortunately, Lilli going to New York had meant that he had more time to spend with Carole and that gave her quite the wrong idea.

It was at this moment that Rex was given the opportunity of appearing in New York in the play, *Anne of a Thousand Days*. It was a wonderful opportunity – and could be the solution to all his problems. On the evening of 4 July 1948 Rex drove over to Carole's house with the script of the play. He talked the matter over with her, explaining as lightly as he could that it would mean a temporary separation for them but he could not miss such a wonderful opportunity. Full of enthusiasm he left just after nine o'clock to go to his friends Roland and Nan Culver and tell them the good news. He stayed with the Culvers at their home, 750 Napoli Drive, until about 1.30 in the morning; he then went home to Manderville Canyon and to bed.

The next morning, 5 July, as Carole's maid Fannie Mae Bolden made her way to the house on the corner of Capri Drive she had a presentiment that something was wrong – something awful had happened or was about to happen. She usually entered the house by the front door but, finding it locked, she made her way round to the back. There she found the door open and her foreboding increased a hundredfold. She found food and dishes on the table, left over from the previous night, and after clearing things up she went into the living room. The whole house seemed strangely quiet. The telephone rang and she answered it. It was a friend inviting Carole to a party. Fannie replied: 'I'm sorry, Miss Landis isn't up yet.' The telephone rang again and Rex asked to speak to Carole. Fannie gave him the same reply. He seemed a little surprised and rang again shortly afterwards to say, 'Tell her I'll be a little late.'

Rex had got up at 9.30 that morning and rang Carole's home at about 11.00. Immediately afterwards Leland Hayward called for Rex; they were going to Maxwell Anderson's home to discuss his play. Rex mentioned that he had telephoned Carole that morning because he had a luncheon date with her. The discussions overran and it was 2.30 before Rex rang Carole's house again.

In the meantime Fannie Mae had taken a peep into her mistress's room. She could see Carole, fully dressed, lying in the bathroom before an open cupboard. She was very nervous and didn't know what to do. Her mistress had always told her she would ring for her when she was wanted ... Fannie Mae went back downstairs without investigating any further.

She was busying herself in the kitchen cleaning this and that when she heard the door open and Rex appeared. He asked if she had gone into Miss Landis's bedroom. She said she had not. Rex said, 'I think she's dead. Let's go up.' Rex, it later transpired, had previously entered the house unnoticed and had found Carole's body. Now he and Fannie rediscovered it, lying in the bathroom that led off the bedroom. Rex ran to the bed, and picked up a note and, reading it, started to scream: 'Oh, darling, why did you do it? Why did you do it?'

The note, propped up among perfume bottles, was written in pencil on Carole's monogrammed stationery and read:

> Dear Mommie, I'm sorry, really sorry, to put you through this, but there is no way to avoid it. I love you, dearly, you have been the most wonderful Mom ever and that applies to all our family. I love each and every one of them dearly. Everything goes to you. Look in the files and there is a will which decrees everything. Goodbye, my angel. Pray for me – Your baby.

Landis's body lay slumped on its left side, her head resting on a leather jewel box, one hand holding the words of the Lord's Prayer printed in gold on a satin ribbon. Underneath her other hand an envelope was found containing one sleeping pill. Her writing on the envelope read: 'Red – quick – 2 hours. Yellow, about 5. Can take two.'

Rex felt for Carole's pulse and said afterwards that he thought he felt a slight beat, but it may have been his imagination or wishful thinking. Understandably confused, he tried to find the telephone number of a doctor and when he failed to do so, he drove home as fast as he could to get the number of his own doctor. Fannie's recollection is a little different. She agrees that they tried to find a doctor but when they failed to do so, Rex walked out of the house saying he would go and tell some of Carole's friends. 'He didn't call anybody, not the coroner, the police, anybody; he left me there and walked out' she was to say later. Not knowing what to do Fannie Mae ran to the nearest neighbours and saw the man who lived there swimming in his pool. She told him what had happened and he jumped over the fence and together they went back to the house and he called the coroner and the police.

Rex, meanwhile, arrived home and tried to reach his doctor who was out; eventually he talked to the doctor's assistant who agreed to come but it would take at least half-an-hour. Rex then rang the Culvers; Roland was out but his wife Nan told Rex to telephone St John's Hospital and the police. Rex did so and when he rang Nan back, she and her friend Judith Fellows offered to accompany Rex to Carole's house. By the time they arrived, the police, the fire brigade and a lot of newspaper reporters had descended on the house and Rex learned that attempts to revive Carole had been unsuccessful. Her body had been removed to the morgue.

There were suggestions that other, undisclosed, notes were left by Carole, and it later transpired that Carole had apparently attempted to commit suicide on several previous occasions. That traumatic evening, once he had been questioned briefly by the police, Rex returned to his home and rang Lilli. 'Something terrible has happened,' he said. 'Carole has killed herself. For God's sake come at once.' Lilli Palmer took the first flight out of New York.

Once reunited with Rex, Lilli lost no time in presenting a united front with Rex. She said she was terribly upset over Carole's death; they had been friends for years. She had heard the gossip but Carole and her husband, she was sure, were just good friends.

Meanwhile Roland Culver made a curious discovery. When

he arrived home, about six o'clock in the evening, he found two small suitcases standing in the drive of the entrance to his house, a drive that was not often used. Attached to one case was a note for Rex from Carole. She had evidently dropped the cases sometime during the night before going home to commit suicide. When Rex opened the cases he found inside all the most intimate possessions of himself and Carole: photographs, letters, presents from one to the other. When Lilli arrived Rex was busy destroying the contents of the two suitcases. The letters were all burnt in the grate and the photographs were burnt in the garden; the photograph albums were hidden in the house with the presents.

Rex's involvement in Carole's death and what he saw of the grotesque Hollywood funeral with its incessant flashbulb photographers and the continual badgering and haranguing that he received from the press by day and by night everywhere he went coloured his views on the film city for years to come. In one interview he stormed: 'So far as I am concerned Hollywood is done with ... Hollywood and I have no future in common and I don't know if Hollywood has any future on its own at all ... it is so egocentric it doesn't know the rest of the world exists, and its social life is one of simply incredible, preposterous boredom.' This outburst provoked a fresh series of personal attacks on Rex Harrison and he was glad to get away, with Lilli, to New York to appear in *Anne of a Thousand Days* on Broadway, but he never really forgave Hollywood for the rest of his life.

At an informal inquiry the coroner stated that there was no doubt that Carole's death was suicide. It appeared that she was worried about her future career and she had financial worries; she was not intoxicated. The funeral took place in the presence of Rex and Lilli on 10 July 1948 with the body of 29-year-old Carole Landis dressed in her favourite evening gown, strapless and made of blue chiffon; in her hands lay a matching blue orchid. Pallbearers included Cesar Romero and Pat O'Brien. The officiating priest said during the course of his eulogy: 'She was a regular and much-loved trouper. I don't think the Almighty will judge her too harshly.' Unfortunately it turned out to be a typically ghoulish Hollywood funeral with over 1,500 fans filing past the open coffin, flashbulbs bursting everywhere and the crowd becoming unruly and pushing and shoving to see the coffin being lowered into the grave at Forest Lawn; some of the 'fans' even snatched flowers from the floral tributes as souvenirs. In death Carole Landis was a more popular attraction than she had ever been in life.

Carole Landis

Rex Harrison at
the time of the
Carole Landis scandal

Marilyn Monroe

-

Every Man's American Love Affair

So much has been written about the life and death of the greatest screen goddess of them all, Marilyn Monroe, that one might well ask: what more is there to say? And yet no book devoted to the subject of death in Hollywood can possibly omit the curious and still puzzling final performance of that insecure 36-year-old who photographed like an angel. Was her death an accident, suicide or murder? There are questions about the sad affair that have not been answered to this day.

Marilyn Monroe had a traumatic childhood by any account — and there are several unsubstantiated versions of her childhood days. Born on 1 June 1926, Norma Jean Baker, or possibly Mortensen (her mother, a Christian Scientist, became Gladys Baker before becoming Gladys Mortensen by marriage), the child saw little of her mother. Gladys was a paranoid schizophrenic and whenever she was in hospital Norma Jean went to live with her grandmother who, Marilyn later claimed, tried to asphyxiate her. She also claimed that for years, from the age of six, she was sexually abused by a foster-mother; that she was raped at the age of nine by a lodger at another foster home; and that for as long as she could remember she had enjoyed sex at any time she felt like it, with just about anybody who asked her, women included. How much of all this was fantasy there is no longer any way of reliably establishing.

The girl who was to become Marilyn Monroe was born, lived and died in Hollywood, 'star struck' for most of her life. As a child she retreated from her sordid everyday life by going to the movies and there in a fantasy world she dreamed of Clark Gable being her father; and soon there were two Norma Jeans as there were to be two Marilyn Monroes, one a cold, ambitious, calculating person who would use all her considerable assets to further her career and the other, a laughing, giggling, insecure and sometimes outrageous but always photogenic and beautiful young woman.

In the early days, when she was struggling to become an actress, she used to watch the cars with famous actors and actresses in them moving smoothly down Sunset Boulevard. 'I used to think', she said, years later, 'that there must be thousands of girls sitting alone like me, dreaming of becoming a big movie star; but I'm not going to worry about them because I'm dreaming the hardest.'

Which Marilyn Monroe you met at any one time depended on what she expected from you; and she could change from one to the other in a flash – she was a Gemini. Most, if not all, of the mystery of Marilyn Monroe is to be traced to her deep need for love. She always needed love desperately and acted on the idea that the more she worked at loving a person, the more that person would love her back; but it rarely worked that way. All too frequently real love eluded her.

At the age of 16, in 1942, she married 21-year-old Jim Dougherty who worked for the Lockheed Aviation Company before he joined the Marines in 1943. His lonely young wife drifted into photographic modelling and eventually into films. When she obtained her first contract, with Twentieth Century-Fox, probably as a result of her relationship with Joseph M. Schenck, an executive producer at the studio and already nearing 70, her name had become Marilyn Monroe. Monroe was her mother's maiden name and Marilyn, suggested by Ben Lyon, seemed to fit. The same week that she obtained her first contract she also obtained a divorce from Jim Dougherty.

Marilyn was to marry Robert Slatzer in 1948, retired baseball star Joe Di Maggio in 1954 and Arthur Miller in 1956. Among her lovers were Johnny Hyde, vice president of the powerful William Morris Agency, who left his wife and four sons in the hope that Marilyn would marry him; Yves Montand, the Italian-born actor who worked chiefly in France and co-starred with Marilyn in *Let's Make Love* (Marilyn wanted to marry him but he returned to his wife Simone Signoret after the affair); Fred Karger, director of music at Columbia Pictures who died

in 1979 on the anniversary of Marilyn's death; also Charlie
Chaplin Jr, Edward G. Robinson Jr, who died an alcoholic
at 40 (choking to death while watching one of his father's
movies), President John Kennedy and his brother Attorney
General Robert Kennedy (she told close friends she had 'made
it with the Prez' at Bing Crosby's house in Palm Springs. 'He
said I made his back feel better'); Henry Rosenfeld, a wealthy
dress manufacturer; Walter Winchell, the powerful columnist;
Damon Runyon, the writer; Howard Hughes, the millionaire
film producer; José Bolaños, a Mexican scriptwriter; Ted
Jordan, a Hollywood actor; and Frank Sinatra. Arthur Miller
(husband number four) believes that Marilyn's promiscuity is
exaggerated. 'Sure she had her men,' he is quoted as saying.
'But not from couch to couch, man to man. Any relationship
she ever had was meaningful to her, built on a thread of hope,
however mistaken.'

I talked with Sammy Davis Jr about Marilyn Monroe. He
said, 'Of course she found a basic enjoyment and inner security
when she made love but she was no whore. Of course she was
unhappy and often insecure; but I never once thought of her
as tragic. She was extremely caring and a very sensitive person
who was easily bruised. She was genuinely one of the sweetest
creatures I ever met.'

The twenty films of Marilyn Monroe owe much of their
quality not so much to her performance as to her presence.
Certainly she could act, witness *The Misfits* (1961), and she
could play comedy, as she did so well in *Bus Stop* (1956) and
Some Like It Hot (1959), but to say that she was not the
easiest person in the world to work with is putting it mildly.
The talented Oscar-winning film director, Billy Wilder, who
worked with her on *The Seven Year Itch* (1955) and *Some
Like It Hot* (1959) said 'Marilyn was mean; terribly mean. I
have never met anyone as mean as Marilyn Monroe, and that
includes Garbo.'

But Marilyn had a lot to contend with. Her early years
continually haunted her; she worried that she would take after
her mother and become mentally ill; she became addicted to
drugs and relied on them more and more as the years passed;
she loved, not wisely but too well and never found the great
love she longed for; she craved for children of her own but
never had any (or possibly one when she was very young,

who was adopted); she had several abortions, and at least one miscarriage, which upset her emotionally and intellectually; she longed to be treated as a serious actress instead of a sex symbol; she had love affairs with people in high places who were unable or who simply refused to acknowledge her; she had three unhappy marriages; she suffered from frightening insomnia; she needed real love desperately; she longed to be more intellectual; and through it all she was expected to appear as a giggly, dumb blonde, inconsequential froth. It couldn't have been easy.

In May 1962, as she approached her thirty-sixth birthday, Marilyn began work on *Something's Got to Give* with Dean Martin. She had little faith in the film but her contract with Twentieth Century-Fox gave her no option but to do it; however she became convinced that the film was her big opportunity, the one that would bring her the critical acclaim that she craved. Sadly, she was already far from well. Henry Weinstein, the producer, later described her as 'one very ill, very paranoid lady'. She had become obsessed with her health and one day walked off the set and went home having learned that Dean Martin had a cold. She harboured suspicions that everyone was trying to upstage her. She thought Cyd Charisse was copying her by having the same hair colour; and even the middle-aged actress playing the housekeeper had to have her hair darkened to avoid any resemblance to Marilyn's. More than once she was seen retching near the studio entrance: this could have been caused by a pregnancy, drugs or slimming, but Henry Weinstein believed it was evidence of her extreme fear of appearing before the cameras. 'We all experience anxiety, unhappiness, heartbreak,' he said. 'But this was sheer, primal terror.'

During the 35 days filming on *Something's Got to Give*, Marilyn only managed to turn up for 12 days and in the middle of working on the film, on 19 May, Marilyn insisted on leaving the set to go to President Kennedy's Birthday Party at Madison Square Garden in New York. She had been asked to sing 'Happy Birthday Mr President' and she did it but her nerve very nearly gave way. She became increasingly drunk as she sought to steady her nerves and she failed to appear on Peter Lawford's first introduction. His second attempt, followed by a drum roll, was no more successful and finally he announced, 'Mr President, the late Marilyn Monroe.' Marilyn was then virtually propelled on stage by Lawford's agent and for thirty seconds, which must have seemed like thirty years, she stood silent before finally singing her lines faultlessly and memorably. She wore a $5,000 sparkling rhinestone dress, with nothing underneath.

Back in Hollywood she celebrated her own birthday with the film crew and they sang 'Happy Birthday' to her. But within days she again became depressed and inconsolable. Her one anchor at this time was Dr Ralph Greenson, the Hollywood psychiatrist who treated and befriended Marilyn in her last years. Desperately she telephoned Dr Greenson and talked to his son and daughter; they said that she sounded heavily drugged and she was crying and saying that she was so very unhappy. They hurried to her new Spanish-style home in Brentwood. There they found her in bed, naked under a sheet, and wearing a black sleeping mask. They realized that she was really falling apart; she said she couldn't sleep (it was the middle of the afternoon); she felt terrible about herself − that she was ugly, worthless, that people were using her. She had no one, nobody loved her and life wasn't worth living any more.

The Greensons noticed an array of pills beside the bed and surreptitiously pocketed them. They did what they could to reassure Marilyn that thousands of people all over the world loved her and looked up to her, but she was inconsolable. Their father was out of the country so they called one of his colleagues and he came over to see her.

For the whole of the following week there was very little improvement and Paula Strasberg, Marilyn's acting coach, told the studio she was too ill for work. Marilyn telephoned her devoted psychiatrist, Dr Greenson, in Europe (she used to say the telephone was her best friend) and a few days later she went for a nose X-ray, complaining of having slipped in the shower and injured her nose. Meanwhile the rushes of *Something's Got to Give* showed Marilyn acting in a kind of slow motion. Director George Cukor was understandably disappointed and there was talk of replacing Marilyn in the film. Dr Ralph Greenson was friendly with Henry Weinstein, the film's producer, and he told Weinstein that he was returning to Hollywood immediately and promised that Marilyn would be on the set and ready for work on Monday, three days ahead.

But he was too late. On the Friday Marilyn was fired. The studio sued Marilyn Monroe for half a million dollars and when Dean Martin refused to work with any other actress, they sued him too. Then the movie was cancelled.

Through June 1962 Marilyn seems almost to have been a prisoner in her own home with only Pat Newcomb (press aide and one-time close friend) and Eunice Murray, (Marilyn's housekeeper and friend) knowing exactly what went on. Both have been strangely reticent about the last days of Marilyn Monroe.

At the end of June Robert Kennedy visited Marilyn at her home. Both Robert Kennedy and John F. Kennedy seem to have been on intimate terms with Marilyn and it is known that Pat Newcomb was deeply in love with Robert Kennedy. By July Marilyn seems to have reached the end of her tether: she saw Dr Greenson on 27 out of 35 days and a Dr Hyman Engelberg on 13 occasions! Peter Lawson was to claim that he and his wife took Marilyn to the Cal-Neva Lodge at Lake Tahoe, where Frank Sinatra was performing, three weeks before her death and the staff there recall her as the occupant of Chalet 52, 'a sad and withdrawn woman who kept herself disguised and stayed in the chalet most of the time'. The switchboard operator remembers that Marilyn usually went to sleep with the telephone at her ear, open to the switchboard, as though it were a way of not being alone. Once the operator heard stertorous breathing and strange grunting sounds and he called the manager who raised the alarm and, it would appear, Marilyn was rescued from oblivion caused by an overdose of pills.

There have been suggestions that Marilyn's despair during her last days was the result of her discovery that she was pregnant. Earlier in the year she had said she wanted to have a child and she talked a lot about babies during her last months. Several witnesses claim that Marilyn said she was pregnant by one of the Kennedy brothers; one friend says she told him that Robert was responsible. If she was pregnant and if either Robert or John Kennedy was responsible, it would be understandable that both the Kennedys would have wanted to distance themselves from the unhappy girl; when she threatened to hold a press conference, with 'world shattering news', they would surely have been very worried indeed.

It is certain that Marilyn repeatedly tried to reach both Robert and John Kennedy during her last days, perhaps even during her last hours, but, as she told a friend, 'They are both ignoring me. I've been trying and trying to reach them but I can't get to either of them.' Robert Kennedy had the number of his private telephone line changed and John Kennedy left instructions that Marilyn was not to be put through under any circumstances.

In her frantic state of mind Marilyn showed her long-standing friend, Robert Slatzer, a cluster of notes from Bobby Kennedy and her small red diary, which he found contained notes of conversations with Bobby and references to political matters of a highly controversial nature. Marilyn said she had made the notes because 'Bobby liked to talk about political things and he gets mad at me because I don't remember what he tells me.' Perhaps by this time the Kennedy brothers had realized the total folly of associating with Marilyn and events were set in motion that resulted in her death. Marilyn Monroe, in the eyes of the Kennedys, had become a definite security risk and it is not beyond the bounds of possiblity that murder may have been considered.

In the last days leading up to her death we know that Marilyn certainly contemplated suicide. She told several people that 'it might be a kind of relief to be finished'. And she managed to obtain a large supply of drugs, possibly with the idea of ending her life.

It was midsummer and sleep became more difficult than ever for Marilyn; days and nights blended together. 'If only I could sleep' she used to say, time after time. Perhaps, some time during the afternoon of 3 August 1962, she may have decided to end her life; perhaps she may have been helped to this decision by someone; perhaps in her confused state she allowed someone to fill her body with drugs that would induce a slow, gradual and very deep sleep, ending in death. It is unlikely that we shall ever know for certain whether the death of Marilyn was an accident, suicide or murder.

One unexplained aspect of the death is the curious position of her legs. The first police officials on the scene said her legs were straight and parallel: she 'looked as though she had been put into that position'.

She could not possibly have died in that position. In the last moments before consciousness is lost, after an overdose of barbiturates, there is pain and there is contortion. The body is

*commonly twisted. You never see a body with the legs straight —
and that statement is based on the evidence of hundreds of suicides
by drug overdose.*

Whatever happened to trigger the event it seems obvious that,
towards the end, she must have realized what was happening
and frantically tried to reach by telephone those friends she
knew and trusted to help her. But no one she reached grasped
the truth of her condition and in the deep narcotics-induced
drowsiness and then oblivious sleep, Marilyn Monroe died alone
and uncomforted, as she had been so often in her tragically
short life.

Dressed in a green sheath dress with a green silk scarf round
her neck, her hair blonde once more, and clutching a small
bouquet of pink sweetheart roses, a gift from Di Maggio, she
was buried in a private wall crypt (Marilyn didn't like the idea
of being buried in the earth) in Westwood Village Memorial
Park with only 24 invited guests present. The flower-covered
coffin went to its last resting place to the music of 'Over the
Rainbow'. Di Maggio's affection for Marilyn never really died
and for years after her death he sent six red roses to her crypt
three times a week. And with her death Monroe became more
famous than she had been in life with more books written
about her than any other showbusiness personality, and a dozen
television shows, and ten plays and three feature films.

Marilyn Monroe was fascinated by death and often talked of
it; sometimes, gazing wistfully at the high blue Hollywood skies,
she would say, 'Wouldn't it be wonderful if there is life after
death? How simply beautiful it would be to spend forever, an
eternity, somewhere like this, for ever and ever.'

Barbara La Marr

-

The Most Beautiful Girl in the World

In the silent era of films Barbara La Marr was one of the biggest stars; she lived a bewildering life of love affairs, marriage, glamorous photographic sessions and exciting personal appearances. She was born Reatha Watson in Richmond, Virginia and her voluptous, feline beauty brought her an early career as a dancer and musical-comedy actress before she entered films. By the time she reached Hollywood Barbara La Marr already had two marriages behind her and, it has been claimed, she had been raped twice, and used and deceived by a number of men, including a would-be bigamist.

In 1921, Barbara La Marr appeared as one of the three principal female roles — the lovely ladies of the court of Louis XIII — in Dumas' *The Three Musketeers.* The following year saw Barbara in another costume drama, with Ramon Novarro, Jean Hersholt, Rudolph Valentino, Wallace Beery and Alan Hale in Rex Ingram's famous 2¼ hour silent film, *The Four Horsemen of the Apocalypse.*

La Marr was suddenly finding her life in Hollywood a constant merry-go-round that had no rhyme or reason; in a town that called her 'the girl who is too beautiful' she played one of the leading ladies in Rex Ingram's *The Prisoner of Zenda* (1922) with Ramon Novarro as the dashing young Rupert. Between films she flirted and had affairs with all and sundry in the heady, unreal world of flickering pictures and bright lights. She donned modern clothes for her film, *The Eternal City* (1923), a drama that featured Lionel Barrymore, Richard Bennett and Bert Lytell. By now the exotic-looking young star was approaching her brief heyday in films and had begun to taste the life of a successful star. She caused something of a stir, even in Hollywood, when she installed in her home an enormous sunken bath in an all-onyx bathroom complemented by gold fittings where she entertained four successive Hollywood husbands. With hindsight it is easy to see that she was totally unable to adjust to the pressures of Hollywood and filming fame and fortune for, apart from her many husbands, she was with good cause the subject of much scandal in Tinseltown. Yet she still found time to play the lead in *Trifling Women* (1924) – which a good many Hollywood people in the know must have thought an ironic title.

In the 1924 Metro film, *Thy Name is Woman*, a First World War drama, Barbara La Marr appeared yet again with Ramon Novarro. They became good friends but La Marr, who used to boast that she never wasted more than two hours a night on sleep – having 'better things to do' – had by this time become a hopeless drug addict and for several years she found it quite impossible to get through a single day without drugs. Ramon Novarro tried to get her to ease off but anything La Marr did, she did to excess: six husbands and literally dozens of lovers during her few brief years of heady fame. She said she enjoyed lovers in the same way that she enjoyed roses.

In her last film, *The Girl from Montmartre* (1926) Barbara La Marr appeared with experienced and sensible Robert Ellis who could see what was happening to the flighty Barbara and he too tried to get her to ease up on the drugs and on her whirlwind lifestyle but by this time her personal life and her film career had become intertwined and very complicated and often she hardly knew where she was or what she was doing.

Among her many escorts was Paul Bern for whom, before his ill-fated marriage to Jean Harlow, it seemed an absolute necessity that he appear in public with the sexiest-looking girls in Hollywood but his physical and mental make-up prevented him from being the great lover he aspired to be and sometimes at the end of an evening he would be seething with frustration. Once, after a date with Barbara La Marr, he arrived home in a frenzy and took out his frustration on his own apartment, literally ripping out the bathroom fixtures, for he had not persuaded Barbara La Marr to let him beat her.

On the other hand Bern could be thoughtful and kindness

itself. When Barbara La Marr was about to marry, somewhat hurriedly, her seventh husband, Bern learned at the last moment that the couple couldn't afford a reception and didn't even have a real wedding ring. Quietly Bern arranged to pay for a wedding ring. He also scoured Hollywood to find a bootlegger who could supply illegal liquor for the newly-weds and their friends.

That year, 1926, saw the last film and the death of one of her lovers, the great Valentino. His last film, *Son of the Sheik* (1926) was a not altogether happy attempt to recapture the glamour, romance and mystery of his first starring role in *The Sheik* (1922). Valentino's funeral service caused riots and the funeral parlour, where his body lay, was nearly wrecked by hysterical and fanatical fans. According to official figures 'thousands' of weeping women gathered at railway stations across the country to watch the funeral train make its way to Hollywood, for he had died in New York.

La Marr herself died two months before *The Girl from Montmartre* was released. She died, after her tempestuous career and many complications in her private life, in her expensive and expansive Hollywood home, of a massive overdose of drugs. Kenneth Anger refers to her as 'Hollywood's most glamorous, if jaded, junkie' and says she 'dabbled in every known variety of dope'. She kept her cocaine in a golden casket on the grand piano and her opium in an equally accessible place.

At first the studios said Barbara La Marr had died as a result of 'over-dieting' but 'the girl who was too beautiful' took either deliberately or accidentally, a massive overdose and died amid the Hollywood glamour that she loved not wisely but too well.

Lupe Velez

The Mexican

Mexican

Spitfire

Wild and impulsive Lupe Velez, a big star in her day and one of Hollywood's liveliest ladies, slipped to second-class movies after some scandalous public behaviour and eventually decided to end it all in typical Lupe Velez style. She was the tempestuous leading lady in a score of films and starred in a stage musical, *Glad to See You* near the end of her life, staged by the undisputed genius of the Hollywood musical, Busby Berkeley.

Towards the end of the silent movie era in motion pictures, the late 1920s, two Mexican actresses came into prominence and lasted well into the following decade. Dolores Del Rio achieved a kind of popularity that briefly rivalled Garbo's but Lupe Velez brought a new exoticism to the movies and her vital, fiery quality carried over into her private life.

Lupe Velez Guadaloupe da Villalobos was born in San Luis Potosi, Mexico in 1909. She was the daughter of an opera singer according to some sources — according to others her mother was a streetwalker — her father was a Mexican Army officer. She made her stage debut at the age of 15 in the raunchy burlesque houses of Mexico City; later she appeared in shows that might be described as 'musical comedies'. According to Budd Schulberg, son of B.P. Schulberg, head of Paramount Studios, stage-door Juanitos panted for her favours from an early age and Mama Velez would sell her for the evening to the highest bidder! Lupe appeared on stage in Los Angeles before appearing in films and she reverted to the stage towards the end of her life. Her first big break in films came when Douglas Fairbanks gave her the lead in *The Gaucho* (1927), the story of an Argentinian Robin Hood.

The passionate and enthusiastic Lupe Velez 'adopted' as her personal protégés those Mexican fighters who fought at the Hollywood Legion Arena and she would cheer them wildly through each round. If the Mexican boxer lost, she was quite likely to climb into the ring to attack the referee physically. She once told John Gilbert, when he was down in the dumps, 'Big baby; you let Hollywood get you down. I say to Hollywood, look out, here comes Lupe. If my heart hurts me, I go to the fights and holler and whoopee. Hollywood says, That Lupe, she is the wild one, nothing ever gets her down.'

The uninhibited Lupe Velez was known to jump enthusiastically on to the table at a restaurant, rip off her dress, and go into some wild Mexican dance – and she habitually shunned the use of underwear. She was soon known as the 'Studio Sweetheart' and she lived up to her name, coming in for a lot of attention. She had a frantic fling with Tom Mix; for a while she and Lawrence Tibbett were said to 'have it bad' during the making of *Cuban Love Song* (1931); but no sooner were rumours of an elopement widespread than it was announced that 'Lupe Velez has gone to New York with John Gilbert.' In the end even the cynical and experienced pressmen and columnists of Hollywood had a hard job keeping up with the romantic exploits of Lupe Velez.

One of her best-known romances was with Gary Cooper, who earned himself the title of 'Hollywood's Greatest Lover'. For a time he moved out of his own home and into Lupe's hideaway at 1826 Laurel Canyon Road. Years after the affair was over Coop told an interviewer: 'I guess I was in love with Lupe Velez. You couldn't help being attracted to her: she flashed, she stormed, she sparkled and on the set she was apt to throw things if she thought it would do any good. She especially objected to being called a spitfire, a word the reporters seemed to favour. But she was also extremely professional in her approach to her craft and totally reliable.'

At one stage of her torrid romance with Coop it was noticed that Lupe was wearing a wedding ring as well as an engagement ring: she claimed that she and Coop had 'slipped into Mexico' and been married. Coop made a formal statement to the press saying he was not engaged and not even thinking about

marriage to Lupe or anyone else, although Lupe and Coop
continued to be together night and day, whenever it was possible
without attracting too much attention. Eventually, when the
affair did peter out, the studios arranged for Coop to leave
quietly by train on a five-week rest. Somehow Lupe got to
hear of his departure. She reached the station just as Coop
was boarding the train. 'Gary, you son of a bitch', she shouted
and took a shot at him with a revolver but missed. Coop hurried
aboard, slammed the carriage door and the train pulled out, but
a lot of people witnessed the event which apparently was never
reported by the papers.

Lupe Velez was wild and uninhibited and often embarrassed
everyone by talking loudly and with great enthusiasm about
very private and very personal matters but there was another
side to her, apart from her dedicated and professional conduct
while she was working. She loved children, and Lenore Coffee
the scriptwriter wife of director William Joyce Cowen, in her
book of reminiscences, *Storyline* (Cassell, 1973), has revealed
a completely different Lupe Velez from that which she publicly
flaunted.

One day Lenore Coffee's husband rang home to say that
there were two chimpanzees on the lot and she ought to bring
their five-year-old daughter to see them because they would be
gone next day.

*Neither of us had ever taken our children to a studio, but
he was so insistent that I agreed and decided we would
have lunch in the commissary. We found a table on the
exclusive screen porch, but no sooner were we seated than
Lupe appeared. She saw there was an extra place at our
table and over she came. My heart sank, knowing what
her conversation could be, but I introduced them. Lupe was
delighted and addressed herself entirely to my daughter, as
if I were not there. 'You have already ordered your lunch?'
My little girl shook her head. 'Oh, good — perhaps we have
the same thing? That would be fun?' This time she got
an enthusiastic nod and much conferring went on, Lupe
reading the menu and making little jokes and finally a
joint menu was decided upon; my child enchanted with all
this grown-up attention. I suddenly realized that I had two
five-year-old children at my table! Lupe's face and voice*

*were so sweet, so tender and yet so full of fun that I was
filled with gratitude and wonder. They chatted all through
lunch, then Lupe looked at her watch and said she must
run and have her make-up repaired. I watched to see if
she would kiss my daughter goodbye, but she took her
little hand and gave it a gentle kiss and was gone, leaving
the child's face glowing. This is the same Lupe who was
to take her life – her wonderful sparkling life – because
a man refused to marry her so she could have a legitimate
baby.*

After a turbulent five-year marriage to Johnny Weissmuller,
surely the best of all the Tarzans, the unhappy Lupe's film
career took a downward plunge as did her personal life: she
had flings by the score – and not only Hollywood stars but
cowboys, stuntsmen, cameramen and stage hands all boasted
of the fun and games they had enjoyed with the Mexican
Spitfire.

In 1944 Lupe was thirty-six, heavily in debt, and she realized
that her latest paramour, one Harold Ramond, was the father
of her unborn child. A devout Catholic, (!) convent educated
Lupe Velez could not consider an abortion and Harold didn't
want to hear about it. He did tell Lupe's manager that he
would agree to a mock ceremony on condition that Lupe
signed a document stating she knew he was marrying her solely
to provide a name for her baby.

One evening Lupe invited her two best (female) friends,
Estelle Taylor (ex-wife of Jack Dempsey) and Benita Oakie
(wife of Jack Oakie) to dinner at her pseudo-hacienda home
on North Rodeo Drive. They shared a hot Mexican meal and
afterwards she told them: 'I'm tired of life. I've had to fight
for everything. I'm so tired of it all. Ever since I was a baby
in Mexico City, I've been fighting. It's my baby. I couldn't
commit murder and still live with myself. I would rather kill
myself.'

By three o'clock that night Lupe was alone again. She dressed
carefully in her favourite silver lamé gown and climbed the
wrought-iron staircase to her bedroom. There she had prepared
a memorable scene for her own death. The room was full of
beautiful flowers, gardenias and roses especially, and it was all
arranged like a shrine. There were masses of scented candles

which she now carefully lit and when everything was to her satisfaction she wrote a farewell note:

> To Harold. May God forgive you and forgive me too
> but I prefer to take my life away and our baby's before
> I bring him into the world with shame. Lupe.

On the back, almost as an afterthought, it seems, she wrote:

> Harold, how could you fake such a great love for me
> and our baby when all the time you didn't want us?
> I see no other way out for me so goodbye and good
> luck to you. Love, Lupe.

It was to be a perfect death scene and after a final check that all was to her satisfaction Lupe Velez opened a bottle of Seconal tablets that she had placed on the table beside her bed. Then she picked up a glass of water and swallowed seventy-five of the pills. She stretched out on the satin bed beneath the great crucifix, joined her hands over her breast in a last prayer, closed her eyes and slept.

Next day the *Los Angeles Examiner* reported: 'Lupe Velez was never lovelier, as she lay there, as if slumbering ... a faint smile, like a secret dream on her face.' It would be nice to think it had been like that but it was not to be. The hot Mexican food did not digest well with the tablets and when the maid entered Lupe's bedroom next morning she found the bed empty and the aroma of scented candles and a hundred flowers could not mask the smell of vomit. A trail led from the bed to the tiled bathroom and there was the body of Lupe Velez, her head jammed down the toilet bowl, ignominiously dead.

2

The Matter of the Heart

-

DEATH FROM
HEART ATTACK

Heart attacks can strike anyone at any time and the history of the stars of Hollywood reflect the sometimes sudden and sometimes drawn-out deaths that occur from heart attacks or heart disease.

Some of the stars in this chapter were born with a heart defect and lived their lives with the knowledge that death might come at any time, others had no inkling the day before they died that it would be the last time they would bask in the sun. Oblivious to when the great reaper was coming their way, they lived their lives to the last moment.

Stress can cause heart failure, and stress, worry and the spectre of what might or might not happen has often haunted those who find themselves enmeshed in the twinkling and uncertain world of film acting.

Merle Oberon in 1932.
Her mother was Eurasian
but the star insisted that
she was white

Merle Oberon in a scene from *Wuthering Heights* (1939).
Also shown are Laurence Olivier and David Niven

Merle Oberon

-

The Magical Presence
with a Mysterious Past

Possessing a curious, irresistible beauty and an insatiable sexual appetite Merle Oberon rose from obscurity in India to the highest pinnacle of international stardom, basking in the warm friendship of the highest in the land as Lady Korda.

In contradiction with many reference books, Merle Oberon was born in Bombay, the daughter of a Eurasian girl who had had an earlier child when she was only 14 ½ years old. Finding herself pregnant again, she married the father, a mechanical engineer from England. Their child, named Estelle Merle O'Brien Thompson, came into the world on 19 February 1911. She was born with a heart defect that would kill her 68 years later. Her father died during the Somme offensive in the First World War and Merle never knew him.

Merle Oberon has been called 'one of the magic presences of the twentieth century'; it is no exaggeration. Dr Paul Tabori, who wrote the first biography of Sir Alexander Korda, whom he knew for fifteen years, told me that her beauty was breathtaking. She lit up a room when she entered; she always looked radiant and incredibly beautiful; and she always seemed to be cheerful, kind and helpful. She was enormously popular with film crews and yet all her life she lived under the threat of exposure. She had to pretend to be white and she had to pretend to have been born into a wealthy family. Paul told me a lot about Merle Oberon and about the Korda family that he did not include in his biography of the flamboyant Hungarian director.

From early days in the shabby Khetwadi district of Bombay,

Merle Oberon rose to the dizzy heights of fame as a screen actress, married four times (including six years as Lady Korda), and became a close friend of the British royal family.

In her late teens, in Calcutta, the already beautiful and sensual girl would frequent the popular Firpo's Dance Hall. She had many admirers and there were stories of her being little more than a prostitute. Certainly she was very hard up at that time and it has to be said that similar stories circulated years later when she lived in London. She was an independent young lady who enjoyed an 'extraordinary line of romantic affairs, as her biographers put it. Among her known conquests were 'Hutch' (Leslie A. Hutchinson, the singer), Turhan Bey, Eddie Fisher, Richard Tate, Miles Mander, David Niven, Leslie Howard, Robert Ryan, George Brent, Joseph Schenck and a score more.

Film Director Victor Saville, a member of my London club with whom I frequently had lunch in the 1960s, told me that when he and Michael Balcon were preparing to cast *A Warm Corner* (1930), he saw and met Merle (then using her real name Estelle Thompson) when she was a hostess at the glamorous Café de Paris in London. 'I decided immediately that this very young, very beautiful girl should be given a break and I engaged her immediately and her first real film part was as an extra in that film.' Years later, when Merle became almost paranoid about her past she went out of her way to avoid Victor Saville; she was never sure just how much he knew. She always claimed to be psychic and perhaps she was because Victor Saville knew far more about Merle's early life than she could ever have guessed.

Other bit parts followed before Alexander Korda put her into *Wedding Rehearsal* (1932), more by luck than judgement — although he never admitted as much. The fact is that Ann Todd, who had already been cast, was involved in a car accident and Merle was rushed in to replace her. In her autobiography Ann Todd tells of being so badly cut and smashed in the accident that when the ambulance men took her away they covered her up with a sheet, thinking she was dead. Years later she did in fact 'die' for a short while but that is another story. Happily she recovered on both occasions and has charmed us over the years with dozens of memorable film and stage performances.

When Merle appeared in another Korda picture (*Men of*

Tomorrow, 1932) Korda began to fall in love with the outstandingly lovely girl but he had no wish to have an affair with an obscure, aspiring actress and he told himself he would build her up into a star; then perhaps, if he still felt the same way, he would declare his love. The chance to put Merle on the road to stardom came when Korda put her into his classic film, *The Private Life of Henry VIII* (1933), although it was touch and go whether she would be able to appear in the picture.

Production had already started when Merle fell ill. She had, it seems, experienced increasing pain during intercourse with various men and now she discovered inexplicable bleeding. She consulted a gynaecologist who said she had cancer and he should operate at once, for the disease was located in one of her fallopian tubes. In fact during the operation the surgeon discovered that both tubes were affected and he removed them. This meant, of course, that Merle could never bear a child but she was not told this devastating information because peritonitis then set in and her body was beginning to be flooded with poison. Happily her considerable general strength, courage and will to live pulled her through in the days before antibiotics and afterwards she went to Margate to recuperate.

Meanwhile Korda, about to wrap up *The Private Life of Henry VIII*, thought he might add a sequence depicting the execution of the king's second wife and he decided that Merle would be perfect for the part of Anne Boleyn. Merle received the offer enthusiastically and, although the part was small, she decided at the outset to make the most of it. She studied everything she could about the ill-fated queen who was ambitious, promiscuous, flirtatious, beautiful, courageous, stylish, charming and with coloured blood in her veins − just like Merle herself! Korda was thrilled with her performance and it was generally accepted that Merle had out-classed and out-acted all the other wives who included Elsa Lanchester, Binnie Barnes and Wendy Barrie.

In the months that followed, when she worked with Charles Boyer in *The Battle* (1934), with Douglas Fairbanks Sr in *The Private Life of Don Juan* (1934) and with Leslie Howard in *The Scarlet Pimpernel* (1934), Merle lived life to the hilt and it was only when she suffered, notwithstanding all her precautions and efforts, a recurring skin problem that had repeatedly affected her in India, that she cooled down and began to worry about her complexion.

The trouble was caused, she was told by the best experts she could find, by a combination of her mixed blood and her use of a highly toxic and heavy make-up that was designed to whiten her face. This is particularly noticeable in stills from the Henry VIII film. Merle was frantic when her perfectly shaped face began to break out in rashes, especially around her mouth, and there were times when she literally locked herself away for days at a time in her apartment in Upper Montague Street near Baker Street.

The problem was that her skin trouble seemed to ease when she was able to relax but this was difficult as she worried about her career and about how long she would be able to stay at the top were she able to get there — conversations with actors and actresses began to convince her that the shortest route to fame in films was to go to Hollywood. Douglas Fairbanks told her that the big Hollywood producer, film executive and head of United Artists, Joseph Schenck, was coming to England, and Merle saw her chance.

At a dinner party at the Fairbanks' London home Merle and Schenck met for the first time. He was instantly attracted and Merle set out to captivate him with her considerable charm and her carefully cultured voice. Merle had seen to it that Douglas Fairbanks had promised Schenck would not learn from him of the 'loose' reputation Merle had acquired in London.

Before long Schenck was showering Merle with presents including a diamond necklace and a mink coat, and soon he was imploring her to marry him. She agreed to their becoming lovers but kept him dangling on the question of marriage. The important thing was that Schenck would be her ticket to Hollywood and that he procured for her a major part in an ambitious film. Everything seemed to be falling into place when he began to talk of his plans for an expansive and important film about the Folies Bergère. Then suddenly Schenck had to return to America on some urgent business and while he was away Merle began an intense affair with Leslie Howard. Once, Howard's long-suffering wife, Ruth, walked into her husband's dressing room to find him and Merle energetically coupling on the floor!

Word reached Schenck that Merle and Leslie Howard were

more than 'just good friends'; and he hurried back to England. At the Savoy Hotel he saw Merle and suggested that she marry him at once, that she forget the Folies Bergère film and in fact give up her film career; in exchange he would offer her a life of luxury in California as his respected and doting wife. Merle said no, they had a verbal contract that she would appear in his film and on the matter of marriage she had now made up her mind: she eased off the diamond engagement ring he had given her and handed it back to him.

That same evening the deflated Schenck sold the ring to Douglas Fairbanks who immediately put it on the hand of his mistress Lady Sylvia Ashley! Schenck then returned to America and Merle returned to Leslie Howard and to work for Alexander Korda again who, somewhat reluctantly, granted her special leave to make the Folies Bergère film in Hollywood.

After *Folies Bergère* (1935) with Maurice Chevalier she made several other films in America before returning to England to work on the ill-fated and uncompleted *I, Claudius* (1937) with Charles Laughton. Robert Graves himself told me that he thought it *could* have been a great film. After four more films, Merle gave one of her best performances in *Wuthering Heights* (1939) with Laurence Olivier and David Niven. Fine reviews effectively put Merle at the very forefront of her profession.

Thereafter Merle was to make more than 25 first-class pictures. In her final film, *Interval* (1973), she played opposite Robert Wolders who was to become her fourth and final husband.

In the forty years remaining to her after her great success in *Wuthering Heights* Merle Oberon was to know the heights of happiness and the depths of despair; she would experience remarkable strokes of luck and fortune but also unfair and unexpected troughs of bad luck would come her way.

Her idyllic affair with Leslie Howard who she had hoped would divorce his wife and marry her, foundered and collapsed when Howard, who was one of the few men Merle really loved, became ill with a mysterious and severe attack of boils that virtually covered him from head to foot. In his agony and despair he turned to Ruth his wife and not to Merle, who soon began an affair with David Niven, at that time practically penniless while Merle was already earning thousands each week.

In 1935, during the making of *Dark Angel*, Merle suffered

a severe shock to her mental system when she was rejected by Gary Cooper, known as 'Hollywood's greatest lover', who was making *The Wedding Night* on a nearby sound stage. Merle found Cooper wildly attractive and decided to have an affair with him but, as his co-star Anna Sten was to say later, he was utterly uninterested in Merle because, beautiful as she was, she was simply not Coop's type and at the time he was emotionally involved elsewhere.

At that time Merle became ill and the doctors diagnosed that her heart murmur was playing up. She was probably lucky to recover quickly and once the shooting of *Dark Angel* was completed she deliberately relaxed among her friends Robert Young, Ida Lupino, Irving Thalberg, Norma Shearer and of course David Niven, now the love of her life, who proceeded to entertain her as she lay in his arms in her newly acquired Malibu beach cottage, with hilarious stories of the off-the-set clashes between Nelson Eddy and Jeanette Macdonald, then making *Rose Marie* in which Niven also appeared.

In London in 1936, ostensibly to appear in the *I, Claudius* débâcle, Merle discovered that Alex Korda was desperately in love with her. Korda enjoyed royal esteem; he was proud and generous with his professed wealth and he lived ostentatiously; he was also a courageous man and he was widely believed to be sexually impotent. As she mulled over the pros and cons of marriage with Alex and comforted Charles Laughton who was known to go into Merle's dressing room without warning, give her a pathetic look of hopelessness and lay his head in her lap and cry like a baby, Merle bought a Georgian house in York Gate, London and furnished it exquisitely with antiques and beautiful articles, especially mirrors, from every part of the world.

While working on *I, Claudius* Merle was involved in a car accident. She was flung heavily to the floor of the car and badly cut over her left eye and ear. She was rushed to the Middlesex Hospital moaning faintly, 'Is my face disfigured? Will it show?' She was in hospital for four weeks and recovered remarkably well but two weeks later, at the end of August 1937, she found herself at the deathbed of her mother, whom she had passed off as her coloured servant, and attended her burial in an unmarked grave at Micheldever in Hampshire.

Soon after the death of her mother, Merle had a picture

painted depicting a woman with brown hair, blue eyes and white skin; a portrait that always hung in a prominent place in her various homes for the rest of her life and should anyone ask who the beautiful woman was, Merle would reply, without batting an eyelid, that it was her beloved mother. During her mother's lifetime Merle took away her mother's identity and she did the same thing after her mother's death.

The following year, 1938, Merle returned to Hollywood and soon appeared in *Wuthering Heights.* For Merle personally the making of the film was a terrible ordeal, because of the gruelling San Fernando Valley locations and the poorly heated and ill-ventilated studios where many of the scenes were shot. In the middle of the film Merle became ill, shivering and trembling and having great difficulty in breathing. Rushed to hospital, she vomited with violent convulsions and her temperature soared. Night after night she endured sleepless misery until eventually, far from fully recovered, she forced herself back to work. When the picture was released she was acclaimed as the perfect Cathy.

Now at the peak of her career Merle's thoughts turned again to Alex Korda. She was now widely regarded as one of the greatest female actress in films and he was indisputably the greatest figure in the film work in England. She sailed back across the Atlantic, met up with Alex and the couple travelled to the south of France for a holiday together in that ideal spring of 1939. They planned a wedding in June but suddenly Korda's ex-wife, former film star Maria Corda, surfaced in Hollywood where she told everyone who would listen that she had never been legally divorced from Alex. In spite of everything Merle and Alex were married by the Mayor of Antibes and Alex presented his new wife with a wonderful necklace of diamonds and emeralds that had once belonged to Marie Antoinette – the genesis of the quite exceptional collection of jewellery that Merle acquired over the years that followed.

The war clouds were gathering over Europe and the newly-wedded Kordas already had their own private war. Within two days of their wedding, according to Joan Korda (wife of Zoltan, Alex's brother) the pair were 'locked in tigerish quarrels' with violent words flung back and forth even before they returned to London. There Merle found a pleasant house in the Denham area, but they both lived to regret Alex's decision to move the whole family into the house with them: Zoltan and Joan, Vincent (another of Alex's brothers) and his wife Gertrude, and David (Zoltan's son) and Michael (Vincent's son) and Peter Korda, Alex's son by Maria. Merle was far from popular with Alex's brothers and sisters-in-law and she soon found the atmosphere stifling. She found the amount of food and drink that they consumed revolting as she did the cigar smoke that always hung heavily in the air in the vicinity of Alex and his brothers. Merle, always inclined to be worried about her heart and, even at the age of 28, fearful of growing old, began to rise early, take the lightest of breakfasts and steal out for a walk or swim before any of the Kordas were about.

As the summer lengthened into autumn Merle became increasingly depressed. She did not know the cause or what would be the final result but, always sensitive, psychic and often aware of impending disaster, she was in agony for weeks until on 3 September the blow fell and the Second World War began.

Alex, somewhat against his better judgement, left for Hollywood, where he knew he had to go if he wanted to continue making films, and where he was also employed to work for British Intelligence. He disclosed some of his official commitments to Merle, who was later co-opted herself to help in the same work, and they bought a huge English-style property on Copa del Ora Road in Bel Air.

In the latter months of 1939 Merle was again troubled by a sense of impending doom although she forced herself to start work on *Till We Meet Again* (1940) with George Brent and Pat O'Brien. During the first week of December she found herself acutely distressed and she hardly knew how to drag herself anywhere and her depression increased when she heard that her good friend Douglas Fairbanks Sr was ill with heart trouble. All day on 8 December she had the unmistakable feeling that something awful was about to happen. After lunch that day, as she talked to George Brent, she fainted and that evening, feverish and vomiting and feeling dreadful, she learned that Douglas Fairbanks had died.

Desperate to complete *Till We Meet Again* she struggled on, only to collapse on 14 December. She was sent home for a week and then returned to work. In January she was ill again and the studio was not amused. Although she always hated taking antibiotics, she now felt she had no alternative but immediately she had the injection she felt sick and a swelling developed on her face making filming impossible. A few days later she collapsed again. The director talked of cancelling the picture and Merle agreed to more injections, hoping against hope that they would work.

Next morning she woke up and found her face unbearably itchy and sore. When she looked in the mirror she became hysterical. Her entire face was covered with hundreds of red and oozing pustules. The last dose of drugs combined with the toxic make-up she was always using had finally erupted in the most frightful way.

As soon as he learned what had happened Alex flew over from Britain, where he had been working, and he discovered that the only effective treatment was something known as dermabrasion, an almost unbearably painful process used only in the most extreme cases. Merle felt she had no option and after resting and trying to build up her strength she submitted to the ordeal which consisted of dyeing and freezing the skin and then, using something like a dentist's drill with a burr, the surgeon literally ground off the surface of the skin. At the same time, to ensure that the skin was completely removed, an acidic jelly was applied until the whole of Merle's face was an exposed and bleeding mass.

Days of indescribable suffering followed as the skin began to grow back, accompanied by the most severe itching, until Merle's hands had to be tied to the bed to stop her from scratching. And even then the ordeal was not over. The treatment was not successful until two further complete courses of the hideous treatment were completed and even then Merle was left with distinct pitting and indentations of the skin on various parts of her face. It was years before all traces of the terrible disfigurement disappeared and this was only due at all to Merle's dedicated and constant and lengthy treatments to her face.

Merle began to feel her film career might be over and her thoughts turned to giving Alex a child. When no child appeared she had a gynaecological examination and then learned for the first time that both of her fallopian tubes had been removed years earlier.

Alex was in one of his financially embarrassed periods. Merle paid for the costs of producing *Lady Hamilton* (1941), a film Winston Churchill had asked Alex to make. Unlike Alex, Merle was shrewd in her investments and by the time she was thirty she was a millionairess.

The failure of *Affectionately Yours* and to a lesser degree *That Uncertain Feeling* (1941) seemed to Merle to be serious setbacks for her and she became bitter with Alex. During the long period of her suffering from the skin disease things had been difficult between them and the knowledge that she could never have a child finished any romantic dreams that involved Alex – and Merle became involved with a new man.

Richard Hillary was an Australian, eight years her junior. He had been serving with the RAF and his face and body bore terrible witness to the agony he had suffered. Merle felt an overpowering sympathy and warmth towards him and in the weeks and months that they were together, Merle succeeded in restoring Richard Hillary's virility and in finding a rare and lasting love. They arranged to meet the following year but Hillary had found another girl – and then, in January 1943 – he was killed when he crashed in his aeroplane together with his navigator. Arthur Koestler told me that Richard Hillary, whom he knew well, had told him he could not endure his uselessness in the war and Koestler was convinced that Richard Hillary had committed suicide. Koestler and his wife committed suicide themselves when they found incurable disease too much to bear.

Meanwhile Alex was made a Knight Bachelor in reward for his services to the Crown and Merle watched as King George VI performed the ceremony at Buckingham Palace. It was perhaps the most exciting moment of her life; she was now Lady Korda. But soon she experienced those awful feelings of foreboding and doom again and this time it turned out to augur the death of her former lover, Leslie Howard, shot down in a Dutch plane on a journey from London to Lisbon. Merle was again deeply affected and then she learned that Alex, like herself, was suffering from a severe heart murmur.

The cameraman on *The Lodger* (1944) was to become Merle's next lover, a part-Cherokee Indian named Lucian Ballard. Much of this affair took place at Merle's beach house, Shangri-La but, in the midst of her physical happiness, she had to face social difficulties. Class snobbery has always existed in Hollywood and Merle found herself no longer being invited to parties given by people like Louis B. Mayer and Sam

Goldwyn. They, and many other big names in the film world, drew the line at entertaining a film cameraman. Although Merle was 'completely besotted' (as Louis B. Mayer's daughter put it) she realized that she would have to maintain some sort of standard as long as she was Lady Korda. Merle wrote to ask Alex for a divorce.

Eventually she obtained a divorce from Alex in Juarez, Mexico in June, 1945 and almost immediately she married Lucian Ballard. Three years later at a party on the Isle of Capri, accompanied by her husband, Merle met an Italian aristocrat, Count Giorgio Cini, who claimed direct descent from the Doges of Venice. Once she met a man to whom she was strongly attracted nothing and no one could stand in her way; and as Merle looked at Giorgio and he looked back at her, they both knew that what would follow was inevitable. Within an hour they were in bed together. Next day they disappeared to Rome where they occupied the royal suite at the Hotel Excelsior; then the couple flew to Hollywood, then back to Europe, to New York, Monte Carlo, Venice − and all the time Merle was desperately trying to get a quick divorce from Ballard.

In August 1949 the divorce went through. Meanwhile Count Giorgio had been trying desperately to overcome his family's opposition to film actress Merle. In September they were in France and Giorgio decided to fly to Venice for one last attempt to get the family on his side rather than marry without their consent, although Merle doubted whether that was possible. That evening Giorgio told Merle that a few days earlier he had been to see a fortune-teller who had warned him against flying. That night Merle, to her horror, recalled a story he had told her earlier: when he had been at school an astrologer had cast some of the students' horoscopes but he had refused Giorgio; later that evening one of Giorgio's friends had told him why. The astrologer had said: 'What is the point? In eleven years he will be dead. Why tell him? There is nothing he can do. It is in the stars.'

Merle had always been superstitious and deeply interested in mystical subjects, spiritualism and fortune-telling fascinated her and she had herself consulted many mediums over the years; she was completely convinced of survival after death and the foretelling of the future. Now she begged Giorgio to travel by

train and not to fly but he refused. Overcome by a premonition
at the airport Merle began to cry as Giorgio set off. Within
minutes one wing of the plane hit the top of a tree and snapped
off; the plane burst into flames and Giorgo died. Merle wanted
to die too. She screamed, she was hysterical, and she had to be
restrained from swallowing a fatal dose of pills. In her agony
Merle turned again to spiritualism on the advice of her friends
Mary Pickford, a convinced spiritualist, and Norma Shearer
who was deeply interested in the subject.

It was arranged that Lady Gillian Tomkins, whom Merle had
known for many years, would visit a medium in London under
an assumed name. Messages were received that Merle accepted
as originating from the dead Giorgio. She came to accept the
notion of life after death, saying at the time: 'Now I know that
Giorgio isn't really dead but alive in another world.'

As Merle approached forty she became more and more
obsessed with vitamin pills and dieting and ever more anxious
about showing any signs of ageing. She decided that she must
have a doctor with her on all her frequent travels and she was
delighted to make the acquaintance and then the deep and
lasting friendship of Dr Rex Ross, a fashionable Beverly Hills
physician. They soon became lovers and for a time they talked
of marriage. Dr Ross gave up his medical career in Hollywood
and was Merle's constant companion for the next five years.

At the end of 1955 Merle was saddened to hear that Alex's
heart condition had deteriorated and she discovered that he
had never forgotten her and that he kept many mementoes of
their years together. She rushed to be by his side. The end was
difficult and protracted. After suffering a severe heart attack
somehow Alex survived and seemed to cling desperately to life
until, eventually, it all became too much trouble and suffering;
he gave up and died in June 1956. Korda's biographer Paul
Tabori told me: 'He wasn't a happy man; but I believe he was
a great man.' Merle would have agreed with that sentiment.

Back in Hollywood later that year Merle accepted, on
impulse, an invitation from Conrad Hilton to attend the grand
opening of the Mexico Hilton Hotel and at the lavish reception
she found herself considerably attracted by Bruno Pagliai, one
of the richest men in South America. A few weeks later Bruno
invited Merle to a New Year's Eve party at his fabulous mansion
in Mexico City.

They were married in Italy on 28 July 1957 and she and Bruno decided to adopt a baby boy and a baby girl from orphanages in Italy. Little Bruno and Francesca began to grow up at Bruno's second home in Cuernavaca, once the palace of Hernando Cortez, the Spanish conquistador. As soon as she entered the place, Merle, always psychic to a degree, knew that the house was haunted.

Many people over the years had been aware of presences in the house; there was in particular an inexplicable coldness in some areas, there were on occasions loud knockings that had no rational explanation, and sometimes the figure of a young soldier had been glimpsed in the vicinity of a very old wall. Merle had the wall taken apart and within a hollow cavity the skeleton of a man was discovered. Thereafter the hauntings were less active.

Unfortunately Merle found the altitude of Cuernavaca distressing; she found it difficult to breathe there, especially at night and on top of this she frequently found herself alone in the great house since Bruno was involved in business activities all over the world. Signora Merle Pagliai began to return to her house in Bel Air from time to time and once, when she was there with the children, she suddenly found herself inexplicably distressed with that awful feeling of foreboding that she knew all too well. Minutes later a fire was discovered, sparks from one of the chimneys having ignited the roof. Fanned by April winds the fire spread rapidly to the rest of the house and Merle fled into the garden clutching the terrified children, sparks literally chasing them. Merle lost dozens of her beautiful dresses, many of her valuable paintings and much of her valued personal correspondence. The house was rebuilt but Merle sold it as soon as it was complete again and bought a splendid house on La Ladera Drive in the Holmby Hills.

By 1960, when she was approaching 50, nothing she did could hide the tell-tale lines that began to form around her eyes and mouth although her forehead remained completely free. Inevitably her neck and hands began to look like those of a woman of her age. As she worried about approaching old age she heard about Dr Paul Niehan's rejuvenation treatments in Switzerland. She went there for the first time in the summer of 1960 and many times after that for booster treatments. She found it wonderful: her skin glowed, her body became tight and strong, the strands of grey hair disappeared and she felt better than she had felt for many years. Of course the treatment did nothing for her heart condition; in fact, by increasing her desire for activity, it tended to put strain on the heart.

In 1966 Merle decided to appear in the film of the bestselling novel, *Hotel* (1967) by Arthur Hailey but it proved to be a traumatic experience. Merle seemed to have lost her way and at times she overacted terribly and in one scene the director, Richard Quine, was unable to get the effect he wanted and he decided to give up. He said they could do without the scene but Merle was immediately up in arms and demanded that the scene be left in. It was cut from the film and when Merle attended the première she walked out and never forgave Quine. She invested all the money she had made from *Hotel* in a playground for an orphanage in Acapulco. She adored children and later built a library there; she also laid out beautiful grounds and made a deal with Pepsi Cola that they would maintain the grounds permanently after her death.

Noël Coward invited Merle to participate in his 70th birthday celebrations in London and at the end of 1969, side by side, Merle and Noël opened the Noël Coward Bar at the Phoenix Theatre and then Coward lectured at the National Film Theatre (where, a month earlier, I had introduced an All-Night Horror Homage to Boris Karloff who had died earlier that year. After spending fifty years in America and many of them in Hollywood, Karloff returned to the land of his birth to die.) Next Noël attended a Midnight Matinee, rehearsed by Wendy Toye, when the whole audience at the Phoenix Theatre, including Princess Margaret and Lord Snowdon sang 'Happy Birthday' and the day after they attended a Birthday Luncheon at Clarence House with the Queen and Princess Margaret. For Coward it was 'the crowning point of his life as a great English playwright'; for Merle it seemed to provide indisputable proof that she was the queen of international society. Two weeks later Noël was knighted in the New Year's Honours List and his fellow knights in the theatrical profession were particularly pleased. As Sir Alec Guinness put it: 'We have been like a row of teeth with a front tooth missing. Now we can smile again!'

Back in Acapulco Merle saw less and less of Bruno. She was approaching 60, Francesca and Little Bruno were in their teens, their schooling divided between Mexico and California and in their holidays Merle took them to England, Italy, France, Greece and she took them to meet her friends Prince Philip and Prince Charles.

With the arrival of the 1970s Merle began to withdraw from society and she began to say that she no longer enjoyed parties. She disliked rock 'n' roll music, she disliked tight jeans and unisex clothing, she disliked the coarseness of life and the way it was depicted on television. By now her marriage to Bruno Pagliai was over and soon they were divorced but not before Merle had met her fourth and final husband, a would-be actor Robert Wolders, a Dutchman and executive of KLM, the Dutch airline, 25 years younger than Merle.

Robert and Merle were thrown together by her friends and she loved his soft speech, his gentleness, his courtesy and his natural grace and good looks. He was equally attracted to Merle and they soon became lovers. In 1972 Merle began work (with Robert Wolders opposite her) in her last film *Interval* (1973), made in Mexico. She was never happy with the way she looked and when the film was completed she supervised the exhaustive work of cutting – and probably ruined the film in the process. The worst reviews were kept from Merle's eyes and she lost close to a million dollars; Bruno lost a great deal more. Merle and Robert took off on a trip to Alaska before cruising to the Orient and Europe. In 1975 they married.

At the age of 64 and back in Hollywood, Merle had a premonition of her approaching death. Her heart murmur began to be more pronounced and she had the distinct feeling that she would not live to see her 70th year. She began to part with material possessions that had once meant so much to her, including a house in Acapulco on which she had lavished considerable loving attention and not a little money.

During their first few years together Merle and Robert lived in a modest house near Coldwater Canyon where Merle's conversation often turned to such matters as the probability of life after death. Merle was utterly convinced of the reality of some form of life hereafter and she was anxious to devise some way to reach Robert after she had passed on; but in any case, she said time and time again, they would eventually be together again.

They travelled again: the South Seas, England and Australia, stopping at Honolulu, for Merle was feeling far from well. Shortly after returning home to Malibu Merle collapsed; she put it down to fatigue after 19 hours of flying but a few weeks later she experienced chest pains and she was admitted to Cedars Sinai Medical Centre for catheterization, an exploration necessary to establish the severity of her condition.

She remained in hospital for ten days and then she had by-pass surgery, on 14 November 1978, an operation that took eight hours. Afterwards came the long and painful recuperation; Merle endured it all without complaint. Sadly when the enormous black stitches that stretched from the top of her breast bone to her navel were removed, instead of the hoped-for red lines on her flesh, the specialists saw the dreaded post-operative legacy: keloids – scarlet raised cables that burned excruciatingly.

In the weeks that followed Merle suffered intense pain from the keloids; and every time she saw her body in the bathroom mirror it was like a knife in her heart. Long days and even longer nights passed but there seemed to be little improvement and Merle felt weaker and weaker and shorter and shorter of breath. Through all this Robert Wolders worked devotedly at her side, never showing his great grief, watching her every need and doing everything he possibly could to help her. Once, when things became too difficult to bear, Merle subjected herself to the dreaded steroids.

As Robert waited for her in a nearby room he suddenly heard the most terrible and heart-rending screams that he had ever heard. He clapped his hands over his ears to try to block out the awful sounds. Afterwards, in the car going home, Merle took his hand very sweetly and said, 'I'm afraid that was me, darling.'

Despite all the suffering Merle did not recover as she should have done and as everyone hoped against hope that she would. She forced herself to travel to one or two functions but everyone said how frail she looked. Back home Robert became worried about being unable to get to a hospital quickly from the house in Malibu if Merle should have another attack and they decided to buy a house in Beverly Hills.

On 25 November 1979 Little Bruno was paying them a visit. His sister Francesca, by this time married, was in Mexico City. Both had a distinct premonition that morning that something awful was about to happen.

After lunch Bruno went to Santa Monica to see a movie and

in the late afternoon Merle and Robert walked along the beach and saw the sunset. It was all very peaceful and Merle seemed fine. She and Robert had not occupied the same bedroom for a year following the operation but they decided to go to bed early that night. Robert told Merle's biographers that Merle went to her room and he went to his. He felt terrible, drained, sick and exhausted, and after drifting off to sleep, he awoke suddenly with the knowledge that Merle was in the room and then he heard her voice. Although it seemed unreal, muffled somehow he heard the words: 'Darling, I love you so much; thank you for the happiest years of my life.'

Robert still felt so sick that to this day he is not sure whether he answered or not but he felt that Merle then went back to her room. Suddenly her bell sounded and he rushed into her room. She was in the middle of convulsions. Bruno suddenly appeared. He had been watching the film when he had an overwhelming feeling that something was wrong and he had rushed back. Neither he nor Robert could find the oxygen tube that had been provided for such an emergency but they had a spare one in the car and Robert rushed to get it while Bruno telephoned for a doctor. As the doctor arrived Merle called out to Robert that she had lost all feeling in her face. The convulsions continued and Bruno remained calm and held Merle's tongue so that she wouldn't bite it; and at last they managed to get the oxygen machine on. An ambulance arrived and Merle was carried out, hovering between life and death. An immediate brain scan showed that Merle has suffered a stroke and that a blood vessel had burst and had leaked into the brain.

Merle was technically dead before she reached hospital but the doctors kept her alive long enough to allow Francesca to see her and the next day, 26 November 1979, at exactly three o'clock in the afternoon, the doctors allowed Merle to pass peacefully from this world into the next.

As Merle's biographers have said, her death left a gap in the lives of many people and nobody who knew her was unaffected by her charm and beauty. It can truly be said of Merle Oberon that we shall never see her like again.

Stan Laurel
and Oliver Hardy

-

Another Fine Mess

Laurel and Hardy are the personification of movie comedy at its best. A slim Englishman Stan Laurel, accidentally teamed up with a tubby American Oliver Hardy, and it all began. They were the best film comedians in the days of silent short movies and they triumphantly made the change to sound. The love and care they poured into their pictures reflects their declared one aim in life: to make people laugh; they did so for nearly a quarter of a century in well over a hundred films and they will continue to do so as long as films exist.

Stan Laurel, whose real name was Arthur Stanley Jefferson, was born in a small bedroom at 3 Foundry Cottages (later renamed Argyle Street), Ulverston, a few miles from beautiful Lake Windermere on the north-west coast of England. The house is marked by a small plaque. In actual fact the house was the home of Stan's maternal grandparents who brought the boy up for the best part of his early years and he always looked back with great affection on his grandparents.

Stan was born into a theatrical family, his father 'A.J.' Jefferson was quite a well-known actor, playwright and theatre manager while his mother, Margaret Jefferson, was an actress of considerable experience. Stan Laurel may have followed his parents on to the professional stage at the early age of ten, in a gala show to celebrate the relief of Mafeking but his first real professional engagement was at the age of 16 at a small music hall where he was billed as 'Stan Jefferson – He of the Funny Ways'.

Early in his career he shared the stage with another great

comedy star, 'Wee Georgie Wood', with whom Stan remained friends for the rest of his life. George Wood was a member of my London Club and I often talked with him about Stan. He would show me letters he had received from Stan who always found time for his friends.

When he was 17 Stan left home to tour with a company of young actors performing parodies of well-known plays and on at least one occasion he shared the stage with another 17-year-old called Charlie Chaplin. When the opportunity presented itself Stan worked as a single act. One thing led to another and one day he was 'discovered' by the successful music-hall impresario of the day, Fred Karno, and Stan became part of the Karno Company where he again found himself in the company of Charlie Chaplin.

Chaplin does not so much as mention Stan Laurel in his lengthy autobiography but Chaplin was very conscious of possible rivals and he could hardly have been unaware of Stan's comic abilities. Towards the end of his life I met Charlie Chaplin briefly and talked to him about Stan Laurel but he professed to remember very little about Stan and hurriedly changed the subject. He became very silent and seemed lost in deep thought. Not knowing the reason for this sudden change in his attitude, I asked him what his plans were for the future, expecting him to outline some new film or other project. Instead he said: 'You know, the older you get, the more you wonder about how you will die', which I thought rather sad.

During their 1947 tour of Britain Stan Laurel became friendly with the spiritualist journalist Hannen Swaffer, who knew Chaplin, and he asked Stan to take to Chaplin in Hollywood a signed copy of his latest book. When he returned to Los Angeles Stan thought he would mail the book and then he thought he would call personally; although they had barely seen each other all the years they had both been in the States, Stan still remembered Chaplin with affection and he duly called at Chaplin's home in Beverly Hills, intending to give him the book and chat for a few moments. In the event Chaplin seemed delighted to see him and the call stretched into seven hours! Afterwards Stan wrote to Chaplin several times but he never had a reply and he never saw him again.

Very early in his career Stan borrowed comic routines, gestures and attitudes from the great Dan Leno who, like many comics, was in reality a tragic figure who had difficulties coming to terms with his limited acting ability and who died an unhappy man. If one is inclined to believe in such things a strong case can be made out for the influence of Dan Leno from beyond the grave. He died in 1904, shortly before Stan's initial appearance on the professional stage. Comedian Peter Sellers always believed that Leno orchestrated his career and there seems little doubt that Dan Leno's image has been seen in his old dressing room at the Drury Lane Theatre by a number of noted performers, including Noël Coward and Stanley Lupino.

Stan travelled to America in the first place with the touring Karno Company and they arrived in Los Angeles before Hollywood existed as a movie centre, although a few scattered 'studios' were already benefiting from the wonderful and reliable Californian sunshine. Stan fell in love with the whole place, little thinking that one day he would settle permanently in the vicinity.

Self-effacing on screen Stan may have been but on the film set Stan was known for sometimes throwing his weight about and it has been suggested that being the one who always messed things up and who was always the recipient of slaps and kicks of all kinds on screen, in private life he rather felt that society owed him an apology. Not that he was a snob, he wasn't; and those who knew him best – writers, directors and film crews with whom he spent a lot of time when he was not actually appearing in films – went as far as to say that he sometimes exhibited what amounted to inverted snobbery in that he went to great lengths to show that he had no pretensions.

Stan seems to have mistrusted women for most of his life although he was always pursuing them and one writer suggested that it is 'something of a wonder that the scandals surrounding Stan's affairs with the ladies did not seriously cripple his screen career'. In fact Hal Roach and his associates, for whom Laurel and Hardy worked for many years, are said to have kept a fat folder detailing Stan's sexual indiscretions which they used to control the huge earnings the pair could have demanded and accumulated had they been independent film-makers like Chaplin and Harold Lloyd. What is indisputable is that Stan was all but overwhelmed by ex-wives and mistresses seeking alimony and settlements and he was not always successful in keeping these activities out of the newspapers.

During his early days in America Stan became enamoured of a somewhat formidable married lady called Mae Dahberg with whom he seems to have lived in disharmony for some years, Mae calling herself Mrs Stan Jefferson. One day Stan, always extremely superstitious, realized that the words 'Stan Jefferson' comprised thirteen letters; at the same time his eye caught a picture of a Roman wearing a laurel wreath and he suddenly caught on to the word 'laurel' and so 'Stan Laurel' was born. Years later Mae was to claim that she and Stan went through a form of common-law marriage ceremony while Stan denied that he had ever been emotionally involved with her!

In fact Stan married four different women in five ceremonies (possibly six): Lois Neilson in August 1926, by whom he had Lois Junior in 1928; Virginia Ruth Rogers in April 1934 (although he was not officially divorced from Lois until October 1934); Illeanor Shuvalova in January, 1938 (a stormy marriage that lasted until May 1939); he then remarried Virginia Ruth Rogers and, in a different ceremony, did so again in 1941, but the marriage still did not last. Finally in 1946 he married opera singer Ida Kitaeva Raphael and it is good to know that she remained with him for the rest of his life and that in his latter years Stan found something like an ideal marriage.

Almost as soon as he became involved in films Stan began to acquire the technical knowledge necessary to put a film together and he also soon mastered direction, camera-work, editing and story construction; all knowledge and experience that stood him in good stead in the years that lay ahead when he would be the one who was involved in every aspect of the Laurel and Hardy films, while Ollie was off playing golf or practising cookery, two of his favourite pastimes.

Some of Laurel and Hardy's best two-reeler silent movies were written and directed by Clyde Bruckman, regarded by many students of the silent screen as a key figure in the history of American screen comedy. Especially memorable are *Putting the Pants on Philip* (1927) which included some outrageous homosexual jokes and *The Battle of the Century* (1927) which contained one of the best-ever custard-pie sequences. Bruckman's other Laurel and Hardy films were *Call of the Cuckoos* (1927) and *Leave 'em Laughing* (1928). Within a few years Bruckman lost out to alcoholism and for years he was a familiar and pathetic sight around Hollywood, more than a little drunk. In 1955 he borrowed a pistol from Buster Keaton, for whom he had been writing scripts, left a note for his wife saying he did not want to make a mess in her living room, went into a café on Santa Monica Boulevard and blew his brains out.

During his early years in Hollywood Stan made a number of short comedies and then he appeared in a two-reeler called *Lucky Dog* (1917) where the overweight and moustachioed villain of the piece was a man named Oliver Norvell Hardy. A few years later Stan was directing a comedy *Get 'em Young* (1926) with the same Oliver Hardy, or rather 'Ollie' or 'Babe' as he was invariably known to everyone in the studios, playing a butler. Ollie scalded himself badly at home while doing some cooking and he was unable to work for a time. Stan stepped in and took over the role. By the time Ollie returned, fit and well, some weeks later, Roach had decided to cast him with Stan in a silent film eventually called *Duck Soup* (1927); the first of the real Laurel and Hardy films. Stan was not entirely happy with the film, which he wrote, and in 1930 he re-made the story with sound, called it *Another Fine Mess* with a fade-out line that was to become immortal in movie history, as Ollie says to Stan: 'Here's another fine mess you've gotten us into!'

The unique way in which the two comedians scored off each other and worked as a team was apparent from the start and the 104 films the pair were to make (silent and sound, two-reelers, three-reelers and hour-plus films) during their 29 years together were to give endless enjoyment and pleasure to millions and become the supreme embodiment of comedy for probably as long as films exist. Curiously the couple themselves were almost completely unaware of their great popularity until their first European tour in 1932.

Off the set the two were friends but their priorities were just about as opposite as they could be. Once filming was over Ollie got into his car and forgot movie-making; Stan, on the other hand, would invariably remain in the studios, sit through the rushes, decide on the retakes, improve the smallest weaknesses and iron out any difficulties. Often he would stay at the studios long into the night and be back there before Ollie in the morning. Not that it was all work and no play for Stan and more often than not a giggling girl would be with him in the darkened screening-room.

Ollie was born Norvell Hardy on 18 January 1892 at Harlem, Georgia, weighing a hefty 14 lbs and already having the enormous hands that were one of his characteristics all his life. The name Oliver was added after the death of his father, a farmer and hotel manager – and veteran of the Civil War. Ollie came from English stock and claimed connections with the Hardy who sailed with Nelson.

When he was 18 years of age Ollie became a projectionist at one of the very first movie theatres, in Milledgeville, Georgia. In 1913 he married a pianist Madelyn Saloshin and the marriage lasted for seven years. His second marriage was to a film actress Myrtle Lee Reeves in 1921 and it lasted until 1937.

During the making of *The Flying Deuces* (1939) Ollie fell passionately in love with the film's script girl, Lucille Jones and he finally won her heart and in 1940 she became the third and last Mrs Oliver Hardy.

Ollie and his second wife Myrtle Lee bought a small estate on North Alton Drive in Beverly Hills and for a time Stan and his then current wife lived at 718 North Bedford Drive, less than a mile away. In the same year as the birth of his only daughter, Alice Ardell came into Stan's life; she was a beautiful, auburn-haired girl with an intriguing French accent and their relationship lasted for more than ten years. Alice was not interested in marriage and enjoyed the admiration of several men at the same time but she and Stan seemed to have found something special and through three marriages, when things built up and became unbearable, he sought and found refuge and relief with Alice.

Perhaps understandably Stan's wife lost a lot of her sweetness when she was forced to contend with Stan's increasingly prolonged drinking bouts, his strange and utter silences that sometimes lasted for days, and the not infrequent whispers and indisputable evidence of his dalliance with other women.

Real sadness entered Stan's life with the arrival of his son, Stanley Robert Jefferson, who was born in Hollywood Hospital on 7 May 1930, two months premature. On the child's sixth day of life haemorrhaging began in the brain and faced with a mentally deficient child, if it survived, Stan went home and drank himself stupid. Three days later, on 16 May, the child died. Stan, who hated funerals and hardly ever went to one (he didn't even go to Ollie's) insisted on cremation and tried to erase the sorry episode from his mind.

Stan and Ollie continued to make many very successful shorts. After receiving an Academy Award for *The Music Box* (1932) they sailed for England. Ollie was accompanied by his wife Myrtle, who was close to a breakdown over her husband's affair with a woman named Viola Morse. Ollie had set her up in a comfortable house and had more or less moved in himself. Lois, too upset with the bleak future she saw for Stan and herself, stayed at home.

Everywhere they went Laurel and Hardy were mobbed beyond their wildest dreams and they were both quite glad eventually to board ship to return to America. One evening a girl knocked on the door of Stan's private state-room and asked for his autograph. He invited her in and learned that her name was Renée and that she came from Houston. When Lois met the boat in New York, hoping no doubt that absence had made Stan's heart grow fonder, she immediately sensed a difference in him and asked whether there was another woman. 'Yes,' Stan told her. 'I met a French girl and I think I'm in love with her.'

By this time Lois was unshockable and, according to Stan's biographer, Fred Lawrence Guiles, she suggested to Stan that he get the young woman an apartment and live with her until he was tired of her. She also suggested that Renée be found work as an extra at the studio so that she could contribute to the cost! Stan followed her advice on both scores. Within a few months Stan did tire of Renée and seems to have made a definite attempt at reconciliation with Lois. He never had any intention of marrying Renée, he told her; 'How could I marry a girl who'd sleep with me the first night I met her?'

For a while Stan and Lois and Lois Junior seemed to be putting things together and then, gradually but unmistakably, Stan began to suffer long bouts of moodiness and he again got into the habit of disappearing into the night with his gold-lettered overnight bag and Lois knew he had gone to spend the night and probably longer with Alice.

Once Stan came home sobbing and mumbling that there was something terribly wrong with his mind. Lois discovered that he had somehow got hold of the idea that people who could not help having unmeaningful sexual adventures must be 'out of their minds'. A psychiatrist examined him over a period of several weeks and came to the conclusion that Stan was over-tired and had a poor tolerance for alcohol but he was certainly not mad. Eventually Lois decided that she had had enough and, faced with the inevitable, Stan gave Alice up – only to become involved with another girl almost immediately.

Stan and Lois and their daughter moved out of their house and took a suite at the Beverly Wilshire Hotel, attempting a new start, but somehow it was all too late; things could never be the same between them and the lawyers were called in. Lois got the Beverly Hills home, two $100,000 trust funds, and support for herself and five-year-old Lois Junior. Thanks to her undoubted business sense this generous settlement eventually became more than a million dollars, making Lois by far the wealthiest of Stan Laurel's former wives.

In some ways Stan must have been relieved to see the end of his marriage to Lois, although he told many people that he had lost all he really cared about when he lost Lois. Be that as it may the next film he made, *Fra Diavolo* (1933), was one of the most successful of all Laurel and Hardy films in commercial terms and probably the best comic opera ever made into a film.

After *Fra Diavolo* Stan and a companion, Bill Seiter (director of *Sons of the Desert*, 1933) were sailing off Catalina Island when they waved to a couple of pretty girls making the crossing on a steamer. The girls were Virginia Ruth Rogers, a beautiful blonde widow of twenty-nine and her friend Gladys. Since they did not receive a brush-off the two men were waiting to greet the girls when the ship docked. They all had lunch together on the men's sloop and Stan quickly became friendly with the very attractive Ruth, mentioning in passing that he was in the process of getting a divorce. It was not until some tourists passed and some children recognized Stan and called out to him, that it dawned on Ruth and Gladys whom they were being entertained by.

Such was the beginning of the relationship between Stan and Ruth Rogers, regarded by people who should know as the most significant of all Stan's feminine conquests; he could not have known that immediately ahead of him were the finest achievements of his career and undoubtedly Stan's three-year marriage to Ruth was a relaxing and beneficial time for him.

Usually Ruth stayed out of the way and did not interfere with Stan's professional work, although it has to be said that *Way Out West* (1937), directed by Stan, might never have been made had she not kept saying that he and Ollie should make a Western. It turned out to be their most successful film since *Fra Diavolo* and among the several songs in the film Laurel and Hardy sang was the one most associated with them: 'In the Blue Ridge Mountains of Virginia, On the Trail of the Lonesome Pine'. Sadly and perhaps unfairly, Ruth was no longer a part of Stan's life when the film was eventually released.

While Stan and Ollie went their infectiously humorous way in such films as *Them Thar Hills* (1933) and the remarkable *Babes in Toyland* (1934) Ruth ran a successful dress shop. Stan was still not legally divorced when he met Ruth and his vast earnings (something like $4,000 a week) were being steadily eaten up by legal fees and the huge settlements he was forced to make, so there could be no possibility of another marriage for the time being.

All this was hard on Stan who might be moody or angry or unnaturally silent by turns and one day Ruth had an urgent call from Stan's lawyer, Ben Shipman, asking her to go at once to the Roosevelt Hotel where Stan was threatening to jump from a window. Ruth hurried to the hotel and as soon as she walked into the room where Stan was perched on the window sill, he seemed to snap back to normality. He and Ruth had a pleasant lunch at the hotel and the episode was forgotten.

Having lost the Bedford Drive house to Lois, Stan rented a house on Palm Drive in Beverly Hills where his brother Teddy and his wife Betty joined him. Within a few weeks Teddy complained of severe toothache and Stan suggested he consult a dentist he knew personally. Teddy was given an anaesthetic in preparation for an extraction and died from heart failure in the dentist's chair.

Ruth helped Stan with the funeral arrangements and although, predictably, Stan dodged the funeral service, he invited the mourners back to his house for drinks and it was at this time that Stan revealed in public his firm belief in reincarnation, arguing forcefully on the basis of such mysteries as child performers and infant musical geniuses.

The night of Teddy's funeral could almost have been taken from a Laurel and Hardy comedy. Ruth, having acted as hostess at the after-funeral reception, left for home but torrential rain caused her to turn back. There she found Stan, still drinking heavily, but more than a little relieved to see her. 'I'm having trouble with Betty,' he said, referring to Teddy's very recent widow. 'She told me to forget about you; said she'd be my sweetheart — and she's been trying to get into bed with me. I hope you can stay the night?'

Ruth stayed the night (there were four other bedrooms in the house) and in the morning Stan told Betty Jefferson she must find other accommodation immediately and he helped her financially to do so.

Stan was by this time drinking heavily with some regularity and sometimes he acted violently. On one occasion he chased Ruth from room to room with a carving knife until a friend arrived and took Ruth home. He was appearing in *Sons of the Desert* at the time and on several occasions he was too drunk to turn up for work and his friend and director Bill Seiter was forced to shoot sequences that did not require Stan, sometimes for days at a time, until Stan was fit for work again.

When *Sons of the Desert* was finally completed Stan and Ruth were married by a Mexican Justice of the Peace at Aguascalientes in Mexico. They found a small Mediterranean-style house in Glenbar Avenue, Cheviot Hills, a comparatively new development of luxury homes outside Culver City and there, for a time, there was order and comfort in Stan's life. In the years to come they were to be married twice more.

Initially the marriage seems to have been a lot of fun and, when they knew Ruth could not have children, the couple talked of adopting a child but nothing came of the idea. Meanwhile Lois Junior visited them regularly. In fact Ruth became very fond of Little Lois (as she was sometimes called) and they remained friends always, Ruth leaving her most of Stan's estate when she died in 1976.

After less than two years Stan's roving eye lighted on a 19-year-old girl. Ruth soon learned of the affair and in the heat of the moment she picked up a riding crop and set out to surprise the couple. Once again it could have been a Laurel and Hardy comedy. At the house Ruth was met by the girl's grandmother who informed Ruth, not knowing who she was, that Stan was indeed inside the house and he was engaged to be married to her granddaughter! Ruth shouted to Stan to come out of the house and take his medicine but Stan remained out of sight and eventually Ruth went home.

In 1935 the final decree in the divorce of Lois and Stan came through and Stan and Ruth made their marriage absolutely legal by marrying again. Work then started on *The Bohemian Girl* (1936), prompted by the success of their previous operetta, *Fra Diavolo*. Thelma Todd was again the leading lady but when she was found dead, after the film was completed (see Chapter 4), Stan decreed that most of the footage in which she appeared should be deleted. He felt it would be morbid to leave her in as one of the stars of the film, 'in view of what had happened'. His superstitious nature was probably working overtime and telling him it would be unlucky to have a suicide, if suicide it was, in one of his pictures.

1936 saw Laurel and Hardy as two unsuccessful hitchhikers in *On the Wrong Track*, cameo roles in a vehicle for Charlie Chase who starred and also directed the film. He was to die in Hollywood five years later from a heart attack. With hindsight it can be said that 1936 and 1937 were the highlight years in the careers of Stan Laurel and Oliver Hardy. For whatever reason (and many have been suggested) from 1938 onwards it was downhill all the way for Laurel and Hardy.

In the marriage stakes things began to go the usual way for Stan. Ruth had by now got used to the sight of Stan's back as he hurried out of the door carrying his black bag. At such times she knew he was likely to be gone for several days. But one evening she decided enough was enough and she walked out too.

Stan left Hollywood and travelled around for some weeks, spending time in New York before returning home where he found Ruth had not only moved out, but had taken the house with her – every stick of furniture, every rug and curtain, every ornament and utensil was gone; his home was completely empty. He folded up and wept.

On Christmas Eve 1936 a divorce settlement was signed by both Stan and Ruth whereby she was to receive 5 per cent of all his future earnings until her death or remarriage. Ruth also had the house, two of their three cars and an annuity for the rest of her life together with a bank account totalling $17,000 and also some real estate. Stan had to face the fact that for a second time in less than four years he had been taken to the cleaners in no uncertain way by a wife.

Before long Stan was visiting his ex-wife in her new home at Hancock Place, furnished with things from their old home and he became jealous when he learned that Ruth was seeing other men. 'You're too nice a girl for that,' he told her and somewhat surprisingly Ruth agreed not to see any of Stan's friends or anyone Ollie knew or anyone from the studio. When she found that one lonely evening followed another, she told Stan she had decided to leave Hollywood for a time and visit relatives in Kansas City. Stan said he would go along too and he went!

The newspapers got hold of the story and said the couple were on a 'second honeymoon'. Stan felt that Ruth's lawyers were probably responsible for the story and he was all for leaving but in the end it was Ruth who left and Stan stayed on with Ruth's relatives − yet again it could have been a scene from a comedy film!

Around this time Stan ran into difficulties with the tax authorities and he asked Ruth to help with a loan; she immediately agreed but then suddenly all communications with Ruth ceased for Stan had met an impressive Russian singer, a statuesque blonde named Illeana Shuvalova.

In December 1937 there was more trouble for Stan and this time from an unexpected quarter. His early lover for several years, Mae Laurel (as she called herself) after a decade of silence, suddenly sued Stan for maintenance, claiming that they had been common-law man and wife for nearly ten years. In the event Mae Laurel's case was settled out of court but at the same time Ruth obtained $750 temporary alimony, which Stan could ill afford as he had recently acquired a Mexican canning company. Mae left Hollywood, remarried and eventually died in a nursing home in 1969.

On New Year's Day 1938 Stan married the redoubtable Illeana in Yuma, Arizona and yet again the event might have been part of a comedy script. When Ruth, on holiday in Phoenix, heard on the radio that Stan planned to marry 'a Russian countess' she immediately contacted her attorney and, notwithstanding the seven-page carefully detailed divorce agreement between her and Stan dated 24 December 1936 which was extremely generous to Ruth, she maintained that the divorce was not legal.

Ruth sent a cable to Stan at his apartment on Franklin Avenue, informing him that she was on her way to Yuma to stop the wedding. 'Sober up', she told him. 'I am your wife Mrs Stan Laurel.' By the time the wire reached Stan, he and Illeana were already married and had returned to Los Angeles while Ruth was booked into the Del Sol Hotel, Yuma, where Stan and Illeana had recently vacated the honeymoon suite! Stan immediately sent Ruth a reply which did not hide his obvious annoyance. 'Divorce papers perfectly legal. Defy you or anyone to prove otherwise. Why don't you sober up. You are not my wife or ever will be. I am very happy now so please leave me alone.'

But within weeks Stan began to wonder what he had taken on in marrying the fiery Illeana. He discovered that her 'title' was dubious to say the least and her background, which included an eight-year-old son and a somewhat curious mother, was distinctly murky. Illeana was lively and unpredictable and she usually produced fireworks wherever she went. In night clubs and restaurants she would suddenly burst into a song and become wild and unmanageable and drink too much for her own good; several times she was arrested – and sang all the way to jail! Soon she was ordered to leave Beverly Hills for persistent public drunkenness and stories began to circulate that she had been arrested in the past for persistent prostitution and that she had been deported from Hong Kong; most of these stories Stan discovered to be based on fact.

That first summer together (in fact their only summer together) Stan and Illeana and her mother moved to a small and rather run-down cottage in Canoga Park. Stan probably hoped that away from the frantic life of busy Los Angeles and her overbearing Russian friends – bogus royalty and the like – he might be able to save the already foundering marriage, but these strange people would turn up at all hours and often stay for days at a time, disrupting Stan's quiet routine. In the end he took to the bottle again and was soon drinking to a really alarming degree.

Still Stan tried to preserve his marriage and at the same time keep some sort of privacy for himself. He built a high wall around the property and called the place Fort Laurel. By this time Illeana claimed that incessant telephone calls from Ruth were driving her to the brink of a breakdown. In April a restraining order forced Ruth to stop pestering Stan and Illeana with her stories of an impending reconciliation and urging him to come to his senses and return to her. Ruth's wishful thinking turned to reality in her mind and she continued in such fantasies for the rest of her life.

Alongside these and other devastating assaults on his private life Stan continued to play enduring comedies with Ollie; indeed some vintage features were made at this time, *Swiss Miss* and *Block-Heads* (both 1938) to be followed by *The Flying Deuces* (1939), *A Chump at Oxford* (which saw Stan in his only real change of personality in more than a hundred films) and *Saps at Sea* (both 1940).

By the time *Block-Heads* was on the screens all semblance of peace for Stan and Illeana dissipated. After a fight that lasted practically all one day Illeana went out with friends in the evening and Stan was preparing a meal for himself when a thug broke into the house, attacked Stan, forcing him to open the safe, and made off with some $10,000 in cash. Stan only noticed that his assailant had very dark hair but rumour has it that the culprit was Illeana's husband, Shuvalova, whom she had never bothered to divorce. It certainly seems to have been the work of someone in the know for the intruder not only knew that there was a large amount of cash in the safe that particular day but knew of the safe's whereabouts and only needed Stan to open it.

When Stan came to his senses the thug had gone and Stan in what could have been yet one more scenario for a farce, raced outside, jumped into his car and set off to pursue the thief – and nearly crashed into a police car as he raced along the dark street on the wrong side of the road! Arrested for driving a car while drunk, Stan spent the only night of his life in a real jail. Always the gentleman and invariably protective to those with whom he was emotionally involved, Stan said that Illeana was so late that he had become worried and went to look for her – but in private he admitted that Shuvalova had been threatening him.

Incidentally one of the technical crew on *A Chump at Oxford* (whose cast included Peter Cushing), was James Parrott, brother of comedian Charlie Chase. Parrott had co-written and directed many of the Laurel and Hardy films and was found dead in Hollywood when the film was still incomplete.

Stan now ran into more personal difficulties. He decided to sue the Roach Studios for $700,000, $200,000 due to him and $500,000 damages. During the legal tussle Fort Laurel lived up to its name with the gates locked and Stan hiding from the world and producing a cross between a potato and an onion (which nobody would eat!) and ducks that had no voice. Eventually Roach Studios said Stan had been 'uncooperative and had violated the morals clause of his contract'. He had 'brought himself into ridicule and contempt and failed to have regard for public conventions and morals and had shocked and offended public morals and decency'. Stan was visibly shocked at these charges. He had always regarded himself as a very moral person and he certainly believed in marriage, perhaps too firmly for his own good.

Thinking it over, Stan could see the damage his wives had done to him with their headline divorces and subsequent activities; first Mae, then Lois, then Ruth and now Illeana. He knew the Laurel and Hardy films were popular and successful but he felt jinxed by women — but not for any longer, he vowed. He ceased escorting Illeana to parties and became something of a recluse, shutting himself up alone at Fort Laurel for days on end. By the spring of 1939 he was practically broke: he had not made a picture for over a year and the word, true or not, that he was 'difficult' spread through the studios. The gossip columnists even said there was a rift between Stan and Ollie which was certainly not true; in fact Ollie was at Fort Laurel very often to help and reassure Stan in those difficult days. Stan had earned well over a million and a half dollars in the thirteen years he had worked at the Roach Studios; now it had all gone, most of it to his ex-wives.

In May 1939 Stan divorced Illeana. For eighteen months she had turned Stan's life inside out and severely damaged his standing in the film community. After the divorce Illeana Shuvalova drifted into acute alcoholism and drug addiction; her liver became affected and she died before reaching her 45th birthday.

In his near paranoid depression Stan saw the emergence of Bud Abbott and Lou Costello who borrowed a lot of their act from Laurel and Hardy; and one night at the start of the Second World War he telephoned Ruth and asked her to go back to him. Although she agreed to do so, she found him subject to moods of deep depression and things were difficult between them. Sometimes at dinner parties Stan would not say a single word from beginning to end. Soon there was a resumption of the walk-outs with the black overnight bag, but nevertheless Stan and Ruth remarried in 1941 in Las Vegas and for a while the horizon looked brighter. The long and profitable association between Laurel and Hardy and Hal Roach came to an end but they made *Great Guns* (1941) for Twentieth Century-Fox and *A-Haunting We Will Go* for the same company the following year and *Air Raid Wardens*, *Jitterbugs* and *The Dancing Masters* in 1943. It became increasingly clear to everyone, including Laurel and Hardy themselves, that short films were pure Laurel and Hardy and in feature films the comedy was more diluted and very difficult to sustain for an hour or so. But there was no turning back, for the world had changed and shorts were no longer profitable.

The marriage of Stan and Ruth now finally disintegrated. Stan had his distractions but Ruth had a wisdom tooth extracted and this was followed by a prolonged and painful infection and she became something of an invalid. In fact she never fully recovered and for the rest of her life she was inclined to cough up a green mucus. The divorce was granted in Las Vegas in 1946 and Ruth eventually died in 1976.

After *Jitterbugs* (1943), which introduced Vivian Blaire, who became a Broadway star five years later in *Guys and Dolls*, Laurel and Hardy's careers went into a steeper decline. Stan began to feel, rightly or wrongly, that the scriptwriters had their characters confused and Ollie was getting words and actions that should have gone to Stan. There were other things too, personal and public, that troubled him, and these all turned Stan, never the happiest of men, into the somewhat sad and forlorn figure of his film portrayals. Their final film (apart from an unsuccessful and unhappy French production, *Atoll K*, which they had been told would take twelve weeks and took twelve months with Stan collapsing half way through filming with a growth on his prostate and Ollie developing pneumonia and suffering a mild heart attack) was *Nothing But Trouble* (1945), a prophetic title for a film that brought Laurel and Hardy no pleasure in the making and no pride in the finished product. Sadly it was their last American film.

Soon afterwards the fifty-five-year-old Stan began to complain of fatigue and listlessness and the doctors diagnosed
diabetes. For the rest of his life, some twenty years, Stan was
to be under the care of doctors for most of the time and the
fact that the disease he was subsequently found to be suffering
from might have been the cause of the bouts of temper and the
depression he had endured was little consolation; nor was the
fact that for the first time in years both he and Ollie were free
of all Hollywood commitments. A personal appearance tour
was set up but Stan was not well enough to take part in such
a profitable project until the following year.

One evening Stan was having dinner with some friends at The
Moskwa in the San Fernando Valley when he caught sight of a
cheerful blonde with blue eyes at a nearby table. He encouraged
her to join his party and Ida Kitaeva Raphael came into Stan's
life, at just the right time.

Next day Stan sent Ida a big box of roses; they met again
and before long Stan, who said he was 'resting', took to driving
Ida to and from the studio where she was appearing in Harold
Lloyd's last film, *Mad Wednesday*. Ida loved Fort Laurence
and in May 1945 the couple drove to Yuma and were married.
It was almost a film comedy scenario yet again for Stan lost his
way in the darkness and that was no fun in open cattle country.
By the time they reached their destination they had to get the
Justice of the Peace out of his bed to marry them! When the
newspaper reporters found the couple honeymooning at the
Grand Hotel in San Diego, Ida faced them and said in no
uncertain terms: 'There will be no more divorces for Stan
Laurel.' Whether she believed what she said at the time or
not, her words turned out to be true, and Stan and Ida lived
more or less very happily for the rest of their lives.

Married to an unselfish woman who cared for him and
forced by his illness to slow down, Stan became the mellow
and charitable man who is today remembered with affection
by the many people who knew him during his last years. His
drinking all but ceased now that he was no longer under the
pressure of film-making. They sold Fort Laurel and moved into
a two-storey property in Sherman Oaks, off Mulholland Drive,
but before they had time to get settled Laurel and Hardy had
the opportunity to appear at the London Palladium where they
took part in a Royal Command Performance and played to full

houses. Stan, Ida and Ollie journeyed over on the *Queen Mary*, but Ollie's wife Lucille was recovering from an operation and was unable to accompany them.

At Southampton they had tea in the reception hotel on the docks in a room that remained virtually unchanged for more than forty years. During the course of a visit to the building for a broadcast in 1990 (for years the property was occupied by the BBC) I was shown the atmospheric tiled and pillared room and it was not difficult to image it crowded with people and Stan and Ollie and Ida holding forth over tea all those years before.

On this memorable visit to England the famous pair were welcomed into the charitable show business organization of The Grand Order of Water Rats, their admission being proposed and sponsored by Will Hay: and they went on to make a highly successful country-wide tour with Stan visiting his birthplace and Ollie enjoying English beer and English food. They went on to Paris, where they played the Lido and were just as popular as the famous nude girls, and then they toured the Low Countries and Scandinavia.

Back in Sherman Oaks, Stan and his wife attempted to resume their comparatively quiet life but Stan had become a kind of elder statesman of screen comedy and he was always keen to meet his fans: since he was listed in the telephone book, they were always calling at the house. Sometimes Stan's health would not permit a personal meeting or the confrontation had to be a brief one for Ida now took it on herself to protect her husband and look after his interests in all things, which she did with courtesy and quiet efficiency. Stan began to spend hours watching the new entertainment craze, television, with the various comedy shows always his favourites. Soon Laurel and Hardy shorts were shown to great acclaim but without any financial reward whatever to either Laurel or Hardy.

In 1952 and 1953 the boys carried out more successful tours of Britain but then Ollie, who had been having circulatory problems with his legs and had not been enjoying the best of health for some time became unwell. He had suffered heart murmurs the year before and was dieting to lose weight in accordance with doctors' orders. Stan seemed almost his old self although many of his fans were surprised at the yellow colour of his skin.

Meanwhile an American actor, John McCabe, produced a book on the two comedians and their films: *Mr Laurel and Mr Hardy* (New York, 1961) and the resulting acclaim from all over the world resulted in the formation of an international appreciation society, The Sons of the Desert, and a flood of correspondence from fans to both Stan and Ollie. The latter, who was ill by this time and in any case never seems to have felt the same obligation to his fans that Stan had, found this all something of a nuisance but Stan answered every single letter himself. A spectacular *This is Your Life* television show followed, featuring both artists but it proved to be their last public appearance together. Ollie suffered a second heart attack complicated by gall bladder trouble and a kidney infection and he had to go on a severe diet; within weeks he had lost 150 lb and the sad old man with folds of excess flesh was not the Ollie everyone knew and loved.

Ollie and Lucille moved to a smaller house they owned on Woodman Avenue and there Lucille obtained a hospital bed, set it up in the living-room, and saw that Ollie occupied it without missing anything that was going on. But soon he was experiencing breathing difficulties and Lucille obtained a portable oxygen tank. Gradually Ollie's health seemed to improve, though a newspaper photograph of him at this time shocked his fans who sent hundreds of letters expressing concern. Although they were written with the best of intentions Ollie was dreadfully upset and he refused to leave the house. The only people he would see were Stan and Ida, his lawyer Ben Shipman and a couple of old friends.

Stan knew that the team of Laurel and Hardy was the most successful screen comedy duo ever formed but with Ollie in the state he was it made Stan sad and despondent to realize that it was all over. During this period of anxiety and depression Stan suffered a stroke that temporarily paralysed his left arm, leg and hand, and his memory became fogged. But with the loving help and support of Ida he fought back and he was soon walking again, albeit with a slight limp. His memory cleared and he was again able to use both his hands and arms.

Lois Junior, Stan's daughter, was by this time married with a family and lived in Tarzana and one Sunday when Stan had virtually recovered and Ollie was mobile, she invited her father and Ida and Ollie and Lucille for the day. Also included in the party was a persistent young fan, Andy Wade, who brought along a movie camera and began shooting. Ollie obviously found it an effort to take part and Stan's limp was all too evident and everyone at the family gathering had the feeling that this would be the last movie the immortal pair would ever appear in and so it proved to be. Both Stan and Ollie only consented to appear on condition that the film would never be shown in public.

That pathetic movie was a sad finale to Laurel and Hardy's career. On his way home from the gathering Andy Wade was killed and the film found its way to a comedy film buff named Bob Chatterton who loaned it to a third party who committed suicide after the film was in his possession. Within months of the movie being shot, it was on sale to the public. All this greatly distressed both Stan and Ollie.

On 15 September 1956 Ollie suffered a massive heart attack that left him completely paralysed and unable even to talk. After a month in hospital everyone said he was unlikely to improve there and Lucille had him moved to her mother's house at 5421 Auckland, North Hollywood. There an extra room was fixed up exactly like the hospital room with its own bath and separate entrance. She hung pictures on the wall from their own home, and in the same positions so it is unlikely that Ollie was ever aware of the move.

Lucille told John McCabe that Ollie was able to move his left arm and leg just a little and there always remained his expressive eyes. When she felt he was trying to say something to her, she would put her face next to his and say, 'I love you', and she was sure he said the same to her with his eyes.

By January 1957 Ollie had professional nursing round the clock and sometimes he would look at a photograph of Lucille within his sight line and cry. The nurses knew the tears meant he wanted Lucille and they would fetch her. Stan, far from well himself, visited Ollie when Lucille said her husband's mind was a little clearer than usual and when there was a good chance that he would recognize Stan.

The last time Stan saw Ollie they had no common method of communication but Stan recalled Ollie at one point clearly indicating with his eyes and slight body movement, 'Look at me, isn't this appalling?' Lucille and Ida withdrew and left the two old friends alone for what was to be their final meeting. Stan wept as Ida drove him home.

During the evening of 6 August 1957 Ollie suffered a series of small, convulsive strokes; then his body was racked with great spasms. Lucille got into bed and put her arms round him tightly. She stayed like that all through the night and next morning all movement ceased and Ollie died. When she knew there was no life in her beloved Ollie, Lucille said: 'Thank you God, for taking him away from his suffering.' Lucille lived on for 30 years, re-marrying and living 25 happy years with Ben Price, a retired businessman. He died in 1986 and Lucille followed him the next year.

Meanwhile Stan and Ida left their house and moved to a sort of motel known as The Oceana in Santa Monica where they occupied one bedroom, a sitting room and a dining area. The apartment had a balcony overlooking the Pacific and Stan grew to love it there.

Stan never could bring himself to attend a funeral and Ollie's was no exception but Ida went and Lucille understood. Stan never really recovered from Ollie's death but he settled into a sort of routine and there were always the hundreds of admirers who called and who today treasure the time they were permitted to spend with him on the balcony overlooking the sea.

During those last happy years Stan bathed in the adulation of his fans and the admiration and respect of his friends and correspondents inside the entertainment industry and outside; President Kennedy, for one, sent Stan an inscribed photograph which he much valued. Stan was in fact the only truly old-time film comedian who was available to the public. Charlie Chaplin did not encourage visitors to his home in Switzerland; Harold Lloyd positively dissuaded any approach to his heavily guarded Green Acres; sad-faced Buster Keaton did not have the same following or appeal at that time; and that left Stan Laurel, the last of the originals and he always seemed to be available. In a way Stan spent his last five years saying goodbye to his fans.

In 1961 Stan was honoured with a Special Academy Award for 'creative pioneering in the field of cinema comedy'. The award was accepted on his behalf by Danny Kaye, watched by Stan and Ida, sitting at home hand in hand. Stan's eyes were beginning to trouble him, possibly a side effect of poor circulation from which he had suffered for years, and he cried off receiving the award in person at the last moment, saying that he feared the bright lights might injure his eyes.

In the middle of February 1965 it was Stan's turn to suffer a heart attack. The faithful Ida, who had been nursing, caring and protecting him for years, sat silent and helpless as the nurses did what they could for him. On 23 February Stan's failing health showed signs of deteriorating beyond recovery but Ida still stayed by his side, her eyes full of tears, her heart like lead, and sad as she had never been before at her inability to help her dear Stan who, in Ida, had found gold at the end of the rainbow.

Soon Stan knew his time had come and he beckoned a nurse to his bedside. 'I'd rather be skiing than doing this' he told her. 'Do you ski, Mr Laurel?' the innocent nurse asked and Stan summoned up the strength for a last joke. 'No, but I'd rather be trying than doing this,' he replied and the next moment he was dead.

'Maybe people loved us and our pictures because we put so much love into them,' Stan used to say and perhaps he was right; today Laurel and Hardy are more popular than when they were making their films; lasting tributes to comedy that will never be replaced.

Bela Lugosi

-

Count Dracula Personified

Bela Lugosi was a famous actor in his native Hungary and he made his film debut there before fleeing the country after an uprising and going to America where he toured in the play of Bram Stoker's famous story of a Transylvanian vampire. When Lugosi was chosen to appear in the subsequent film he did so with incredible authority and ingenuity, and for his work on that film alone he achieved world renown.

Bela Lugosi was born in Hungary in 1882 and he appeared in several Hungarian films before the 1919 uprising when he escaped to Germany and appeared in *Dear Januskopf* (1920), an adaption of Stevenson's *Dr Jekyll and Mr Hyde*, Lugosi playing the dual role. Shortly afterwards he emigrated to the United States where he soon appeared on stage and screen; first touring with a Hungarian company and then appearing on the stage in New York. One of his stage successes was as Count Dracula and he obtained the lead in the 1931 film version, directed by Tod Browning, which became the top money-making film of the year. It was a role that was to type-cast Lugosi for the rest of his life and attract an enormous public following. After the remarkable success of *Dracula* for Universal, Lugosi ought to have gone on to bigger and better things but, as Leslie Halliwell put it, 'his somewhat limited acting ability and his lack of foresight were against him'.

In 1928 Clara Bow, a sizzling redhead who was to end her days in a mental institution, saw Lugosi when he was touring in *Dracula* and the unlikely pair had a steamy romance. Lugosi is also said to have had affairs with a number of other young and attractive girls; as his biographer, Arthur Lenning, puts it, 'If nothing else, it was a pleasant way to learn English.' In fact Lugosi's halting speech and heavy accent were to be considerable assets to him in the film career that lay ahead.

He appeared, somewhat unevenly, in a number of individual films in the 1930s and while none of them can be described as earth-shattering, they were rarely dull, for Lugosi had a compelling presence that came across in most of the films in which he appeared and when he was on the screen the story seemed to come to life: there was something mesmerizing about the commanding tall figure with the measured voice. With films that featured zombies, mute furry creatures, mad scientists, misshapen retainers, hypnotic sorcerers, villain-ous orientals, scheming murderers and of course vampires, Lugosi left a legacy of remarkable horror films but, although in his heyday he was a much-sought-after actor, he always scorned the horror films that had brought him fame and resented the typecasting of himself as the villain.

The man himself had a mysterious, hypnotic quality, particu-larly in his deep-set eyes; and one had the feeling that Lugosi might have probed deeply into the occult. For some years he lived in an almost inaccessible retreat in the Hollywood mountains and he was rarely seen in public. He once said, during the course of a rare interview: 'I have lived too completely, I think. I have known every human emotion: fear, hate, hope, love, rage, despair, ambition – all are old acquaintances of mine but now they have nothing left to offer me. Only study and reflection remain.' For years Lugosi was an unhappy man, given to unaccountable moods and spells of silence during which it almost seemed that he was aware of some unseen presence.

By the time he became resigned to his fate as a screen master of menace his career suddenly evaporated and he became addicted to drugs as he sought to console himself. In 1955 while committed to the Metropolitan State Hospital in California, for a minimum of three months and a maximum of two years – after admitting he was broke and had been taking narcotics for twenty years – he received many encouraging letters from his still-faithful fans and one of them, Hope Lininger, a lady in her late thirties employed in a film studio editing department, wrote to him again and again. Her letters gave him hope and encouragement and four months later he passed the necessary health examination and was released from hospital. One of the first things the 72-year-old actor did was to visit Hope, the woman whose letters, he felt, had helped him so much.

Three weeks later the couple were married. This was Lugosi's fifth and final wedding and it took place at a private house in Hollywood; the actor's 17-year-old son, Bela Junior, acting as best man. Manly P. Hall, the writer and philosopher, was also an ordained minister and he conducted the ceremony. It was the same Manly Hall who hypnotized Lugosi for a scene in the film *Black Friday* (1940). The happy couple moved into an apartment in Hollywood.

The following year, 1956, Lugosi started work on *Plan Nine from Outer Space* (eventually released in 1959). As the film opens Bela Lugosi is standing by the open grave of his wife, Vampira. Wearing his Dracula cape, Lugosi spreads his arms, looking for all the world like a giant bat, for the last time on film. A few days later, in the middle of shooting the film, he was dead.

Lugosi was at home, resting, on 6 August 1956, and his wife went out to buy some groceries. She returned home around seven o'clock in the evening to find her husband dead, from a heart attack. Afterwards, according to Barry Brown in his *Drug Addiction* (n.d.) she said:

> *He didn't answer when I spoke so I went to him. I could feel no pulse! Apparently he must have died a very short time before I arrived. He was just terrified of death. Towards the end he was very weary, but he was still afraid of death. Three nights before he died he was sitting on the edge of the bed. I asked him if he were still afraid to die. He told me that he was. I did my best to comfort him.*

In accordance with his last wishes his wife had Lugosi interred in his Dracula cape in Holy Cross Cemetery. Among the sixty or so mourners at the funeral were directors Zoltan Korda (Sir Alexander's brother) and Edward Wood Jr who was directing *Plan Nine from Outer Space*. Lillian, one of his former wives, and his son, Bela Junior, were also present.

One of the mourners said afterwards, 'It was so strange for we had seen Bela lying in a coffin so often that it seemed a familiar sight.' The simple headstone on his grave in the beautiful grotto section of the cemetery reads: 'Bela Lugosi, 1882–1956. Beloved Father'. But to everyone who ever saw him as Dracula he will be remembered as The Count.

3

The Big C

-

DEATH FROM CANCER

If overwork, stress, disillusionment, frustration and profound unhappiness can cause or spark off cancer, then it is not to be wondered at that the dreaded and dreadful disease has resulted in an enormous number of deaths in Hollywood.

Although the cause of cancer, in its various forms, is still largely unknown, it is probable that different causes may operate and that when a particular set of circumstances affect a person a virus causation is set in motion. Such circumstances are likely to be extreme irritation of various kinds; the consumption of certain foods, exposure to radium, X-rays and ultra-violet rays; deprivation of oxygen; heredity; and stress of one form or another resulting in the poisoning of cells, the units of which living forms are composed.

In this chapter we will look at the lives and deaths of such well-known, well-loved and respected figures as Gypsy Rose Lee, Charles Laughton, Sammy Davis Jr, Humphrey Bogart, Lilli Palmer, Gary Cooper, Jack Benny, Susan Hayward, John Wayne and others.

Gypsy Rose Lee

-

Queen of the Strippers

The name of Gypsy Rose Lee is synonymous with striptease. A hardworking realist who always insisted on a big salary and star billing, she owned a large Rolls-Royce and lived for years in a 28-room mansion in Manhattan, New York, and she possessed beautiful furniture, jewellery and clothes. All this did not prevent her from always pleading poverty and invariably cooking her own meals and occupying cheap motels and caravans whenever she could, for she was obsessed with the horror of being poor.

Perhaps surprisingly Rose Lee was actually a very modest woman and ever since her earliest performances in burlesque (in common with all conjurers and illusionists) she always insisted that no one should be at the back of her when she performed. Her act was designed to be seen from the front and she had no intention of stage-hands or musicians or anyone else seeing parts of her that she did not intend to be seen. Like her mother she was eminently practical; her mother was always saying to both Gypsy and her sister June Havoc, who was a year and a half older: 'God will protect you, but to make sure always carry a heavy club.'

For years Gypsy's nightclub acts involved changes of costume and for a while this entailed her paying someone to perform while she changed. This went against the grain and she soon evolved the idea of what she called 'a shadow box'. This was a collapsible frame of aluminium 6ft wide, 4ft deep and 8ft high which was assembled on stage before her act. A translucent drop sheet, decorated round the edges, was stretched across the front and a spotlight carefully sited behind enabled Gypsy's shadow to be seen within the box. The sides and back were draped with opaque satin.

Her young son Erik would help her change in the shadow box. About half-an-hour before each show he would sneak into the box and remain there until about half-an-hour after each show. Gypsy liked to give the impression that she was helped in her dressing by a maid so Erik had to be careful that only his arms were seen in silhouette.

Gypsy, in common with many stage performers, was extremely superstitious. She would never allow anything green or faded flowers in her dressing room; she would never allow any hats on her bed; no whistling in the dressing room and she always liked to eat twelve grapes on the twelve strokes of midnight each New Year's Eve for luck. All this superstition seemed to have stemmed from an event which took place when she was a child. She had read the tea-leaves for one of her fellow performers in their old vaudeville act and had seen a violent death. Three days later the boy was killed in a car accident. She never read the tea-leaves again.

Gypsy, a woman ahead of her time, arrived in New York in 1932, an unknown stripper, but her knack of obtaining free publicity for herself soon resulted in her becoming established. One night she saw Walter Winchell in her audience. He was probably the most important columnist in New York in those days and his comments were known to have made or broken even an established star, let alone an unknown. After the show Gypsy sent a hurried note to Winchell, apologizing for her poor performance, which she blamed on being awed by his presence, and imploring him to come back the following night and give her another chance. He did so and saw a completely different show — based on his column published only that morning; Gypsy had written the complete script that afternoon! Walter Winchell was charmed and after that he frequently and favourably mentioned her in his column. Gypsy Rose Lee was really on her way!

It is probably true to say that in reality Gypsy was a comedienne with a gimmick that enabled her to introduce humour into her act. That gimmick was striptease and all her life there was nothing she enjoyed more than appearing before a live audience. She was, of course, excessively vain about her personal appearance and not once but many times she resorted to plastic surgery. Her son has described her recovering from one session, 'with hundreds of tiny black stitches around her eyes, across her forehead at the hairline, and under her chin ... she looked like a musical comedy version of Frankenstein's bride'.

In 1937 she made it to Broadway, co-starring with Fanny Brice in *The Ziegfeld Follies* and when Darryl Zanuck, the former screenwriter of Rin-Tin-Tin stories who had by then risen to be head of Twentieth Century-Fox Film Studios, saw her he immediately offered her a contract. Gypsy had dreamed of becoming a great movie star and she didn't hesitate, especially when Zanuck said he would pay the producers of the stage show $20,000 to release her.

However, they had both overlooked William H. Hays, the czar of Hollywood's powerful self-censorship board, the so-called Hays Office, set up in 1922 after scandals like those affecting Roscoe 'Fatty' Arbuckle, whom Will Hays steadfastly refused to allow to return to the screen as an actor. His singular power was still awesome and he was outraged at Zanuck's signing a 'strip woman'. He therefore publicly declared that no film in which she appeared would be allowed a general release. Zanuck saw Hays and they came to a compromise: she could appear in films but not as Gypsy Rose Lee. So Gypsy used her maiden name, Rose Louise Hovick, but it was her stage name that drew the public and without it she had little appeal. Zanuck lost interest in her and she subsequently appeared in five B-pictures, after which her film contract was not renewed.

Another disappointment for Gypsy Rose Lee was in 1944 when she was called back to Hollywood to star in the major International Pictures production, *Belle of the Yukon*, with Randolph Scott – and under her own stage name, taking second billing. The trade reviews gave her and the film excellent notices and the critics generally agreed but the public didn't go to see the picture and the long-term contract that was being negotiated fell through. Gypsy had arrived in Hollywood to considerable press coverage but when she left, her departure went completely unrecorded. Hollywood has never had time for the unsuccessful.

Gypsy Rose Lee married three times; first to Bob Mizzy, a dental supplies manufacturer; then to Alexander Kirkland, a handsome young Broadway actor; and finally to a Spaniard, Julio de Diego, a tall, flamboyant, talented and hardworking painter in the modern school; but the great love of her life seems to have been another flamboyant character, Mike Todd, who was to prove yet another disappointment.

Gypsy met the showy, cigar-smoking impresario, whose real name was Avrom Goldenborgen, when he had already made and lost a fortune; and he would make and lose several more before his untimely death. In 1940 he hired Gypsy to appear with Abbott and Costello in *Streets of Paris*, a show he produced at the New York World's Fair. Gypsy never forgot that Mike pictured her on 40ft high placards that dominated the park. It was the most successful show of the Fair.

Two years later Mike Todd decided to revive burlesque on Broadway and his star was to be Gypsy Rose Lee. Gypsy and Mike wrote the show, *Star and Garter* and it opened to rave reviews. At about this time they embarked upon a love affair, and soon she was urging him to get a divorce and marry her, but even as she asked she knew it was impossible. Mike's wife at that time had already threatened that if he ever divorced her, he would never see his son again and Mike thought the world of his son. So the relationship between Gypsy and Mike continued; she demanding, he promising and postponing. Gypsy always said she only threatened to marry Alexander Kirkland to make Mike jealous and get a divorce, never really thinking that she would have to go through with the wedding. She told her son that she spent most of the wedding-day at the window, waiting for Mike to ride up and carry her off. When he didn't turn up she went ahead with the wedding, at 12.30 at night, the latest possible time she could. Her son understood that Kirkland was his father.

In 1958 Gypsy had agreed to attend a Friar's Club Dinner at the Waldorf Hotel in New York in honour of Mike Todd. For weeks she had been looking forward to the event and she had a really spectacular gown for the occasion. She never gave up hope that Mike, now married to Elizabeth Taylor, would eventually return to her. Mike Todd did not attend the dinner; he and his friend Art Cohn were killed instantly in an aeroplane crash.

Gypsy Rose Lee, according to her son, remained locked in her room for three days, mourning the death of Mike Todd.

Whenever his name came up in conversation in the long years that followed his tragic death, Gyp (as she was known to many of her friends) would always go quiet and say, 'Mike was the most exciting and vital man I have ever known.'

Several people close to Gypsy have said that all her life she exuded 'a psychic warmth', and not only a psychic one perhaps for although she was always careful to save on heating the rest of the house, her personal room was always at least half as hot again as anywhere else in the house. It was a room cluttered with Victoriana which she collected from all over the world.

Gypsy the musical based on her autobiography, was a considerable success. The cast received a standing ovation at the opening and Gypsy, who was in the audience, left the theatre not only famous but on the way to becoming a legend. The *New York Herald-Tribune* said it all: '*Gypsy* is the best damn musical I've seen in years.' It was to be the basis of prosperity for the real Gypsy for the rest of her life.

On the crest of the success Gypsy decided on a visit to Europe in the grand style and accompanied by her son Erik, who had travelled everywhere with her since he was a baby, and the Rolls in the ship's hold, she set out visiting France, Yugoslavia, Switzerland, Italy, Austria, Germany and England, where she took a furnished apartment in Knightsbridge.

In 1960 Gypsy Rose Lee bought a beautiful Mediterranean-style house, with lots of big windows, on a hill on a winding road in Beverly Hills. It was a very private place, invisible from the neighbouring roads, and it seemed to exude the air of a slightly tarnished past, reminiscent of Hollywood's silent days with its tall cypress trees, three-car garage, wrought-iron gates, a passage lined with statues, huge living room with black marble fireplace and the fountain and goldfish pond. The views were really exceptional, taking in practically the whole of Los Angeles and, although the house had been unoccupied for over seven years, Gypsy fell in love with the place and lived there for the rest of her life. Outside she had 'Gypsy Rose Lee' painted in florid script on the mailbox. Son Erik wrote: 'Looking back it seems almost mystical, as though Mother and the house were kindred spirits destined to come together.'

One day she told her son that his father was Otto Preminger. It was after Mike Todd had died. She said she had felt so alone and had decided to have a child, someone that no one would ever be able to take away from her. As soon as she met Otto Preminger she sensed that he was a good man and decided that he should be the father of her child.

Before long Erik and his father met in Paris where Otto was opening his latest film. He, it seemed, knew about his son by Gypsy ever since the birth and he had offered to maintain and support her and the baby but Gypsy had refused to take any money, being determined to be independent. Their affair had been a short one. They had met at a party and afterwards used to meet in Gypsy's dressing room or in the bungalow where she was then living. Later, learning that she was in hospital in New York, he joined her there. 'Congratulations,' she told him. 'We have a son.' Otto and Erik hit it off immediately and for a time Erik worked as Otto's assistant. He always remained close to his mother and whenever his work took him to Los Angeles, they would meet.

One day Gypsy telephoned her son and announced out of the blue: 'Erik, they've found a spot on my lung and they want to operate immediately. I've told them to wait until you get here ... when can you come?' When he heard the news Otto told Erik to go at once and stay as long as he was needed.

When Erik arrived at the house he learned that his mother was already in hospital. There she told him it was cancer. They did not know how serious it was until they had operated but 'from the X-rays, they think they will be able to get it all out'.

After she had been wheeled away Erik went back to the house and three hours later returned to the hospital, expecting his mother to be in intensive care. Instead, he found her back in her private room. 'They took one look and sewed me back up,' she explained. 'It has spread too far for them to operate. They say there's a good chance they'll be able to knock it out with radiation.'

Erik saw the doctors and asked to be told the true position and the prospects. He was told that the cancer would kill his mother for sure but they refused to say how long it might take. Erik explained that he lived in New York but could arrange to move if it would be a year or less; he was told, however, that she might hang on for years. Later Erik learned that nine months would have been a miracle and in fact she died within five months. Erik always blamed the doctors for denying him those months with his mother; instead he made a dozen short visits, thinking there was still a long way to go.

Each visit was a painful one. Gypsy visibly deteriorated but she was allowed to go home and at first was able to get around the house and walk in the garden that she loved. After a while she needed a wheelchair; then she was completely bedridden. Soon came the oxygen tanks, the electric bed, the round-the-clock nursing and the constant attention that comes with serious illness.

She never gave up. Sometimes Erik would find himself wishing she would accept the inevitability of the fight and that they could make their goodbyes but she insisted, time and time again, 'I'm going to beat this thing, Erik. I'm going to beat it.' Everyone, those close to her and the medical staff, helped in the conspiracy, even to the extent of putting a foot on the scales when she was being weighed to make her think she was gaining weight.

In fact, of course, she was losing weight to a frightening degree and she became little more than skin and bones. The pain became constant and unbearable as she was literally being eaten away from inside. She had injections of nerve-blocking drugs to help her but nothing could hide the awful smell of the illness. Gypsy tried to hide it with perfume, which only made it worse.

Sometimes, late at night, she would call for her son and he would lie next to her and they would talk. She would doze intermittently and suddenly start, awakened by the pain. 'Nurse, isn't it time for my shot?' was the question she asked a thousand times: causing those in her room at the time to hide their faces in pity. 'Just a little longer,' she would be told when there was still an hour or more to go. Erik argued with the doctors about the pain-relieving drugs she had: why couldn't she have more if she needed it? He was told that if she had all she asked for, she would curl up in a ball and sleep her life away. Yet, Erik asked himself, would that have been such a bad thing? Instead she spent her last days watching the slow passing of the hours and asking and waiting for the next medicine.

'But it hurts so,' she would cry repeatedly. 'Oh God! It hurts so,' until she mercifully dozed off but moments later she would be awake again.

Once she said to Erik while he was close to her at her bedside:

'It hurts so much, Erik, and I'm so tired. I don't know how much longer I can fight the pain. It's awful.' Erik thought she was finally realizing that she was dying and without thinking he said, in kindness, 'It'll be over soon.'

Immediately she was her old suspicious self. 'What do you mean?' she demanded, alert and clearly frightened. Erik knew then that she must not, could not, accept the inevitable and he lied to her and said he meant it was almost time for her next shot. As things turned out that was the nearest he came to saying goodbye to his mother. Not long after this, in 1970, she died in Hollywood as he was on his way to see her. He has no parting words to remember but he always recalls what she said on one of her first visits to the radiation clinic, the night before her 65th birthday. As she walked past the patients waiting for their treatment, she said quietly, 'You know, Erik, when I look at all those people I can't bring myself to complain about having this horrible disease. I've had three wonderful lives, and these poor souls haven't even lived once.'

She was undoubtedly an original, an elegant maverick who transformed a low-brow entertainment into art with her intelligence and humour.

Charles Laughton

-

The Man Who Knew Too Much

The unmistakable features, the ambling gait, the petulant lower lip and the watching eyes of Charles Laughton were the hall-marks of a rare stage and screen actor whose greatest talent lay in portraying complex personalities: Henry VIII, Captain Bligh, Claudius and Rembrandt, to name only a few.

Charles Laughton was born at the Victoria Hotel, Scarborough, on the east coast of England; it still exists, an emblem of the actor as King Henry VIII outside. He lived in a hotel and was himself in the hotel business for the first 25 years of his life and the Laughton family progressed to the splendid Pavilion Hotel near by.

The preparatory school that Charles attended was a Roman Catholic one; he then went to a French convent in Filey and finally to Stonyhurst College, the Roman Catholic public school for boys where the Jesuits informed their young charges that eternity was 'as if this world were a steel globe and every thousand years a bird's wing brushed past that globe – and the time it would take for that globe to wear away is all eternity'. Charles grew up to hate snobs of all sorts and he liked to call himself just an ordinary man.

At first there was talk of a career for him in the Navy but eventually and perhaps inevitably, as the eldest of three boys, he found himself absorbed into the family business, for the Pavilion had become well-known and fashionable and its clientèle included the Sitwells, who stayed there while Renishaw Hall, near by, was in process of being refurbished. Charles spent

a couple of happy years at Claridges Hotel in London, where
he discovered the theatre.

At the age of 18, in the last year of the First World War,
he enlisted as a private and saw service at Vimy Ridge. The
horror of the trenches was agonizing for the fat, sensitive boy.
He was gassed in the last week of the war and the memory of
it all was never to leave him; the gassing damaged his larynx
and reappeared periodically as rashes on his back. He was never
happy with his physical body and used to say that he had a face
that would stop a sundial and frighten small children!

Returning from the war to run the Pavilion Hotel when his
father fell ill, Charles threw himself into the work which he
nevertheless came to dislike and he consoled himself by joining
and eventually running one of the local amateur dramatic soci-
eties. The time came when he walked out of the family business
and sent in his application to the Royal Academy of Dramatic
Art. There he was auditioned by, among others, Claude Rains,
ten years his senior. He was enrolled two days later. Less than
five years after he returned from the war to end all wars, he was
at the Academy and had already received a Special Honourable
Mention for his participation in a curriculum that included
fencing, dancing, gesture and elocution. Fellow students and the
Academy principal were astonished at the hard work Laughton
put in. Sometimes, unobserved, they would watch him as he
moved about one of the Academy's rehearsal rooms: he seemed
to people the room with his impressions and variations. 'It was
sheer magic,' one of them said. His end of the year report
stated, under Acting: 'Laughton is sometimes too brilliant.
He'll persevere and prosper.' One trustee of the Academy,
the formidable George Bernard Shaw, went to see Laughton
in *Pygmalion* and said to the budding actor afterwards: 'You
were perfectly dreadful as Higgins but nothing will stop you
from getting to the top of the tree and I predict a brilliant
career for you.' Before leaving the Academy Charles Laughton
won the coveted Bancroft Gold Medal, the highest award given
by RADA, and within six months he was working on the West
End stage.

Even his early work in the theatre was noticeable and I recall
Alan Dent telling me how excited he, already a hardened
theatre critic, had been by the 'astonishing, new, young, plump
comedian' he had seen in a production of *The Cherry Orchard*.

Before long, with the help of people like Ivor Novello, Charles Cochran and James Agate, Laughton obtained more or less continuous employment in a variety of parts in a variety of theatres.

Already within a relatively short time of his stage debut there were references to the 'sleepy eyelids, the modulations of the indolent, caressing voice, the slow-moving, velvet hands' and the all-important power of attracting attention whenever he was on stage. According to Simon Callow, in 1927, the year he left RADA, Charles Laughton played seven featured roles in seven new West End productions; surely a record that is unlikely ever to be surpassed.

Soon he was at the Royal Court Theatre in Arnold Bennett's *Mr Prohack*; 'a performance of exceptional artistry, one which lifts Mr Laughton to the front rank of actors', said the staid *Theatre World*. Of a later play, *Beauty* (1929) one reviewer said Laughton's character 'weeps once in every act and, Mr Laughton being one of our finest actors, very possibly during the intervals as well'. In the role of Mr Prohack's secretary there was a pert and quirky red-haired young actress named Elsa Lanchester, who had trained with Isadora Duncan. Slowly and shyly at first but with growing enthusiasm on both sides the youngsters found in each other's company what they had both unconsciously been looking for: companionship, deep friendship and only occasionally any sexual or emotional involvement.

At first they lived apart but after Elsa had an abortion they moved into a flat in Dean Street, into Karl Marx's old house in fact. Although Charles always had homosexual leanings and desires, he may have hoped that marriage would obviate such desires, but this was not to be the case. Furtively he began to seek out young men with similar inclinations and occasionally he took them home with him, when Elsa was away. He never told her of these nocturnal encounters or of that dark and forbidden other self of his.

Among his idiosyncrasies Charles Laughton was always careless of his appearance (Elsa used to describe him as 'anything but well-dressed') and of his personal hygiene. All his life he dressed sloppily whenever he could and he revelled in the character Ginger Ted in *Vessel of Wrath* (1938), a beachcomber, sot and reprobate. Charles only seemed to bathe when he had to.

Elsa learned to live with such foibles but in Hollywood Tallulah
Bankhead is reputed to have refused to shake hands with him on
their first meeting, because of his dirty fingernails. During the
rehearsals for *On the Spot*, perhaps the greatest triumph of his
stage career and written especially for him by Edgar Wallace,
on one occasion the whole cast, with the exception of Laughton,
was gathered on stage at Wyndhams with Edgar Wallace in
charge; for he was to direct the play. Calls and enquiries went
out but of Charles there was no sign. Eventually Wallace's
secretary was sent to the stage door where the doorkeeper
said the only person he'd seen had been a tramp whom he
had thrown out several times. Miss Reissar opened the stage
door and there was Laughton, smirking, looking more like a
tramp than a prominent actor. He went in and the read-through
began; as always Charles read brilliantly and then left as quickly
as he could to vanish again into the murky London of 1930.

During rehearsals for his next play, *Payment Deferred* (St
James's Theatre, 1931) Charles's homosexuality fell like a bomb
between him and Elsa. Late one night Charles arrived home
accompanied by a policeman and writer Jeffrey Dell who had
adapted the C. S. Forester story for the stage. Overwrought
Charles said he must speak to Elsa privately. When they were
alone he told her that there was a homosexual streak in his
makeup which he occasionally indulged. A young man with
whom he had been consorting had harassed him for money, a
policeman had intervened and this was the outcome. Elsa was
to say years later that prior to this time she had no indication
whatsoever that Charles 'liked young men' but in spite of the
frightful shock she had had, she immediately told him it was
all right, she would stand by him. She did ask whether he had
had sex with the man in their house and when Charles said he
had, on the couch, ever-practical Elsa said they would get rid
of the couch. In later years, of course, Elsa knew that Charles
'indulged his weakness' but she turned a blind eye and in public
they always supported each other – they were loyal friends up
to the end; but of course things were never quite the same after
that dreadful night.

After a run of three months it was decided to take *Payment
Deferred* to Broadway; an idea welcomed with open arms by
both Charles and Elsa. It would be an escape from the scene
of turmoil and unhappiness, a change that might enable them

to come to terms with the events that could well have shattered their marriage.

Things were hectic during the Laughtons' first visit to America and before long Elsa, who was unemployed, returned to England. As soon as his play came to an end, Charles followed but before the boat left New York harbour he received a telegram offering him a three-year, two-films-a-year contract from Paramount, with the right to choose his roles. No sooner did they meet in England than Charles and Elsa returned to America.

Laughton returned again to London, ostensibly to appear in a season at the Old Vic Theatre but meanwhile he was to star in one of the two films for which he will always be remembered: Henry VIII in Alexander Korda's *The Private Life of Henry VIII* (1933). Korda, as ever, had great difficulty in finding the money to make the film and although every part had been filled by experienced actors – Binnie Barnes, Merle Oberon, Wendy Barrie, Robert Donat, John Loder and of course Elsa Lanchester – it was a constant headache because the money kept running out.

> *During the making of that film* [Laughton said afterwards] *we were often apprehensive that while we were saying our lines the flimsy sets would collapse and smother us. We finished the picture in five weeks and we were all fairly satisfied with it but never for a moment did we think it would be the great financial success that it was. We would have sold it to the first bidder; but there were no bidders!*

The banquet scene was truly memorable with Charles demonstrating Tudor table manners as they have never been demonstrated before or since. Real food was used; every day the chickens and boar's head and the rest were freshly prepared and sent to the studios from the Savoy Hotel; and the actors really had to eat the food and some of them almost choked. But it was a performance that Laughton revelled in and he made it one of the great scenes in film history.

As he sailed for America once again he could hardly have guessed that some of his most memorable film and stage performances were still in front of him.

The delicate Irving Thalberg first had the idea to re-film *The Hunchback of Notre Dame*, Dumas' famous novel that had been such a success in the 1923 silent version for its star Lon Chaney. Thalberg was ecstatic when he discovered that most of the spectacular Tod Browning sets used in the original production were still available.

Laughton was at once equally enthusiastic. Perhaps he saw something resembling himself in the deformed and tortured Quasimodo. In any case he entered into the project wholeheartedly and eventually became involved in various aspects of the production of the film. The grotesque mask he would wear in his characterization enthralled him and the final masterly composition was largely due to his conception and ideas. Ever insistent on reality, Laughton made sure that the hump on his back was really heavy. Chaney's, he pointed out, had been made by the 'man of a thousand faces' himself and weighed half a ton. Laughton needed his to be just as heavy and unwieldly, a constant reminder of the pain that Quasimodo lived with.

Laughton need not have worried about reality in his portrayal. The summer that saw the outbreak of the Second World War, 1939, was a real scorcher and in temperatures of well over 100°F, Laughton sweltered and sweated and laboured day after day; only to stagger home to find it too hot to sleep. After tossing and turning for a few hours he would get up around four o'clock in the morning to be at the studios and be made up for the next day's filming. So it went on day after day; and strange stories went round the lot that Laughton was really enjoying his painful role. During the scene where he is lashed on the wheel, it was said, he asked one of the assistants to twist his foot roughly so that his pain and suffering was real. Of that scene the director, William Dieterle, was to write later: 'When Laughton acted that scene ... he was not the poor crippled creature ... but rather oppressed and enslaved mankind, suffering the most awful injustice.' Certainly, the terrible events that were happening in Europe brought back to Charles Laughton the agonies he had suffered in the trenches of France twenty years earlier.

The Second World War was declared on the day of the shooting of the scene where Quasimodo rings the bells for Esmerelda, high up in the bell tower. According to the script it was supposed to be more or less a love scene but something very odd happened that was felt by everyone there. An atmosphere of doom pervaded the whole set to the background of the doleful pealing of the bells and the fact that a film was being shot seemed to be completely forgotten. When Dieterle called out 'Cut' at the end of the scene Laughton went on ringing the bells until, after what seemed an eternity, he was completely exhausted and he stopped.

Nobody spoke, nobody moved and for everyone present it was an unforgettable and unexplained moment. Afterwards Laughton said: 'I couldn't think of Esmerelda in that scene at all. I could only think of the poor people out there, going to fight in that bloody war! I was trying to arouse the world to stop the terrible butchery. Awake! Awake! That's what I felt when I was ringing the bells.'

When the Laughton property in Gordon Square was bombed, the only house in the square to suffer, Laughton was uncharacteristically philosophical: 'I should be glad to sacrifice twenty houses if German dive bombers would smash themselves to bits on them,' he said, in a piece published in *The New York Times*. 'To Hell with the cash ... it was a glorious end for the house.'

Laughton's performance in *The Hunchback of Notre Dame* (1939) was one of the finest things he did on film; it was acting at its very best and most accomplished. It gave stage and TV impressionists their third gift from Laughton, the other two being his Henry VIII and Captain Bligh, but it was the last time he was to risk physical and mental collapse for the sake of art as he saw it. Thereafter he set out to like and be liked. As his biographer puts it: 'He climbed down from the cross, pulled out the nails, and made with uncertain steps for real life.'

Almost thirty films followed for Charles Laughton and seven plays, including *A Midsummer Night's Dream* (Bottom) and *King Lear* both at Stratford in 1959, and the films included *The Tuttles of Tahiti* (1942), *Hobson's Choice* (1954), *Witness for the Prosecution* (1957) – with Tyrone Power in his last film – and Laughton's own last film *Advise and Consent* (1962). Marilyn Monroe appeared briefly as a streetwalker with Laughton on *O. Henry's Full House* (1952), her last role before stardom came her way, and she said afterwards, 'Charles is the sexiest man I've ever seen.' Judging by his make-up in the film, she probably had her tongue in her cheek! And yet Marlene

Dietrich is on record as having said, 'I would rather play a love scene with Charles Laughton than any other man in the world.'

During his latter years Laughton gave highly successful readings; started a Shakespearean group; and one way and another became one of the best-known and best-loved figures on the American scene. He had a remarkable and sometimes soothing voice and there is a story that one day during the making of a film in which a baby was involved, the baby chose not to stop crying. Eventually Laughton went over to the baby and murmured into its ear for a few moments and the baby fell asleep. On being asked what he had whispered to the baby that was apparently so effective, Laughton replied, 'The Gettysburg address; it has such a wonderful rhythm, you know.'

He loved books and always said a library was a wondrous place for him to be. 'I think of all the wonderful tales I will never know and I wish I could live to be a thousand years old.'

In fact, time was running out for Charles Laughton. The strain of it was beginning to tell and during the whole run of *King Lear* he was troubled with horrific nightmares. For a time he turned to television, but the strain of skimped rehearsals and instant transmission was too much for him and suddenly he suffered a heart attack, which he was told originated in a diseased gall-bladder, for which he underwent surgery in 1960. As soon as he was more or less fit he devised a one-woman show for Elsa that was remarkably successful. The programme credit for himself read, 'Censored by Charles Laughton'. So effective was the show that Elsa continued playing it for the rest of her working life.

By the beginning of 1962 Charles Laughton seemed to be distinctly unwell most of the time but he undertook yet another reading tour and then, at Flint in Michigan, he fell in his bath and broke his shoulder. The real trouble proved to be cancer. He never really recovered from that fall and died in the last month of the year.

After two operations he was so weakened that he barely had the strength to appreciate the reviews of *Elsa Lanchester – Herself*; and shortly afterwards the pain and depression became so bad that he threatened to kill himself. He seemed convinced that he would soon die but in fact he recovered sufficiently to go to Japan, with a young man friend, and to Hong Kong.

The months that followed Laughton's return from the East were full of agony as the cancer of the bone, which seemed to have originated in the kidneys, began to make its fatal journey round his tortured body.

Soon the actor was paralysed below the waist and although he had an operation on his spine that restored the feeling to his lower limbs, he was never able to walk again unaided. His weight decreased and continued to drop until the familiar bulky form that everyone knew weighed less than seven stone. Before long his condition was such that every movement was excruciatingly painful. Everything that might help was tried including several new 'wonder' drugs but nothing alleviated his deepening misery and progressive pain. Finally he slipped into unconsciousness and a few weeks later he died.

Laughton was taken home to 1825 North Curson Avenue on 30 November 1962 and for a while, even then, he sustained the idea that he would make a new film, *Irma la Douce* playing Moustache. Billy Wilder went to see him and found him sitting in a chair by the swimming pool. He had been dressed, shaved and was even wearing a little make-up. 'Look at me,' he said. 'Do I look like someone that's going to die?' And he got out of the chair and walked round the pool. Elsa said it must have been a tremendous effort and must have caused considerable pain but what he was really saying was: 'Wait for me.' Billy Wilder said, 'It was one of his finest performances and I was very touched.'

Elsa devoted herself to Charles totally for the last year of his life and during that hideously painful time for both of them, there were inevitably times of tension. At times Elsa almost seemed to hate Charles and at times he seemed to hate her but they remained married for over thirty years and although there were occasional murmurs of divorce, those close to them never felt there was any serious prospect of Charles and Elsa breaking up permanently. In Britain and in Hollywood they were always very much a couple, a somewhat eccentric couple perhaps, but still a couple. Both Charles and Elsa hated Christianity and the do-gooders and his death-bed conversion, which really annoyed Elsa, was nothing more nor less than a trick played on a man in a terribly weak and distressed condition, wearily endorsing something that he had vehemently repudiated all his adult life.

Charles's brothers Tom and Frank believed that for Charles to accept religion would help him and one evening when Elsa was out shopping a priest was hurriedly summoned and gave extreme unction; when Elsa returned the weary Charles told her: 'I think I've joined the gang!' What a pity that it had to end in an awful, agonizing death with the top half of his body twisted on its side and his face pushed into the pillow. Better to remember the wonderful and undying characterizations that Charles Laughton left behind and to recall with affection Charles and Elsa, that 'strange pair; no, not mad, my dear; but strange, I grant you,' as Ernest Thesiger once put it to me.

Rembrandt (1936) played
by Charles Laughton

Charles Laughton in
The Private Life of Henry VIII
(1933)

Sammy Davis Jr

-

Mr Showbusiness

He was a man without any formal education, a man who forced himself to succeed and to go where no black entertainer had ever been before. In a professional career that spanned more than half a century he appeared successfully on stage, in films, on television and in four Royal Command Performances. His charity appearances raised millions of pounds and he became one of the highest paid and most popular entertainers of all time. He was the friend of presidents and of the famous on both sides of the Atlantic; he fought for right as he saw it and he died still fighting.

Arguably the most accepted black entertainer of all time, a candid, vulnerable and likable man who survived problems of drink, drugs and debt, Sammy Davis Jr was nothing if not an original and a showman, but a showman with class.

Walking tall on shiny, built-up shoes, hair slicked back to patent leather perfection, the famous toothy smile creasing his face, Mr Showbusiness himself, one of the highest paid entertainers of his day, was almost modest and retiring when I met him during one of his visits to London to launch the Music for Pleasure record label.

He was born in Harlem, New York City, of showbusiness parents and he joined their double-act while still a small child but already a bundle of energy. He used to say he had travelled ten states and played in over fifty cities with his father and grandfather by the time he was four!

In later years he said he never spent a single day in school in his life. His philosophy was summed up in his autobiography:

What have I got? No looks, no money, no education. Just talent. Where do I want to go? I want to be treated well — want people to like me. How do I get there? There's only one way I can do it with what I have to work with. I've got to be a star! I have to be a star like another man has to breathe.

In November 1989 he celebrated 60 years in showbusiness and within a few short months he was dead, having put up a fantastic fight against cancer. The Anniversary Celebration was Sammy's big Hollywood night: Bob Hope, Dean Martin, Frank Sinatra, Michael Jackson, Ella Fitzgerald and Mike Tyson were there, to mention only a few.

Sammy Davis Jr fought many battles during his lifetime and one of the most difficult was the colour prejudice that still existed in American showbusiness and which he fought with considerable success. Michael Jackson always gave Sammy Davis the credit for helping black artists: 'He showed us the way forward and we are eternally in his debt,' Jackson said in 1989.

In the 1950s, when Sammy did his first show in Las Vegas, he wasn't allowed to occupy a room in the hotel where he was appearing. As he put it: 'I was considered good enough to sing and dance my butt off, but not fit to sleep in one of their bedrooms.' Sammy altered all that when he married Mai Britt, the blonde Scandinavian actress, in 1960. At first all he received was hate mail — far more than congratulations, but the marriage made a world of difference to the colour problem in America.

Sammy and Mai were married for eight years and they produced three children, Tracey, Mark and Jeff, all now grown up. At the time of the wedding mixed marriages were almost unheard of and much frowned upon. The thing that hurt Sammy most, he told me, was when President Kennedy, for whom Sammy had campaigned countrywide tirelessly, withdrew an invitation to his inauguration because of the furore that surrounded the marriage.

Sammy knew Jack and Bobby Kennedy and Martin Luther King and he was devastated when they were each assassinated. When Jack Kennedy was shot, Sammy closed the show he was appearing in for that night and he did the same when Luther

King died at the hand of an assassin. When Bobby Kennedy was shot Sammy was appearing at the London Palladium in *Golden Boy*. It was the second night of the show and the management pleaded with him to keep the show open and to go on and the cast told him their careers would suffer if he stopped the show so he did the first half, with tears streaming down his face. During the interval he went on stage, told the audience what had happened, adding: 'For once in my life my heart is not in this wonderful theatre; it is somewhere in America where one of our last dreams has just been murdered' and he walked off for the night to respectful applause.

Letting the audience down in this way really saddened Sammy but he was so broken up that there was nothing else he could do and it was sad for him because he always said that London had a special place in his heart. 'I love London more than any other place on earth,' he told me. 'If my business people would let me, I'd willingly live here for the rest of my life.'

After the marriage to Mai broke up Sammy, having had battles with drink and drugs, accepted that he had to bear a lot of the blame. 'I'm not saying that it was just colour prejudice that pulled us apart but the hate mail sure didn't help; neither did the fact that I wanted to be out on the town every night while Mai wanted me to stay at home.' 'People think of me as having a big ego,' Sammy once said revealingly. 'But if I have, it's just there to hide my insecurity. I've always had an uphill struggle, just to get a decent break; fight and run, fight and run, that was the story of my life. And when I finally made it, achieved all my ambitions, there was nothing left to struggle for so I went to party after party.' Sammy had by this time become a member of the renowned Hollywood Rat Pack with Dean Martin and 'the one and only' Frank Sinatra who, Sammy always admitted, 'kicked open a few doors for me in the early days'. At some of the nightspots that Sammy frequented there was a lot of drinking, and cocaine and other drugs were available.

Sammy was a real film buff and he even pandered to this obsession by writing a book, full of affectionate praise for actors, actresses, films and filming, which he called *Hollywood in a Suitcase*. He calculated he had spent a third of his life watching movies. He built his own personal cinema with the help of Howard Hughes in his home in Beverly Hills and during his life he collected copies of literally thousands of films. He once said to me, when we were reminiscing, that there were probably 10,000 films in circulation or available to television and many thousands more in various archives and, in all modesty, he thought he knew every magic moment worth remembering in all of them.

The first film he ever saw was the original *Dracula* and he always had a soft spot for horror movies; he even loved the 'cheap' Hammer productions and was present whenever he could get in as a guest when some of the Hammer Horrors were produced. He became friendly with Peter Cushing and Christopher Lee and he used to say that after watching every Hammer film a hundred times he knew Chris Lee's face better than the actor did!

Inevitably he came to know a lot of other movie enthusiasts including Mel Torme, Lionel Blair, Buddy Rich, Elvis Presley – who all 'lived and breathed movies' – and Jack Haley Jr (the man who conceived and produced the nostalgic hit, *That's Entertainment* for MGM). Haley built a projection room in his moderately sized house in Beverly Hills that took up about half the living area! He always said his idea of heaven was to live in a cinema.

In his house with its couple of acres in Beverly Hills Davis exhibited his treasured showbusiness memorabilia: things like a letter from Fred Astaire and a suit he had worn; Leslie Caron's corset which she wore in *Gigi*; James Dean's red jacket from *Rebel Without a Cause*; a pair of Marilyn Monroe's high-heeled shoes; a pair of Gene Kelly's shoes and a hat, gun-belt and six-shooter worn by John Wayne.

In 1954 Sammy was involved in the car crash that could easily have ended his life; in the event he got away with little more than losing one eye. For a time he adopted a rhinestone eye-patch, which was copied by other people including politician Moshe Dayan of Israel. Humphrey Bogart eventually talked Sammy into throwing the eye-shade away.

So, after Mai Britt, after the drinking sessions, after the drugs and after the car crash, Sammy Davis Jr took stock; and he was brutally frank with himself. 'I don't have a lot going for me in the looks department,' he used to say; but in a career that spanned 60 years he was literally willing to sacrifice everything for the love of his audience. Sammy liked to play a round of golf now and then, especially with his old friend Bob Hope. One day Bob asked Sammy what his handicap was and quick as a flash Sammy replied: 'I'm one-eyed, I'm Jewish and I'm black; what's yours?'

He made nine movies, none of them earth-shattering, but he was always proud of his first film, *Anna Lucasta*, which was little more than the story of a promiscuous woman, played by Eartha Kitt, leaving home when her boyfriend finds out about her love life; it never received rave reviews but it was accepted and made a lot of money over the years. If the film had really taken off Sammy and his partners planned to go into independent production but that was not to be.

Sammy's special friend Laurence Harvey knew he was going to die (also of cancer) and he had all his friends to a last supper in Hollywood, telling them he had only a few months to live. Sammy said, as cheerfully as he could that one day, just for Larry, he would 'swing a great party and remember the good times'.

Exactly a year after Larry Harvey died Sammy held his party and a medium present swore that Larry was around. Everything was exactly as Larry would have wished it and, as Sammy said afterwards, 'We gave him the send-off he deserved – and everyone who knew him has marvellous memories.' It almost seemed that Larry Harvey *was* there that night as a peculiar hazy light came up over Los Angeles. Sammy often talked of that night and felt as he had never felt before, a sense of yearning, of companionship, of a rare magic that he felt was what the movies and Hollywood was all about. 'If I could pack a little of that in my suitcase each time I leave home,' Sammy mused, 'it won't matter what town I'm in; Hollywood will be with me.'

Sammy always credited his second wife, Altovise, with a lot of the happiness and peace that he found in the latter part of his life. On two occasions he had been so low that he had tried to commit suicide but Altovise had talked him out of it. He and Altovise married in 1969 and they enjoyed nearly twenty years of happiness before he was diagnosed as having throat cancer.

He underwent weeks of painful radiotherapy and was forced to cancel what might have been a very profitable tour. His weight, never enormous, plummeted, but even in the early weeks of 1990 he thought, as he was meant to, that he had the disease beaten, especially when doctors told him he was clear; but a month later, in February 1990, he had to go to hospital again for further treatment.

Everyone knew that Sammy was dying and all his friends did what they could; Frank Sinatra, for example, said he would pay all hospital bills and he also paid for the funeral and is said to have given Sammy's widow, who had by that time financial difficulties, a cheque for $50,000. So Sammy continued to fight his final battle as he had fought all his life until, in a particularly awful way for a man whose voice had given so much pleasure to so many people, the throat cancer took the life of Sammy Davis Jr, an entertaining singer, an actor of enormous vitality and a rare human being, on 16 May 1990.

Humphrey Bogart

-

Here's Looking at You, Kid

The son of well-to-do parents who wanted him to be a surgeon, Humphrey Bogart chose acting and came to be associated with cold and ruthless gangster roles; tough and yet vulnerable characters; and also a new kind of anti-hero or outsider; but it is for his gangster films of the 1940s that he is chiefly remembered and admired, roles that have made him part of cinema mythology.

Humphrey DeForest Bogart often claimed to have been born on Christmas Day although in fact he was born on 23 January 1899. His father Dr Belmont DeForest Bogart was a third-generation American who was proud to trace his family back to 1500. A prominent physician and surgeon in a fashionable West Side thoroughfare near Riverside Drive, New York, Bogie's father was a natural athlete and a superb shot. His mother, the former Miss Maude Humphrey, had a ready wit and was herself also a third-generation American; she had studied art in Paris under Whistler and by the time she was 30 she was one of America's best-known magazine illustrators. Thus Bogie's early years were spent in comfortable and well-to-do surroundings, a far cry from the world of gangsters portrayed in most of his cinematic roles. The solid Bogart home stood across the street from the old Hotel Marseilles whose wealthy permanent residents included Sara Delano Roosevelt, the President's mother.

The couple's first child was named Humphrey, after his mother, and DeForest after his father. Two daughters followed, Frances (known as Pat) and Catherine (known as Kay). Their son, the Bogarts decided, would be a surgeon and he would go to Yale. His mother had made a portrait of her boy with blue eyes and an appealing smile, which was bought by a baby food manufacturer and used extensively in their advertising, becoming one of the most popular baby pictures of its day.

In later years Bogie was to recall that his parents fought a lot, usually over money. Dr Bogart was never happier than when he was hunting, shooting, fishing and sailing, which he did at the expense of his medical practice; and by the time he was ten young Humphrey was quite an expert in sailing, a pastime he enjoyed for the rest of his life.

Humphrey attended the ancient and select Episcopal institute for young gentlemen, known as Trinity School. and in his early and impressionable teens Humphrey's best friend was a Trinity classmate, William Brady, who lived near by. His father, who had once managed heavyweight boxers 'Gentleman' Jim Corbett and Jim Jeffries, had married an actress and the family often had free passes to Broadway shows. By this means Humphrey was to see such shows as *Peg O' My Heart* and *Bella Donna* and such accomplished actresses as Laurette Taylor, Maude Adams, Nazimova and Sarah Bernhardt. He also remembered seeing an act way down the programme that featured a comic juggler named W. C. Fields.

Humphrey's parents, in common with the fashion of the day, tended to look down on the acting profession who courted the attention of the press and more than once Humphrey was to be reminded of the old saying that a gentleman's name appeared three times in the papers: when he was born, when he was married, and when he died. Soon Humphrey's father decided it was high time his son left Trinity and enlisted at his old school, Phillips Academy at Andover, Massachusetts, in preparation for enrolment at Yale.

Humphrey never liked Phillips Academy and it seemed not to like him. His fellow students he found dull and unadventurous, 'bookworms', he called them. The feelings were mutual and one of them has recalled: 'If there's one thing I remember about Humphrey Bogart in those days, it was his sullenness. I got the impression that he was a very spoiled boy; when things didn't go his way, he didn't like it one bit.'

During his second term the headmaster wrote to Dr Bogart to inform him that Humphrey had not extended himself and since it seemed that he had no intention of doing so, he must leave the school at once.

The boy's homecoming was stormy. His father in particular was deeply disappointed and realized that there could be no question now of Humphrey going to Yale. Humphrey was told in no uncertain terms that he was on his own.

The United States had by this time entered the First World War and after a few weeks moping round the house Humphrey decided to enlist in the Navy. There he first spent a year aboard the *Leviathan*, making perhaps twenty Atlantic crossings.

On one occasion, the ship was sighted by a German U-boat and a splinter of wood from a burst shell pierced Bogie's upper lip. According to Joe Hyams, a nerve was damaged and the lip was left partly paralysed. Another story has it that one night when he was on guard duty, Humphrey was escorting a hand-cuffed prisoner from one place to another when the prisoner attempted to escape, and in suddenly bringing up his hands, he hit Bogie in the face and split his lip. Whatever the origin the scar is apparent in photographs where there is no make-up and the partial paralysis gave his mouth the tight-set look that was to become a dominant feature of his screen appearances; it also affected his speech and thereafter he spoke with a slight lisp. The accident may also have been the original reason for the twitching of his mouth which he was to use to such advantage in his various gangster roles.

After two years' service in the Navy, at the ripe old age of 20, Humphrey was given an honourable discharge and for a while he returned to his family home; but Dr Bogart had gone downhill and had taken to signing on as ship's doctor on freighters and there were rumours that he had become addicted to morphine, a not infrequent catastrophe for members of the medical profession at that time.

During the following months Humphrey tried a number of jobs but it was the early days of the Roaring Twenties, of Prohibition, of the Jazz Age and even the occasional gangster shoot-out in broad daylight. Humphrey and his girlfriend of the moment went slumming in Greenwich Village, smashed up Dr Bogart's car, received more than one summons for speeding, and generally did little to be proud of. It was all empty and unfulfilling and Humphrey began to complain that job after job was leading nowhere and felt the future looked bleak and hopeless.

One day one of his friend's sisters, Alice Brady, sowed a

seed in Humphrey Bogart that was to flower beyond anyone's expectations. Her father, a prominent theatrical producer, was starting an independent movie company, World Films, and was looking for assistants and staff. Humphrey was hired as an office boy and promised, should the opportunity arise, that he would be 'given a chance'.

Towards the end of a picture called *Life* the boss, Bill Brady, discharged the director and eagerly Humphrey Bogart said he would direct the picture. He did try to do so but found himself hopelessly out of his depth. Brady fired him and completed the picture himself.

Humphrey agreed that he was no good at film directing but he felt that he might be able to construct a film story and eventually he submitted his effort to Brady, who thought it was interesting enough to pass to his assistant, Walter Wanger. But Wanger hated it and threw it into the wastepaper basket. This did not prevent Wanger from saying, many years later, 'Bogie once wrote for me.'

Continuing his stage and film career Humphrey worked behind the scenes on a play and one day the producer's wife, actress Grace George, asked him to stage-manage her new play, *The Ruined Lady*. During the run the juvenile lead fell ill and Humphrey hastily made himself ready for his first professional appearance, but then Miss George fell ill and the play closed.

However Humphrey's stage debut was not long delayed. A play called *Drifting* had a Japanese houseboy with one line of dialogue and that was Bogie's start. Dr Bogart was in the audience and was suitably impressed by his son's performance. Brady must have been equally affected for he gave Bogie a juvenile part in his next production, *Swiftly*, which starred Frances Howard, later to become Mrs Sam Goldwyn.

During rehearsals for this play Bogie learnt a valuable lesson. His speech was slightly handicapped by his lisp and the promoter, sitting at the back of the balcony, kept shouting out, 'What?' 'What?' with such regularity that Bogie soon learned never to mumble.

The producer of *Swiftly*, Rosalie Stewart, liked Bogie and offered him a part in *Meet the Wife* which she was producing with Mary Boland and Clifton Webb heading the cast. Bogie had the part of a newspaperman and the show ran for thirty weeks. During the months that followed Bogie alternated between actor and stage manager.

In 1924 Bogie appeared in a play called *Nerves*, with Paul Kelly and although it ran only a few weeks he received favourable notices; and during the run he fell in love with Mary Philips.

Bogie next worked for a time on a play that starred his friend Alice Brady and when she suddenly fell ill he hurriedly found a talented redhead named Helen Menken as a replacement. She was older than Bogie and far more successful but within weeks there was talk of marriage.

Mary Boland was appearing in the comedy *Cradle Snatchers*, also in 1925, with Edna May Oliver, when she offered Bogie a part in the play. This time one of Chicago's leading critics referred to Bogie as 'as young and handsome as Valentino and as graceful as any of our best actors'. But Helen Menken had done even better. She was now the toast of Broadway in *Seventh Heaven* and she still wanted to marry Humphrey Bogart. She had a friend in Alec Woollcott, an important critic of the day, and she set about helping to further Bogie's career.

Bogie put his doubts behind him and he and Helen were married on 20 May 1926 at the Gramercy Park Hotel in New York, both bride and groom giving their ages as 26 years. Helen's parents were deaf-mutes and the rector who performed the ceremony was deaf but he had learned to talk and read the service in a horrible, hilarious sing-song voice while at the same time using sign language for the benefit of the bride's parents. After the ceremony Helen had hysterics.

That first Bogart marriage was not a happy one. 'We quarrelled over the most inconsequential things', Bogie was to say in later years. 'What started out to be just a little difference of opinion would suddenly become a battle royal, with one or the other of us walking out in a rage.'

They tried to patch things up, several times, but after a monumental fight in which Helen claimed her husband had blackened both her eyes, she left and sailed for England to appear in *Seventh Heaven*. After a year and a half of marriage, during which they had lived together only a few months, they were divorced. By this time Bogie was already a heavy drinker. His biographer says, of this period of Bogie's life: 'When he was not working, his life was one extended hangover.'

One night Bogie went to see the first talking film, *The Jazz Singer*, and afterwards went backstage at a nearby theatre to where an actress he knew, Mary Halliday, was appearing. Already talking to Mary was another actress who looked familiar and it turned out to be Mary Philips, with whom Bogie had appeared in *Nerves* three years earlier − and a girl he had thought he might be in love with. She remembered him and they began frequenting bars together but Mary was no fool and she told Bogie, when he talked to her of getting into the 'talkies', that the real actors were to be found on Broadway and not in Hollywood. Gradually their drinking sessions decreased and their circle of friends became serious showbusiness people where the talk was all about acting and the theatre.

Helen Menken had waived alimony when she and Bogie were divorced and soon Bogie and Mary Philips were married at her mother's home in Hartford, Connecticut. Years later Helen told Lauren Bacall, 'I was to blame for the breakup of our marriage. I put my career first and our marriage second.'

In 1929 David Belasco was casting *It's a Wise Child* and he gave Bogie a role along with Sidney Toler who was to become a reliable screen character actor. The comedy was successful and while it was still running Bogie heard from his brother-in-law Stuart Rose, then story editor for Fox Films and married to Bogie's sister Frances. The studio was casting *The Man Who Came Back* and Rose had suggested Bogie might be right for the lead. The test went well and with a contract and a train ticket for Los Angeles in his pocket Bogie hurried home, hoping Mary would leave her play and go west with him. The most he had earned up to that time was $500 a week; the film contract he now had called for him to be paid a regular $750 a week − but Mary refused to consider leaving New York where her career looked more than promising. They agreed that while they were apart they could each have friends of the opposite sex without questions being asked.

On arrival at Los Angeles Bogie was surprised to run into two actor friends Bobby Ames and Kenneth MacKenna, who were amused to learn that Bogie had come to play the lead in *The Man Who Came Back*; they had both arrived in Hollywood having been promised the same part! Eventually the role went to Charles Farrell with Bogie assigned to be Farrell's voice coach!

Once he had completed that task Bogie obtained a role in *A Devil with Women*, starring Victor McLaglen, released in 1930. Bogie played a rich young man in this, the first of the 75 films he was to make.

Before he appeared in *The Petrified Forest* (1936), one of his most famous roles and the film that convinced him that he should remain in Hollywood, he had appeared in films with Spencer Tracy, Charles Farrell, Elissa Landi, Myrna Loy, Conrad Nagel, Bette Davis, Zasu Pitts, Slim Summerville, Edmund Lowe, Bela Lugosi, George O'Brien, Joan Blondell, Guy Kibbee, Warren William, Ann Dvorak and Henry Hull.

But at first, things were decidedly difficult, in more ways than one. For a while, without much enthusiasm, Bogie and Mary resumed their marriage while Bogie made unnoticed appearances in several plays. It was the Depression and the outlook was bleak. It seemed a time to try to forget all their difficulties and they both began to drink far too much. The Bogarts moved to New York in the hope of finding stage work but there was little acting work to be found anywhere.

For a time Bogie, a good chess player, sat in the window of an amusement arcade and took on all-comers. It was while he was there, one day in September 1934, that he heard that his father was dying. Bogie hurried to the hospital in Manhattan, only to find that his father had already died. Bogie always felt sorry that his father had not lived long enough to see his success. In fact his father's death burdened Bogie with debts which he was eventually to pay off, selling almost everything he possessed. All he kept was an old-fashioned ring which he wore for the rest of his life.

While playing the villain in *Invitation to a Murder* on stage Bogie heard that Arthur Hopkins was looking for an actor to play a gangster in an important new play, *The Petrified Forest*. He did a reading but the author, Robert E. Sherwood, was not sure if Bogie was the right man for the part; however, Leslie Howard, the star of the show, thought Bogie's flat and world-weary voice just right and his opinion finally settled the matter. The success of *The Petrified Forest* enabled Bogie to pay off all his own debts and those of his father and still have a fairly healthy sum left. He deposited that remainder in what he called his 'F.Y. Fund', which he added to whenever he could: money that enabled him in the years to come to refuse films he didn't want to do.

Joe Hyams has pointed out that Warners had signed Leslie Howard for the film of *The Petrified Forest* and had chosen Edward G. Robinson for the gangster role. When he learned this Bogie remembered that Leslie Howard had promised that if the play were made into a movie, Bogie would get the role himself. Bogie cabled Howard in Scotland and next day Warners received Howard's ultimatum: either Bogie played the gangster or *The Petrified Forest* would be made minus Leslie Howard. The rest, as they say, is history. Bogie's Duke Mantee was hypnotic; nobody could take their eyes off him because they were never sure when he might shoot up the place.

After *The Petrified Forest* (1936) Bogie signed a long-term contract with Warner Brothers and began appearing and re-appearing in gangster roles. Off-screen, as Alan Barbour recounts, Bogie began to imitate his screen image, acting tough and drinking more than he should.

Bogie and Mary moved to the Garden of Allah, a group of bungalows built around a pool on Sunset Boulevard. The 24-hour bar service was only one of the attractions at this centre for many of the hard drinkers of Hollywood. Before long the Bogarts were enjoying a kind of non-stop party that continued from bungalow to bungalow.

In a way perhaps Bogie's portrayal of the trigger-happy gangster in *The Petrified Forest* was *too* good. Warners could not see Bogie in any other kind of role and he made 28 gangster films in a row.

When Mary returned to New York to appear in a stage play, *The Postman Always Rings Twice* Bogie was furious. Things had not been going well between them and perhaps they knew they were coming to the parting of the ways. While Mary was away Bogie became friendly with a tough, hard-drinking show-business girl, then in the midst of her second divorce. Mayo Methot was in the cast of Bette Davis's film *Marked Woman* (1937) which Bogie was currently working on and they hit it off at once. Both were equals when it came to fighting, drinking and throwing insults but the making-up was all the sweeter. Mayo was soon joining Bogie for weekends on his boat and before long she moved into the Bogart bungalow at the Garden of Allah.

This was the situation that Mary discovered when she returned to Hollywood and although Bogie told her he didn't want to marry Mayo, Mary insisted that he choose between them. Bogie was the last person to be presented with an ultimatum so Mary returned to New York to get a divorce.

During the course of an interview at this time Bogie said: 'The reason Mayo and I get on so well together is that we don't have illusions about each other. We know what we're getting, so there can't be any complaints on that score after we're married. Illusions are no good in marriage and I love a good fight, and so does Mayo.' On 20 August 1938, just a few days after his divorce from Mary was made final, Bogie and Mayo were married in Beverly Hills. The ceremony was a fitting prelude to the turbulent marriage that was to follow.

Among the diversions at the wedding Mischa Auer, the Russian character actor and comedian, suddenly stripped off and did a Cossack dance naked; and the wedding night augured what was to follow during the stormy seven-year marriage of 'the battling Bogarts' as the couple were soon dubbed. The pair had one of their usual fights so Bogie went off and got drunk and Mayo spent the night with a friend.

The Bogarts bought a house on Horn Avenue, east of Sunset Boulevard, and there, amid numerous birds, dogs and cats, they seemed to perfect the technique of marital disharmony. Bogie called Mayo 'Sluggy'; and they named their home Sluggy Hollow; their boat was named *Sluggy* and so was one of their dogs.

Mayo was a truly tough lady and she loved a real fight; Bogie liked nothing better than a shouting match but he was not a naturally violent man and he hated the sight of blood. Peter Lorre, who became a close friend after *The Maltese Falcon* (1941) witnessed many Bogart battles and had a dozen tales to tell about the fights and their aftermaths. He was himself to die a lonely death in Hollywood.

One night at Sluggy Hollow things got out of hand and Mayo stabbed Bogie with a kitchen knife. Bogie collapsed but a hurriedly summoned doctor said the actor was lucky, only the tip of the knife had gone in. It cost Mayo more than $500 to keep the matter quiet.

Another time Mayo set the house on fire but the studio police quickly and quietly took charge and again there was no publicity. Among her other accomplishments Mayo could drink most men under the table; a feat that Bogie greatly admired and during that third marriage he progressed from being a moderate drinker to a heavy one. Bogie was one of the few actors (W.C. Fields was another) who never tried to conceal the fact that he liked to drink.

Mayo had her virtues. She went out of her way to do all she could for Bogie's mother, who lived with them for a time; and for his sister Frances who suffered a nervous breakdown in New York and moved to Hollywood to be near them. His other sister Catherine died in 1937. Bogie's mother died in Hollywood at the age of 75 and it was Mayo who took charge of things and made all the funeral arrangements. It was Mayo too who insisted that Bogie have a business manager, but the sad truth is that Mayo's mental health deteriorated steadily during her marriage to Bogie.

When British actor Peter Cushing visited Ida Lupino on location at Big Bear Lake during the making of *High Sierra*, he met Humphrey Bogart. He described Bogie to me as 'a most charming and intelligent person' who, upon Peter's request, 'demonstrated his superb marksmanship and quick draw with a revolver, tossing coins high up into the air and, nine times out of ten, scoring a bull's eye before they reached the ground!' Despite his difficult home life Bogie was always a conscientious actor and it is said that he was never known to keep anyone waiting or to be late for an appointment.

During the filming of *Casablanca* Mayo became very difficult. She thought Bogie really was in love with Ingrid Bergman and she attempted suicide. Bogie took her on an extended foreign tour and for a while things were better but then he made *To Have and Have Not* and this time Bogie really did fall in love with his leading lady, Lauren Bacall, a new discovery, in her first film.

Betty Joan Perske was modelling for *Harper's Bazaar* when Howard Hawks's wife sent her husband pictures of the model. The producer told his secretary to get some background information on her and in error she sent the 19-year-old an air ticket. Howard Hawks said in 1974: 'This young girl appeared, very eager but totally inexperienced, with a high nasal voice. I told my secretary to get her a pass to two or three studios and then send her home. Instead she stayed in Hollywood. I had no intention of teaming her with Bogart although I could see she had something and I improved her voice a lot by taking her up into the Hollywood Hills and making her bellow across the valleys for three weeks.'

In the event the casting of the Hemingway novel — Bacall's smouldering and intelligent young personality opposite the already established and experienced Bogart — was brilliant. 'Bogie went overboard to help her,' Hawks added. 'We virtually made *To Have and Have Not* and *The Big Sleep* (1946), Bacall's second film with Bogie, back to back but by then he was letting her steal scenes from him. Making the film was a joy because Bogie was so happy.'

In later years Bogie himself was to recall that the days when he courted Lauren (Betty) Bacall were the happiest of his life. There was an age difference; he was 44 and she was 19 and Bogie did have misgivings. His friend Peter Lorre helped Bogie to make up his mind: 'It must be better to have five good years than none at all,' he said and Bogie smiled and knew that his friend was right for this was a rare love on both sides. Mayo couldn't win this one and she and Bogie were divorced on 11 May 1945. Six years later she died alone in a hotel in Hollywood. Ten days after the divorce Lauren Bacall became the fourth and last Mrs Humphrey Bogart. It was a good marriage, cemented by two children, a son Stephen born in 1949 and a daughter Leslie, born in 1952.

With a stable marriage Bogie stopped seeing many of his former drinking companions and he cut down on his own drinking. Betty Bacall has always thought that Bogie's drinking was caused by insecurity. 'When he realized he had security, emotionally as well as professionally, he found he could control his drinking.'

In 1947 a Federal Grand Jury indicted ten Hollywood writers as alleged Communists for refusing to answer when asked whether they were members of the Communist Party. Betty and Bogie were promptly in the forefront of the Hollywood contingent of stars who travelled to Washington to protest. From time to time, as the years passed, the Bogarts did become involved in politics but their real love, other than for each other, was Bogie's boat, the *Santana*, which they sailed as often as they could. Bogie had bought the lovely 55ft sailing boat from Dick Powell. She could sleep eight people comfortably and she was tended by Carl Peterson, a retired fireman known to all and sundry as Captain Pete.

When their young son Stephen was coming, the Bogarts moved to a larger house in the Holmby Hills from where Bogie was to form the Holmby Hills Rat Pack consisting of Betty and Bogie and people like Frank Sinatra, Judy Garland, Sid Luft, David Niven and Claudette Colbert. It all started out as a joke but soon became part of the Hollywood culture – a group of Hollywood celebrities who were friends of the Bogarts and who met at Romanoffs.

Soon Bogie was working on the John Huston film *The Treasure of the Sierra Madre* (1948), a film that was to win two Academy Awards. Bogie, ably assisted by Walter Huston (father of John), gave one of his most memorable performances and this film, like *The Maltese Falcon, Casablanca, To Have and Have Not* and later *the African Queen* (1951), has become a true film classic. A classic film is a motion picture that is retained in the public memory, becoming part of film culture, a film that will live as long as there are films. A few actors and actresses have appeared in one classic film, fewer still in two; how many have appeared in *five*?

One day John Huston rang Bogie to say he had a great story about a skinny missionary spinster and a hard-drinking captain of an old river launch who is persuaded to attack a German gunboat. Bogie thought it a most improbable tale but, when he learned that the author was C. S. Forester, he became interested. *The African Queen* turned out to be a film that is generally regarded as Bogie's best role and it won him an Academy Award as Best Actor of 1951.

The film was shot in Africa, seemingly in the most inaccessible spots that Huston could find. Everyone was ill with dysentery except Betty (who again insisted on accompanying Bogie) and Bogie himself: they both avoided drinking any water and even brushed their teeth with Scotch Whisky! And there were other difficulties: during the filming the old boat they used (since restored and something of a public attraction) sprang a leak and settled on the bottom of the river. This was deep in the jungle and it took five days to raise it. Another time the camp was attacked by a marching army of soldier ants and there were dozens of other problems but in the end the film was made. The famous leeches, incidentally, were made of rubber!

Bogie was always nostalgic about the film and once said: 'We loved those two silly people on that boat and Katie, of course, was absolutely perfect.'

During the making of his last film, *The Harder They Fall* (1956) Bogie complained of feeling different – he always seemed tired and it is from this time, 1955, that Bogie's fatal illness is usually regarded as having begun. However Verita Thompson says that a year earlier, while shooting *We're No Angels*, she noticed a sore on the top of one of Bogie's ears. She encouraged him to have it checked and eventually he did. It was skin cancer but the doctor removed it without complications, or so it seemed at the time. Around this time too Bogie began having a dry cough and occasionally losing his voice. He attributed the symptoms to too many cigarettes but in fact they were the early symptoms of the disease that would prove fatal two years later.

Verita Thompson has revealed that she was a close friend of Bogie for the last fifteen years of his life; his confidante and his lover. From 1942, when he was married to the explosive Mayo Methot until the day he died, Verita was frequently at his side sharing the laughs, sharing the liquor, and often sharing the bed of this complex man. It was a romance that was common knowledge, it seems, within the film fraternity but little known outside and Verita is not mentioned in any of the many biographies written about Bogie to date. She revealed the whole story in a book published in 1983.

Verita Thompson says she travelled with Bogie at home and abroad; she was with him at the studios and on location for all but four of the pictures he made, from and including *Treasure of the Sierra Madre* until his death. She and Bogie had been lovers for two years at the time of their supposed 'first meeting' in 1944 when she walked into his dressing room to fit his hairpiece or toupee. She was introduced to Bogie by Ann Southern who knew about the affair from the beginning and comforted Verita when she learned from the newspapers that Bogie had married Lauren Bacall. A runner-up in a Miss Arizona beauty contest, Verita had come to Hollywood under contract to Republic Studios as an actress; now she was in the wig business and had already worked with many famous stars and such leading men as Charles Boyer, Gary Cooper and Ray Milland.

Three months after his marriage to Lauren Bacall, Bogie got

in touch with Verita and the affair recommenced. Among other things Verita learned to copy Bogie's signature exactly and for several years she signed photographs of him for his fans.

In the spring of 1956 Bogie was still troubled with his throat and after a lot of tests he was told that he had a malignant cancer of the oesophagus — but the doctors told him they thought an operation would take care of it. He had the eight-hour operation which nearly cost him his life and included the removal of a section of oesophagus. After some weeks he was allowed to go home and for nine months he tried to recuperate. For a while his strength seemed to return and he was beginning to feel a lot better, although he was undergoing radiation treatment as an outpatient, and he enjoyed regaling the grisly details of his operation to anyone who would listen. What he did not know at that time was that his condition was fatal.

Gradually Bogie resumed the routine that was very special to him: cocktails at 5.30 at his place, the two-storey, white, colonial house on Mapleton Drive in fashionable Holmby Hills. And his friends would come: the Spencer Traceys, John Huston, David Niven, Truman Capote and many others. These memorable occasions took place in the Butternut Room on the first floor, oak-panelled, spacious and comfortable, with high windows that overlooked the garden and pool.

The bar alcove was Bogie's favourite spot and towards the end of his life he would sit there day after day at the cocktail hour, the highlight of his day; a gracious host entertaining his friends. Later, when he was no longer strong enough to walk downstairs he had the ceiling removed from the dumbwaiter that served the first and second floors and used it as an elevator. He would be wheeled to the second-floor opening, helped on to the stool inside, and lowered to the first-floor where he would be helped out into another wheelchair and taken into the Butternut Room.

Slowly but surely his appearance deteriorated. He lost a great deal of weight and although he was always cheerful and he kept up the cocktail hour, each grew more and more painful for him and more and more painful for his friends. It is unclear whether or not he knew he was dying. John Huston says he was present at one of the later cocktail hours when Bogie suddenly turned to his doctor and said: 'Level with me, Doc, am I really going to pull out of this?' Everyone held their breath while the doctor quietly attributed Bogie's weakness and loss of weight to the treatment he was taking, which was partially true. John Huston says he thought Bogie accepted the doctor's word, but who knows?

Alistair Cooke saw the sick man in his last weeks and he believes that Bogie knew he was dying. Adlai Stevenson saw him too in that last month. He said Bogie was very ill and very weak but he made a most gallant effort to keep cheerful for the two-hour session with his friends. Truman Capote wrote, 'He seemed to bring out the best in all of his friends. He looked awful, so terribly thin and his eyes were huge and they looked so frightened.'

During his last week of life Bogie heard that the press had said he was dying of cancer. 'Get me a lawyer,' he stormed. 'I'm going to sue them.' A lawyer was found and he was asked to prepare a law suit. 'He was full of fight,' the lawyer said afterwards. 'Even though he was obviously very sick.'

Next day, in the evening, Spencer Tracy and Katherine Hepburn went to see him and as they were leaving Dr Brandsman arrived. Katie Hepburn kissed Bogie goodnight as she always did and Tracy put a friendly hand on the sick man's shoulder. Bogie looked up at his old friend and with the ghost of a smile said, 'Goodbye, Spence.'

'You could tell he meant it,' Hepburn said. 'He's always said "Goodnight" before. When we were downstairs Spence looked at me and said, "Bogie's going to die."'

After the doctor left for the night Betty Bacall went in to kiss Bogie goodnight. She said later, 'I don't know why but that night I slept on the bed with him.' Bogie spent a fitful night and in the morning he said to his wife: 'Boy, I hope I never have another night like that.' He never did. Fifteen minutes later Bogie was in a coma and in the morning of 14 January 1957 Bogie took his last, deep gulp of life.

A memorial service was held three days later at All Saints Episcopal Church on Santa Monica Boulevard in Beverly Hills, but Bogie's body wasn't there. In accordance with his request he was being cremated at the same time a few miles away at Forest Lawn in Glendale. In the church, where Bogie's casket might have rested, stood a glass case containing a model of his beloved yawl, *Santana*. There was a minute's silence on the film lots of Warner Brothers and Twentieth Century-Fox.

Tennyson's poem 'Crossing the Bar' was recited and John Huston read a moving eulogy. Today Bogie's ashes rest in a small vault in The Garden of Memory at Forest Lawn instead of being scattered at sea as might have been more appropriate had it been possible.

To those who knew Bogie personally and to those who only knew him through his films John Huston's words were equally true: 'We have no reason to feel any sorrow for him, only for ourselves for having lost him.'

Lilli Palmer

-

Loyal, Talented and Beautiful

A German-born British actress whose real name was Maria Lilli
Peiser, Lilli Palmer, always delightfully attractive and charming,
had stage experience on the continent before moving to Britain
and making her first screen appearance in 1934. She appeared
in a number of Hitchcock films but also continued to establish
a career on the British stage. In 1943 she married Rex Harrison
and they remained married for fifteen years and only parted for
a singular and poignant reason.

Born in Posen in 1914 where her father was head of surgery
at a major hospital, Lilli was the middle sister in the family
of three. Before marrying Dr Alfred Peiser, Lilli's mother
had herself been an actress. When she was sixteen and still
at school Lilli also attended a drama school for two years and
at the end of the course she was rewarded by a twelve-month
contract with the Darmstadt State Theatre, regarded as one of
the best repertory companies in the country.

With the emergence and growth of Nazism Lilli's parents
could see that Germany was no place for young Jewish girls
and Lilli was sent to Paris to join her older sister who had
recently settled there. Lilli's boyfriend, a painter and medical
student six years her senior, soon followed and they all shared
an apartment. As Lilli began to look for stage work in Paris
she changed her name from Peiser to Palmer as it was easier
for the French to pronounce and eventually she and her sister
obtained work in nightclubs as a double act.

In 1934 Lilli's father had a sudden heart attack and died.
The two sisters went at once to Berlin but they were soon

back in Paris with a plan to go to England because Alexander Korda, the powerful film producer, had shown interest in Lilli's stage appearances. Lilli did journey to Britain but there were difficulties with Korda and instead Lilli appeared in a film for Warner Brothers, *Crime Unlimited* with Esmond Knight, made at Teddington. As a result she was offered a contract by Gaumont but she was unable to obtain the necessary work permit and she returned briefly to Paris. On her return to Britain she obtained the contract and a work permit for three months. Lilli promptly sent for her mother and two sisters and they set up house in Hampstead where Lilli had a drama teacher visit her to improve her technique.

Lilli Palmer worked in various films in a variety of situations: with comedian Will Hay in *Good Morning Boys*; with Madeleine Carroll and Peter Lorre in *Secret Agent* and with Margaret Lockwood in *A Girl Must Live*. In between filming she appeared on the London stage in *The Road to Gandahar* and *The Tree of Eden*.

With the outbreak of the Second World War Lilli's contract with Gaumont-British was cancelled but the Home Office granted her a permanent work permit and for a while things were difficult until Lilli obtained a part in Leslie Banks's tour production of *You of All People*. It was at this time that Lilli first met Rex Harrison, also appearing in repertory, in *Design for Living*, and both companies met in Birmingham, in November 1939.

Their relationship slowly blossomed as 1940 arrived although Lilli, as an enemy alien, was forbidden to leave her home after dark and when Rex rented a small cottage near Denham Studios to make Shaw's *Major Barbara*, Lilli moved in with him. She tried to contribute to the war effort, saying she could drive an ambulance, but her status as an enemy alien prohibited her helping in any way. However, she continued to be in demand for films and she enjoyed making *Thunder Rock* with James Mason and Michael Redgrave. In 1942 Rex was divorced from his first wife Collette, whom he had married in 1934 and by whom he had a son Noel; for most of the years they had been married they had led separate lives.

A few months later, in January 1943, he and Lilli were married at Caxton Hall Register Office. 'We had several years of true happiness,' Lilli was to say later. 'We were very much in love and I remember us lying in each other's arms when the bombs were falling and thinking, "Nothing will ever replace this," and nothing ever did.'

Their son, Lilli's only child, was born during one of London's worst air-raids on 14 February 1944. He was christened Rex Carey Alfred but he was always known as Carey. Later both Rex and Lilli became involved in entertaining the troops in a touring show, with Lilli singing and dancing. After the war Rex and Lilli were able to buy a small house in Denham which they called The Little House and Lilli always recalled those days with affection. 'It was our first real home and we were proud of it. I sewed the curtains − very badly − and we had a lovely garden. We were very happy there.'

In 1945 Hollywood called to both of them and each carrying a single suitcase they sailed on the *Queen Elizabeth* in the November of that year; the only civilians among the thousands of American servicemen returning home from the war. They loved California but Hollywood soon brought strains on their marriage; all the ladies threw themselves at Rex and he did not always resist temptation. But Lilli was apparently unconcerned. 'I would have stayed with that one man all my life,' she said.

Within months of their arrival Lilli and Rex were avid party-goers, at least once a week, with Rex eating and drinking and thoroughly enjoying himself and Lilli, who didn't drink, being little more than a chauffeuse. At one party David Niven's wife fell down a flight of stairs and died next day. Rex soon succumbed to the undeniable charms of Carole Landis with the tragic results that we have seen. On hearing the distressing news Lilli immediately travelled three thousand miles to stand by her husband and they faced the barrage of reporters together, but the marriage never really recovered from the Landis affair, and there was talk of a separation. Lilli and Rex were still married, however, when Rex fell in love with Kay Kendall who desperately wanted to marry Rex. Lilli had learned to accept such situations throughout her marriage and she simply kept out of the way.

By Christmas 1956 Kay began to suffer severe headaches, bouts of extreme exhaustion and other worrying signs of ill-health. Rex had at length persuaded Kay to seek medical opinion and one day he was surprised to receive a call from Kay's doctor, asking him to go and see him. Rex had himself been feeling under the weather and had consulted the same doctor, who told him that Kay was suffering from myeloid leukaemia and would be dead within three years. A dazed Rex Harrison wrote to his wife, who was in Austria, asking her to come to New York as soon as possible. Lilli responded immediately and as soon as she arrived they both went to see Dr Atchley, a trusted doctor friend, and explained the appalling illness from which Kay was suffering.

Afterwards Rex and Lilli talked long and hard about the matter and they agreed that the overriding need was for them to get a speedy divorce to enable Rex to marry Kay and give her as much happiness as possible – but it was all very difficult. Rex, according to Lilli, said, 'I cannot do it. You know how I feel about death ... I simply cannot do it.' Lilli told him he had to do it. 'Look on it like a war mission. You simply have to do it.' Rex replied, 'I could only do it if I knew you would come back to me afterwards.' Lilli told him she might well marry an Argentinian actor named Carlos Thompson and Rex replied, 'Well, you can, you can ... And when you get that out of your system, you can come back to me because we belong together.' In London, where she talked to me about the Carole Landis affair, Lilli told me, 'I did pledge myself at that time to go back to Rex.'

Immediately after the quickie Mexican divorce (under the petition Lilli was to have custody of their 12-year-old son Carey and would retain a half-share in their beautiful house in Portofino but otherwise there was no alimony settlement) Lilli returned to Europe and Rex became engaged to Kay. For a time they lived with Rex's old friend Terence Rattigan at his Hollywood home and occasionally they enjoyed a weekend with Bing Crosby in Palm Springs. Kay obviously adored Rex and soon they were married at midnight in New York after a performance of *My Fair Lady*.

While the couple were on holiday in Switzerland Kay felt unwell and then she cracked a bone in a tobogganing accident. Back in London they took a house in Chelsea while Rex appeared at the Theatre Royal, Drury Lane, in *My Fair Lady*. Kay's health continued to deteriorate but she took on a play in Brighton, *The Bright One* with Gladys Cooper as her grandmother. During the second week of the play Kay again fell ill (it was generally assumed that she was suffering from influenza) and she was absent for three days; but in any case the play folded at the end of the week.

Rex ended his stint as Professor Higgins in *My Fair Lady* and then, with the agreement of the doctors, Kay prepared to take the lead opposite Yul Brynner in the film comedy, *Once More With Feeling*, which was to be made in Paris.

Shooting began in the April but Kay's health soon cracked and she was more and more frequently unable to report for work at the studios. Rex took Kay back to London and to the London Clinic for treatment but after only four days she returned to Paris and worked again on the film. By sheer determination on Kay's part — twice the doctors had to fly out to administer heart stimulants — the film was completed and Rex took Kay to Portofino. Although she seemed to improve at first, she soon began to go rapidly downhill and Rex hurriedly brought her back to London and she again went into the London Clinic.

Hardly able to stand unaided, she told waiting news reporters: 'I'm just here for a couple of days.' A few days later she went into a coma from which she was never to awaken. Kay Kendall died on 6 September 1959, aged 32. As Roy Moseley says in his biography of Rex Harrison: 'Her death left a void in the lives of her many friends whose love and admiration for her great courage endure to this day.'

From the Clinic Rex wrote a hurried note to Lilli who was in London herself, caring for her dying mother; Lilli said it was a heart-rending letter asking her: 'Are you true to your vow?' But Lilli was by this time married to Carlos Thompson and Rex went on to marry Rachel Roberts. And so the years passed.

In September 1985 Rex Harrison and Claudette Colbert arrived in San Francisco for a four-week run of the successful comedy *Aren't We All?* They followed this engagement with performances in Washington and Los Angeles where Rex learned that his beloved Lilli was being treated for terminal cancer.

Already she required constant medical attention, day and night, and Rex's immediate response was, 'Don't worry about the expense. I'll pay whatever is necessary.' Later he learned that Lilli, the wife who had stood steadfastly by him for seventeen years, in times of great trouble and even when she knew he was seeing other women, was not expected to live beyond Christmas although in fact that loyal, beautiful and quite remarkable lady, Lilli Palmer, died on 28 January 1986 aged 71.

Rex Harrison continued to work on stage and in films and television and when he was 80 a friend described him to me as 'still young at heart, still upright, and sprightly, still wickedly attractive ...' He lived mostly, during the latter part of his life, at his home in Monaco, keeping up his membership of such clubs as Beefsteak, Green Room, Garrick, Players (New York) and Travellers' (Paris). Sir Rex Harrison died, also of cancer, in New York on 2 June 1990 aged 82, having appeared on stage eight weeks previously.

Lilli Palmer, actress,
authoress, loyal and
heroic wife of
Rex Harrison

Gary Cooper

-

The Gentle Giant

He was the strong, silent, all-American hero to an adoring public; in private he was known for having affairs with his leading ladies, for his unabashed nudity and for his considerable sexual appetite. He was particularly effective in Western films where his tough, resilient, brave and laconic roles endeared him to the film-going public and he won two Oscars, the second for one of his most outstanding roles, Will Kane the ageing marshall who stands alone against a vicious gang in *High Noon* (1952). Cooper's acting abilities may have been limited but there was a sincerity about every role he played and he enjoyed considerable popularity and was much loved for many years. He married only once, in 1933, and apart from a four-year separation, Veronica Balfe, who always made light of his continuous flirtations and widespread affairs, stayed with him until the end in 1961.

Born in Montana, Gary (whose real name was Frank James Cooper) and his older brother were sent, before the First World War, to live with their grandparents on a farm in Bedfordshire, a farm that bordered the vast estate of the Duke of Bedford. Arthur Cooper was a modestly successful lawyer, originally from Bedfordshire, England, and his wife, Alice Brazier Cooper of Gillingham in Kent, decided that they wanted a classic English education for their boys.

While at school Gary was involved in an accident that injured his hip and for the rest of his life he walked with a stiff and distinctive gait. To help the hip injury mend the doctors advised that he take up horse-riding. He sat tall in the saddle and became, more perhaps by accident than by design, an expert horseman.

Back in the States in 1924, with no acting ambitions but longing to mingle among the beautiful and sophisticated people he had glimpsed from time to time at Woburn, the Duke of Bedford's estate, he found work as an extra in the fast expanding movie industry and, as time passed, the tall, personable, handsome and willing young man found that a few bit parts came his way. During his first 18 months in the movies he estimated years later that he appeared in 50 different films.

One day while working as an extra on *The Lucky Horseshoe* (1925) with Tom Mix, the doyen of movie cowboys, Gary decided to see whether he could make a living in films – he always said the deciding factor was the difference in salaries that he and Tom Mix were paid. His weekly salary while working on that film was $50, Tom Mix was paid $17,500. About this time Coop (as he was already known) met Nan Collins, a studio casting director, and when she told him there were already two aspiring actors with the name of Frank Cooper, he decided to change his Christian name and Nan came up with Gary, her home town in Indiana.

The newly named Gary Cooper had a series of photographs taken and even invested in a home-made screen test showing his riding prowess, his agility, his 6ft 3in of masculine appeal. Almost immediately he obtained a starring role in a two-reeler, *Lightin' Wins* (1925) and when Sam Goldwyn was casting *The Winning of Barbara Worth* (1927), with Ronald Colman and Vilma Banky, Cooper managed to land the important part of Abe Lee, a cowboy whose unrequited love for the leading lady brought about his death. Sam Goldwyn's reaction on seeing this incident in the film was: 'Why didn't you tell me that boy was a great actor? He's one of the greatest actors I've ever seen. Put him under contract.'

At the outset of his career Gary Cooper played the good guy who might stray during the course of the story but always redeemed himself by the end of the film; and Cooper was rarely to stray from that formula in all his future films. He signed a contract for $200 a week and immediately it was announced that he would co-star with the talented boop-boop-a-doop girl, Clara Bow in *Children of Divorce* (1927) and then two Westerns, *The Last Outlaw* (1927) and *Arizona Bound* (1927).

Clara Bow, a bubbly redhead who at 16 years of age had won a 'Most Beautiful Girl in the World' contest, had a lifestyle as racy off-screen as she depicted in her films but there was a dark side to her life. Her mother was mentally unstable, perhaps unhinged by the deaths of her two previous children in infancy and one night Clara awoke to find her mother bending over her with a kitchen knife at her throat, threatening to kill her daughter before she let her become an actress. The terror of that moment was to live forever in Clara's memory and perhaps accounted for the chronic insomnia from which she suffered all her life. By the time Clara made her mark in pictures her mother was in a mental institution from which she would never be released. Suddenly in 1926 Clara's career exploded when she filmed *It*, her first starring role and adopted the appellation of 'The It Girl'. Cooper only had a bit part in *Children of Divorce* but he found Clara 'a different type of girl, glamorous, full of fun, a very sexy little girl, so pretty and so cute.' There were already those who said Coop didn't give a second thought to sleeping with anyone who might further his career and he certainly had affairs with many script girls, directors' secretaries and useful females in the casting department before he became involved with Clara Bow, but she was probably his first real love.

During the location shooting of *Wings* (1927: it won the Best Picture Oscar for that year), the cast were quartered in the St Anthony Hotel in San Antonio, Texas and there Gary Cooper discovered that Clara Bow was using the place like a brothel: all the young actors in the film falling in love with her and she took care of their feelings without becoming romantically involved. She also looked after Cooper's passion (she once told Hedda Hopper, the Hollywood columnist that Gary was 'hung like a horse and he can go on all night'). She also responded to the advances of actor Richard Arlen and those of a couple of pursuit pilots in the film and a writer! Director of *Wings*, William Wellman said she handled them all like chessmen; they never ran into one another, never suspected there was anyone else in her life and she made each man feel he was the one man she really cared about and each man was only too happy to accept without question 'the gorgeous little sexpot' and her insatiable and infectious appetite. But Coop became suspicious. When he found that discreet enquiries verified his suspicions he ended the affair, although he did stray back to Clara many times during the years that followed.

Years later, when the world learned the extent of Clara Bow's emotional disintegration and unseemly lifestyle – her private secretary sold the lurid stories of her love-life to a newspaper – Cooper somewhat ungallantly claimed that their relationship was nothing but a publicity stunt. When Clara Bow died of a heart attack in 1965 Hedda Hopper revealed that in her later years Clara would send her a card at Christmas, writing inside, 'Do you still remember me?'

While filming *Wolf Song* with tempestuous Lupe Velez, Cooper moved into Lupe's house at 1826 Laurel Canyon Road. It was the beginning of a long affair that seemed to be kept alive by public brawling and public making-up. Soon Lupe sported an engagement ring and said she and Coop were in fact married, having hopped over the Mexican border for that very purpose. Cooper immediately made a formal statement to the press averring that he was not engaged, nor was he even thinking of getting married. He always knew when to bow out of an affair and yet keep his options open.

When Lupe Velez was filming *The Storm* up in the Californian Rockies, Cooper visited her from time to time and there is a story that on one occasion he used Lupe's lipstick to paint in colour strategic areas of her exposed body, much to the amusement of a large part of the film company. However he found Lupe's home empty without her and he took a flat for himself in 1919 Argyle Avenue in Hollywood, celebrating the new independence by being arrested for speeding at 45 mph in a 25 mph zone on Wilshire Boulevard. Later he was to lease a house in Beverly Hills at 200 North Baroda Drive.

Soon Cooper was making five pictures a year and when the pressure mounted Paramount agreed that their increasingly valuable property should have a five-week break in Europe, providing he went alone. Lupe heard of his departure, turned up at the station too late to speak to him but, as the train pulled out, she pulled out a revolver and took a shot at him. Fortunately it missed its target and Cooper hurriedly made himself scarce and the studios saw to it that the whole episode was hushed up.

In Italy Cooper met the remarkable Countess Dorothy di Frasso, daughter of a manufacturer who left her $12 million and sister of a President of the New York Stock Exchange. The Countess was known to have entertained Crown Prince Umberto of Italy, the English Duke of York, Barbara Hutton and Benito Mussolini — who confiscated her opulent Villa Madama with its frescoes by Raphael as his guest house during the Second World War. The generous hostess took at once to Cooper and introduced him to the best tailors in Italy, to the renowned Italian Cavalry 'to keep him company on his rides', and to Italian society in general. As Mrs Jack Warner put it: 'He went to Rome looking like a cowboy and came back looking like a prince.'

Cooper began to appear in some good films and to be appreciated for his acting. Charles Laughton, his co-star in *The Devil and the Deep* (1932), said of Coop: 'He's the greatest actor in Hollywood; he acts from the inside.' Cooper's anti-war film *A Farewell to Arms* (1932) was particularly well received; *Design for Living* followed with Fredric March and Miriam Hopkins; he was the White Knight in the curious *Alice in Wonderland* (1933) before making the widely acclaimed *Lives of a Bengal Lancer* (1935). By this time Cooper was married for the first and only time to Veronica Balfe, known as Rocky, by whom he had a daughter Marcia. Three years after Coop's death Rocky married Dr John Converse.

Cooper went from strength to strength as he played Wild Bill Hickock in his own favourite film, *The Plainsman*; he joined Marlene Dietrich in *Morocco* (1930); played the crusading millionaire in *Mr Deeds Goes to Town* (1936); he was Hemingway's own choice for the hero of his epic drama *For Whom the Bell Tolls* (1943) — for which Cooper obtained his fourth Oscar nomination, having already won that coveted award for his appearance as the idol of America in *Sergeant York* (1941), and he won a second Oscar for his tense portrayal of the bitter marshall in the memorable *High Noon* (1952). Before his death he was awarded an Honorary Oscar for his services to the film industry.

It was at the presentation of that honorary Oscar that the world became aware that Coop was a sick man. The award was accepted on his behalf by James Stewart who visibly choked back the tears as he made an emotional acceptance speech: 'I'm sorry he's not here to accept it but I know he's sitting by the television set tonight and Coop I want you to know

I'll get it to you right away. With it goes all the friendship, and affection, and admiration ... and the deep respect of all of us. We're very, very proud of you, Coop. All of us are tremendously proud.' At the contemporary Cooper residence on Baroda Drive in Holmby Hills the actor, his wife and their daughter were indeed watching.

In April 1960 Coop had undergone an operation in Boston for cancer and soon afterwards he went into Cedars of Lebanon Hospital to have part of his bowel removed. Before the end of the year it was discovered that cancer had spread throughout his body and nothing more could be done. Within months the pain was with him constantly and it was only when it eased a little that he would sit up in his easy chair and contemplate the beautiful garden and welcome the occasional guest. His wife was a tower of strength and a wonderful help to him at this time. In those last months he managed to act as best man at the wedding of Fred Zinnemann, the director of *High Noon* and he saw a run-through of his last film *The Naked Edge* (1961) to advise on the cutting.

When his many friends became sad in his presence it was Coop who comforted them. 'I have no regrets,' he said many times. 'My life has been full and rich. I've had a wonderful life.'

One of his last visitors has described being shocked to find Coop a wasted and immobile figure lying in a darkened room. It was painful for the actor even to speak and he had to pause between words; sweat poured off him at the mere exertion of trying to speak normally. He converted to Catholicism and it seemed to bring him some comfort. On Friday, 12 May 1961 he received the last rites of his Church. Heavily sedated and in the presence of his doctor, his wife and his daughter, who had brought a rose from the garden for him each day, he quietly died the following day a few moments after midday, and six days before his 60th birthday. In all he appeared in more than 120 films in a career that stretched from 1923 to 1961. The newspapers spread the sad news of his death around the world with the words: 'He lived and died at high noon.'

Jack Benny

-

The Unique Humorist

'The warmest, the most gentle, the nicest human being I ever met in my life'; so said George Burns of Jack Benny, his friend for 55 years. A comedian who specialized in the 'slow burn', a brand of humour depending on skilled and accurate timing, Jack Benny constructed most of his jokes around his own reputedly mean, cowardly and incompetent personality. Most of his work was confined to radio and television but one of his films, with Carole Lombard, showed him to be a stylish comic actor.

He was born Benjamin Kubelsky in Chicago in 1894, his father coming from a small Russian town near the Polish border, who soon found and married a young lady in Chicago, a lady who had also emigrated from Russia.

The family, soon to be increased by a sister for Benny, lived over a butcher's shop. Before long Meyer Kubelsky opened a men's haberdashery store which he ran for the rest of his working life. On his sixth birthday Benny received from his parents a half-size violin. He was so pleased with it that they arranged for him to have violin lessons, hoping against hope that their son would one day become a concert violinist, but Benny hated having to practise. He much preferred to set up all the chairs in the house in rows and play the violin to anyone who would listen. Gradually he began to recite a poem or a little monologue in between the violin numbers and so his act was born.

When he left school Benny persuaded his parents to let him work at the Barrison Theatre, playing the violin in the pit and doubling as an usher; they agreed because they now realized that their son would never be a serious violinist as they had dreamed he might be. Benny loved the theatre; he watched the acts whenever he could and learned many of the tricks of the trade. He was always keen to support any act with his violin music and a formidable little lady named Minnie Marx was so impressed when she brought her sons to the theatre with their act that she invited Benny to join the group to provide the music but Benny's father and mother would not hear of him going on the road.

Soon the Barrison Theatre closed and Cora Salisbury, the pianist, decided to go back into vaudeville. She had been watching Jack Benny, as he now called himself, and thinking she could see talent she suggested they form an act together. This time Benny's parents gave in and so 'Salisbury and Benny – From Grand Opera to Ragtime' first saw Jack Benny facing a paying audience.

The first booking for the newly formed act was in Gary, Indiana and Cora and Jack set off with high hopes. Miss Salisbury, it should be explained, was a mature woman to 17-year-old Jack, and she was like a mother to him. At the end of the journey Jack gave two of his hard-earned dollars to the porter as a tip and when Cora heard about that she upbraided Jack for squandering his money, saying 50 cents would have been quite enough. 'That was the beginning of my thrifty image', Jack always insisted.

When Cora's mother became ill, Cora decided to leave the act that had by that time played successfully all over the Mid West and Jack found a young pianist named Lyman Woods. The partnership of 'Benny and Woods' continued the good work started by 'Salisbury and Benny' and went on for several years, including bookings in New York. The act seemed to improve all the time and life was beginning to be good for the two young men when, in November 1917, Jack was called home when his mother's health gave cause for concern. Her death from cancer when Jack was 23 affected her son deeply and for the rest of his life he had a terrible fear of the disease.

Early in 1918 Benny and Woods performed their last professional engagement in Milwaukee and Jack joined the Navy. He never saw Lyman Woods again and in the seven years that he had been on the professional stage, Jack Benny had not uttered a word.

At the Great Lakes Training Station for the Navy Jack soon heard about the service theatrical company that was being set up to present shows for Navy Relief and he teamed up with a clever young pianist named Elzear Confrey and they formed an act which was a progression from the Benny and Woods routine, with Confrey playing the piano with originality and humour and Jack rolling his eyes and fiddling and fooling.

When the war ended Jack and Zez (as Confrey was called) talked about taking their act on to the professional stage but Jack was discharged first and it seemed that it might be some time before Zez was out and able to join him. Jack therefore thought he would try his hand on his own as a fiddle-playing comedian. He was moderately successful and toured the small theatres of the day.

When Zez finally came out of the Navy he began to write songs and pieces for the piano, like 'Kitten on the Keys' and, seeing that he was on the road to success as a composer, Jack made up his mind to continue as a single act. Gradually, despite the sense of insecurity that dogged him all his life, Jack Benny's act improved; he found comedy more popular than singing or playing his violin and soon the act became a comedian using the fiddle as a prop which was what it remained for the rest of Jack's life.

His act went from strength to strength and soon he married his first wife, Sadie Marks. When she became bored sitting backstage while he appeared in the touring musical revue *The Great Temptations*, he wrote her into the act. She had a very pleasant singing voice and an excellent delivery for the jokes that Jack fed her. One day he heard that Irving Thalberg had seen the show and wanted him for MGM movies! He signed a six-month contract and the couple rented a lovely house in Beverly Hills. Jack soon became the subject of studio publicity and was thrilled to meet most of the big stars like Joan Crawford, John Gilbert, Greta Garbo, Lionel Barrymore, Wallace Beery and Cary Grant.

Jack Benny was never to lose his admiration for Grant with his classy sophistication, poise and indefinable air of breeding. In fact Cary Grant was born Archie Leach in a small semi-detached house with an outside toilet in Horfield,

Bristol; the son of a factory worker who frequently indulged
in affairs with young women and habitually drank himself into
a stupor. His biographers believe that he was the illegitimate
child of a Jewish woman who died in child-birth. Jack Benny
knew none of this and he attempted to incorporate some of the
suave composure and bearing of Cary Grant into his act.

Benny did play in the film *Hollywood Revue* but when
nothing else materialized he went to see Irving Thalberg and
asked to be released from his contract. When the formalities
were finalized Jack and Sadie moved to New York where Jack
found work in the *Earl Carroll Vanities* on Broadway. Afterwards he worked extensively in radio and on television; his radio
programme reaching the No 1 position in the national ratings,
helped by the gravel-voiced coloured servant Rochester. Benny
then made a deal with Paramount to make three pictures for
$100,000 each.

Most of his films, *The Horn Blows at Midnight*, *Road Show*,
Chasing Rainbows, *The Medicine Man* and *Transatlantic Merry
Go Round*, are perhaps best forgotten; or as Jack used to say,
'the less said about them, the better'. But then, having moved
back to California, he made *Broadway Melody of 1936* and *The
Big Broadcast of 1937* and he joined his great friends George
Burns and Gracie Allen in *College Holidays*.

Benny found himself on the Fascist hit list in late 1938,
along with people like Fredric March, Charles Chaplin and
Louis B. Mayer (all members of the Anti-Nazi League) and
he discovered that the Hollywood Fascists were reportedly led
by Victor McLaglen who worked hand-in-glove with the Los
Angeles German Consul of the day. They were days of distrust
and strange bed-fellows.

Towards the end of 1938 veteran showman Earl Carroll
opened his theatre-restaurant on Sunset Boulevard with its
patent-leather ceilings, satin walls, 76 of 'the most beautiful girls in the world' and music by Ray Noble. Over
the entrance an enormous girl's face in neon lights was
surrounded by the words: 'Through these portals pass the
most beautiful girls in the world.' It was hardly likely to
be missed by Jack Benny who was among the glittering
crowd on the opening night which also included Bob Hope,
Errol Flynn, Betty Grable, Claudette Colbert and Constance
Bennett. The new nightclub was so successful that it inspired

a movie and so ensured Earl Carroll a place in the legend of
Hollywood.

More films followed but none of them really took off apart
from the very successful *To Be or Not to Be*, the Ernst Lubitsch
picture co-starring Jack with Carole Lombard, who was to die
tragically a few weeks after the completion of the film. *To Be
or Not to Be* was one of the best anti-Nazi parody films. Set in
occupied Warsaw it was full of typical Lubitschian buffoonery.
All the traditional tricks of farce were utilized to unravel the
complex plot and although the cast included Sig Rumann, Felix
Bressart and Joseph Tura, the film belonged to Jack Benny
who proved himself to be one of the American cinema's most
accomplished light comedians.

At the time, when her long relationship with Alexander Korda
was finally disintegrating, Merle Oberon looked in on the set
of Alex's new picture, *To Be or Not to Be*, and met Jack
Benny. She admired the talent of the great comedian but found
an unhappy and depressed man who was himself seemingly
suffering from many repressed problems. She was captivated
by the delightful Carole Lombard but with Benny Merle was
to enjoy an intense friendship for many years. They shared an
interest in the supernatural that blossomed, in a light-hearted
way, when Jack appeared as a ghost in Raoul Walsh's *The Horn
Blows at Midnight* (1945), Jack playing the angel Athanael, sent
to earth to sound the trumpet of doom.

Tours, television, personal appearances, radio, charity concerts all filled Jack's life; even when he was well into his
seventies (although he only admitted to 39!) he played an
eight-day engagement at the Candlewood Theatre in New
Fairfield, Connecticut, and filled the theatre to capacity every
night. He had not starred in a movie for 28 years but he won
one of the two leading roles in *The Sunshine Boys* and he played
in several symphony concerts during the summer of 1973 but
by the autumn he was moody and irritable; he had no appetite
and he complained of stomach pains and felt sure he had an
ulcer or something more serious. In the November his doctor
gave him a thorough examination and carried out tests over
a three-week period, and ended up giving Jack a clean bill of
health. All Jack's friends were convinced that the pains were
psychosomatic but he still complained of stomach pains and he
began to visit his doctor almost daily.

During rehearsals for a television special Jack picked up his violin to warm up and found that his right hand was numb and he couldn't hold the bow. Doctors diagnosed a stroke and ordered him to hospital although Jack protested that he was all right and he insisted on treating the ambulance attendants to coffee and doughnuts at a coffee shop on the way to the hospital, refusing to lie down in the ambulance. In fact he finished up riding in the front seat with the driver!

He remained in hospital for four days and was delighted when the strength came back to his hand and when all tests were negative. The doctors told Jack he had had the slightest possible stroke that only affected his hand and he was told he would be completely normal in a week or two.

Back in his Hollywood home he was in good spirits for a few days but then the stomach pains returned and became more severe. His daily visits to his doctor recommenced but still no cause was discovered and Jack was given some pills to ease the pain.

He enjoyed a pleasant evening when he was inducted into the 'Hall of Fame' at the convention of the Television Advertising Bureau at the Century Plaza Hotel in Los Angeles and afterwards he seemed to forget the pains. But they returned a few days later and Jack became very depressed as he took more and more sedatives and tranquillizers. Soon he was sleeping most of the day; however he agreed to take part in a function for the Hollywood Women's Press Club. As he prepared for the event he doubled up in pain, but still said he would see it through and with great courage he forced himself erect and walked to the car. He barely spoke on the way and at the pre-luncheon photo session he finally gave in and said, 'Sorry, I can't make it ... take me home.'

Once back in their Beverly Hills home his wife hurriedly called the doctor and Jack Benny was sedated and ordered nursing round the clock. A week or so later his long-standing personal manager and producer found him going over the script of a film. He looked fairly well and seemed in good spirits but later Irving Fein learned that he had been given drugs to relax him. Reading the script with Jack the producer knew at once that it was not going to work. Jack seemed unable to focus properly, he couldn't concentrate and he skipped words and even sentences as he tried to read the first page. He tried and tried to get it right but after half-an-hour he hadn't managed more than four lines of the script. The show was cancelled.

Two days later the doctors made another test and revealed to Mrs Benny the terrible news that Jack had terminal cancer of the pancreas and he probably had less than a month to live. Sometimes called 'the hidden cancer' this particular form of cancer often remains undetected by various tests and it is not unknown for patients to die, seemingly from another cause, until the autopsy reveals cancer in the pancreas.

A week later Mrs Benny was told that her husband might die that night. In the morning he was still holding on but the doctors said he couldn't possibly last through that day. At 11.26 pm on 26 December 1974 Jack Benny died quietly. Millions of people treasure their memories of the gentle, generous man who loved to make people laugh by laughing at himself.

Susan Hayward

-

Spirited Heroine

Susan Hayward was tough and she needed to be. Born Edythe Marrener in Brooklyn in 1918 she would one day be lauded as top female box office star and top money-spinner at both MGM and Twentieth Century-Fox studios. She had thick red hair, a tip-tilted nose, she was glamorous, attractive, intelligent, vulnerable and a sex symbol whose only real competition at the time was the rising Marilyn Monroe.

Susan Hayward always seemed to play characters who were tough on the outside but weak inside. The spirited heroines of *Tulsa* (1949) and *Untamed* (1955), the tragic drinkers of *Smash-Up*, *My Foolish Heart* and *I'll Cry Tomorrow*, the crippled singer of *With a Song in My Heart*, the less than good women of *David and Bathsheba*, *The President's Lady* and *Back Street*, and the murderess in *I Want to Live* (1958) for which she won an Oscar.

Her father was a subway guard, her diminutive mother of Swedish extraction and she had a brother who was born prematurely with a stomach defect. By the time the boy was three years of age he was wearing leg braces and one day when his mother was carrying the boy to get a new pair fitted a total stranger fell into conversation with her and walked off saying, 'Take the braces off; he'll be all right.' Instead of going to the clinic Susan's mother turned round and went home. There she removed the supports and to her surprise the boy took a few steps. Within a month he was running about like any other child.

Susan, like her mother, saw the episode as proof of the supernatural and throughout her life Susan accepted omens, listened to prophecies and believed in astrology. When she was little her father had told Susan: 'An angel sits on your shoulder and protects you.' As she grew older the angel became less real but she always accepted the idea that a beneficent power protected her and as long as she believed that no problem seemed too big for her to meet.

'My father also taught me something else that I have never forgotten', Susan used to say. 'Fight for what you believe in; be like a rubber ball – the harder the hit, the higher the bounce.' One needed such encouragement, for life was hard in the Marrener household; Mrs Marrener kept the four cramped rooms immaculate but the children wore the same grey linen clothes day in and day out – they had no other, and when the shoes wore through cardboard was used to cover the holes.

One day when she was six years old Susan ran out into the road in the direct path of a car. She was thrown ten feet into the air and fell to the pavement with a sickening thud. Everyone who saw the accident thought the child must be dead. Her mother picked up the crumpled and unconscious body and, ignoring the pleas of the distraught driver to let him take her to the hospital, she carried her daughter home and took her upstairs to the children's room. There she found that both legs had been shattered and the right hip severely dislocated, but there was no money for hospital treatment.

Pulleys were fixed up to suspend the broken legs and tight bandages sought to secure the damaged hip. Susan stayed in that position for seven months and then for two years she was pulled about in a wooden truck and taken to a free clinic where her progress was monitored, her mother advised, and the child hobbled about on crutches.

The bones never did really knit together perfectly and the damaged hip left Susan with a sexy hip-swivelling walk that was to become one of her trademarks. Another drawback that Susan used to her advantage was her short-sightedness; she could hardly see anything or anyone more than a few feet away without glasses and she was too vain to wear them in public. Later, of course, contact lenses came to her rescue, but her habit of looking long and searchingly at whoever was speaking to her unconsciously added a dimension to her acting.

In the darkness of the movie theatres that she began to

frequent she had no hesitation in donning her glasses to follow
the films of her favourite movie stars: Bette Davis, Lew Ayres,
Charles Boyer and Katharine Hepburn.

Meanwhile at school Susan began to be interested in acting
and it is significant, in view of the majority of her later screen
roles, that even then her drama teacher recalls her as 'always
choosing the parts no one else would take – but parts with
dramatic possibilities, and she always did well'.

After leaving school Susan decided to try modelling and the
energetic 16-year-old redhead was soon one of the Thornton
Agency's top models. David O. Selznick had already spent
nearly three years and over $50,000 looking for an actress to
play Scarlett O'Hara in *Gone With the Wind*, when George
Cukor picked up a copy of the *Saturday Evening Post* that
diplayed a sweater-clad teenager with knowing eyes and a wealth
of red hair. Cukor lost no time in contacting the photographer,
Ivan Dmitri, and obtaining the telephone number of the stunning
model. The same afternoon Susan agreed to go to Hollywood
but the test for the role of Scarlett O'Hara did not work out.
She was told she needed more experience and she had better go
back to Brooklyn and try acting in stock companies.

'No, Mr Selznick,' Susan smiled, hiding her disappointment.
'I think I'll stay. I like the orange trees.'

The great man was incensed. 'Then turn in your return tickets
to New York at the front office,' he barked.

'Can't,' replied Susan. 'I've already cashed them in to live
on. Bye.'

Susan moved to a bungalow on the outskirts of Beverly Hills
and one afternoon, cycling without glasses, she crashed on to
the lawn of Bunny Medford, one of Hollywood's myriad of
agents. He immediately saw something in Susan and talked to
Max Arrow, one of Warner Brothers talent executives. He too
was impressed and she was sent to the Warner drama school
where she worked with people like Ronald Reagan, Carole
Landis and Jane Wyman. Eventually she made her film debut
in Busby Berkeley's *Hollywood Hotel* (1937) together with 200
other girls; the following year, just before her 20th birthday,
she said a few lines at the beginning of the highly acclaimed
suspense film starring Edward G. Robinson, *The Amazing Dr
Clitterhouse*, and then an even shorter piece, as a telephone
operator in the Bette Davis picture *The Sisters*.

During the following 35 years Susan Hayward was to appear in more than 60 films, some of them successful (*Reap the Wild Wind* (1942), *The Snows of Kilimanjaro* (1952)) but most of them forgotten by everyone but Susan Hayward fans, of whom there were in those days – and still are – a great many.

From about 1971 Susan began to suffer headaches, piercing stabs that seemed to radiate from the centre of her skull, but she put the pain down to her not infrequent over-drinking.

It was at the Hollywood Canteen, the brain child of Bette Davis, that Susan Hayward met the Canteen's master of ceremonies, Jess Barker and she married him in July 1944. Seven weeks later the couple had a noisy slanging match on the front lawn of their Beverly Hills home and Susan went home to Mother. It could well have been the end of the marriage but two weeks later Susan found she was pregnant. There was a cosy reconciliation and she took a year off from films to start her family, giving birth to twin boys in February 1945, Timothy and Gregory. Sadly, however, the shouting matches between Susan and Jess resurfaced and they were evicted from four different residences during the following twelve months for causing noisy disturbances.

Not that it was all unhappiness. They were in fact to share (more or less) a decade together but increasingly Susan and Jess did things separately rather than as a couple.

As the years passed the marriage grew, if anything, more shaky but to celebrate their ninth anniversary, and perhaps in an effort to repair their marriage, they bought a Jaguar car and toured Italy, Spain and France, a trip that lasted three months. But it was a holiday interspersed with bickering and quarrelling and within two weeks of their return to Hollywood the final row erupted, witnessed by friends and neighbours, and the police were called. Susan filed for divorce the next day. They had been married for nine and a half years.

During the weeks that followed Susan found solace with several men including Jeff Chandler, who had known her as a schoolgirl, and powerful and dynamic Howard Hughes who starred Susan in *The Conqueror* (1956) where the cast were exposed to radioactive earth for almost two years. A number of them succumbed to cancer, including Susan.

Susan continued to have trouble with her husband and the couple usually had a row whenever he picked up or returned the twin boys. Susan had become addicted to sleeping tablets; she felt she was unfairly manipulated by men; she had always sought to keep her private life private but now she was constantly being badgered by the press and everything she said or did was distorted; in short she felt her life was a shambles.

Deep in lonely despair at 3737 Longridge Sherman Oaks one April night in 1945 Susan deliberately took a massive overdose of sleeping pills. About twenty minutes later the pills began to take effect – and Susan panicked: she staggered to the telephone and somehow managed to reach her mother.

Within fifteen minutes the police were at the house. Susan was unconscious and was rushed to North Hollywood Receiving Hospital. The doctors hurriedly clamped her tongue and pumped her stomach, although they were doubtful whether they were in time. Susan sank into a deep coma and her life was steadily ebbing away.

Shortly before dawn Susan's own doctor arrived and ordered her removal to Cedars of Lebanon Hospital where Susan recovered after she had slept off the effect of the pills. 'I feel so ashamed,' she admitted afterwards, while insisting that the whole thing was an accident.

In 1955 she made *I'll Cry Tomorrow*, generally regarded as a great film and certainly the most effective one ever made about female alcoholism. In the film she was required to do a drunk scene without make-up and she told director Daniel Mann, well-known for his unpretentious and realistic approach, that she had freckles and couldn't very well do a scene with no make-up. Mann told her he would use a blue light to make her look even more spotted and he explained that the most sympathy would come if the audience could see for themselves how the character had degenerated. Susan saw his point at once, shrugged and accepted the situation. She was a real professional. When the film appeared she was voted best actress of the year and was the only American among the winners at the Cannes Film Festival; but when she missed out on the expected Oscar Susan dissolved into tears.

This time she found solace in the arms of Don 'Red' Barry, the hunky star of a dozen Westerns who had a bit part in *I'll Cry Tomorrow*, but it all ended in tears when Barry's fiancée, blonde starlet Jill Jarmyn, found the two in bed together. The girls began fighting and Barry had to separate them. But the fighting began again and in the end Jill made her getaway and filed an assault-and-battery complaint against Susan, which was eventually dropped. The publicity did Susan no good at all, however.

The following year Susan met tall, dark and handsome Floyd Eaton Chalkley, a lawyer and former member of the Federal Bureau of Investigation who ran his own investigating agency. They were married within a few months of meeting; he was 47 and she was 38. Susan sold her properties in California and the couple moved to Georgia.

In 1959 Susan at last won an Oscar, for her work in *I Want to Live*. As she went back to Eaton's side at their table after accepting the award she revealed her true opinion of Hollywood. 'Finally, dear,' she said. 'I've climbed to the top of the dungheap.' She still had film commitments but in her life with Eaton and the boys Susan found contentment and she was ready to retire. Instead she made 14 more films in the 16 years left to her; including the traumatic experience of *Where Love Has Gone* (1964) where she clashed with temperamental Bette Davis who was playing Susan's mother and who took second billing to the star. Meanwhile the twins were growing up; Gregory was studying veterinary medicine and Timothy was hoping to become something in the music industry. Through her husband Susan met Ron Nelson, a lifelong bachelor who, after heart trouble, had devoted himself to raising funds for heart research. They became good and sincere friends and Ron respected both Susan and Eaton and considered them the happiest married couple he had ever known.

In 1965 Susan went to Rome to make *The Honey Pot* with Rex Harrison and Eaton accompanied her; it was almost like a second honeymoon and Eaton, a devout Roman Catholic, even managed an audience for them with the Pope. Then one morning Eaton woke up in agony. During his service in the Second World War he had been the recipient of a blood transfusion that had caused a viral form of hepatitis and now it had suddenly resurfaced. It was agreed that the filming could be rearranged to shoot round her and Susan flew back to America with her husband.

Within a few days the complaint disappeared and Susan returned to Rome but a couple of months later Eaton was suddenly readmitted to hospital and a week later his condition worsened. Susan rushed to his side but he knew he was dying and asked to be taken home. Within a few days he was dead. 'I sure as hell hope there is an afterlife,' Susan told her friend Nelson. 'I want to see Eaton again.' She sold the houses they had lived in together and tried in a hundred ways to erase the painful memory of what she always referred to as 'the happiest ten years of my life. When you say ten years it sounds like a long time but when you live it and are truly happy, it's no time at all.' Her constant companion in the dark days after Eaton's death was Mate, her black Labrador retriever – and once more she drank.

Then she made *Valley of the Dolls*, from Jacqueline Susanne's infamous novel and the author herself told me she was delighted with Susan Hayward's performance. Most of the critics and just about everyone who saw the picture praised the work of Susan. Ironically both Jacqueline Susanne and Susan Hayward were treated for cancer at the same time at the UCLA Medical Centre.

After a brief spell on the stage in *Mame* Susan became something of a recluse. She continued to drink a lot and she was still friends with Ron Nelson and once a month she would visit the bank and ask to see the $400,000 she kept there in a safe deposit box. One night a smouldering cigarette set her apartment alight and she nearly lost her life. Even so, she was beginning to recover her confidence and when things looked bright for her in television she decided to go back to Hollywood to live; especially when her astrologer who had been preparing daily charts for her for thirty years, told her that the moon was in the 4th House and that a move was in order. She found the house she wanted at 1460 Laurel Way in Beverly Hills.

It had been almost a year since the fearsome headaches had begun to trouble her; headaches she tried to explain away but they became worse and worse and she began to drink even more heavily. At a hospital in Washington she had a liver scan consisting of an injection of a dye which would show up on an X-ray screen.

Moments after the injection Susan's body arched in violent convulsions and the worried doctors hurriedly had to attend to the writhing body on the X-ray table. Later, when she recovered consciousness they told her that the dye must have hit something in her brain to cause the convulsions. They said they would make more tests but Susan had had enough. 'You bastards did this to me,' she lashed out in her anger. 'You injected me with that goddammed dye and I'm obviously allergic to it,' and she stormed out of the hospital.

She did more television work, mostly weepies — by this time she was known as 'the queen of the weepies' — but the headaches worsened and she told Nelson she would have to do something. The doctors performed a brain scan and broke the terrifying news that she had numerous cancerous lesions in her brain. She told them they were crazy and flew to New Orleans to promote one of her films, but little things began to show evidence of something very wrong: she found it difficult to light a cigarette, to remove the cap from a bottle, and she froze whenever the telephone rang: 'It always seems to be bad news,' she said.

For several months she endured the growing pains that blurred her reactions and spoiled everything in her life, only slightly alleviated by pills. And then in April 1972 she collapsed at a friend's birthday party. She was rushed to hospital and for five weeks her life hung in the balance. When she came out of hospital she weighed only 85 lbs and her shaven head was concealed under a red wig. Nobody was told the truth except Ron Nelson. The doctors thought that she would be dead by 4 July, less than two months away.

But Susan had no intention of dying to doctors' orders or schedules. 'I've died a dozen times in pictures,' she said bravely. 'And when it is over I just get up and walk away.' Nevertheless the time had come for full-time nursing. Soon she was unable to stand unaided and her hands shook. She passed the 4 July 'deadline' although several Hollywood papers ran her obituary. Instead Susan and Ron Nelson escaped to the beach at Santa Monica where they dined on lobster, scampi and Beaujolais.

Three months later Susan was still there and she was now convinced that she was in complete remission but one day she began to drag her right foot and collapsed. By Christmas she was dragging her leg more noticeably and the paralysis spread over her entire right side, except for her arm. The doctors said the tumour on the left side of the brain was spreading to the right side and would soon paralyse her completely. Defiantly Susan called a halt to all orthodox treatment and found relief in the controversial drug Laetrile; by February 1974 she was again in remission.

Heartened by her improvement Susan decided to defy the doctors' advice and accept an invitation to take part in the Academy Awards presentations on 2 April; despite the fact that her brain seizures were now occurring almost hourly. She wore a high-necked, full-length gown and her by now paralysed right hand was concealed. Aided by a massive injection of tranquilliser and introduced as 'a medical miracle', Susan laboriously made her way to the podium and performed the necessary presentations. Afterwards she collapsed.

By late summer 1974 Susan was confined to a wheelchair, her legs were in braces to prevent the brittle bones from shattering at the least strain and she could no longer even turn the pages of a book or feed herself.

In September she found it difficult to speak and Ron Nelson learned with horror that within days she would lose her memory, her speech, her ability to swallow – and that would be the end for her since she had explicitly prohibited any type of intravenous feeding.

Nelson was at her Atlanta hospital bed four days later when she suddenly rallied and asked for water. He helped her and asked whether there was anything else he could do for her. She knew what he meant. 'I don't want anyone to push me over the brink,' she said. 'And I don't want anyone to hold me back.' She asked to be taken back to her home on Laurel Way, Hollywood; if the time had come for her to die, she wanted it to be in her home, looking out over the city she knew and loved and hated and had conquered.

As they travelled back Susan said suddenly, 'They think I've got cancer. We know you've had a heart attack. Let's make a deal. If you kick the bucket first, I'll try to be there. If it's me, you be there or I'll haunt you for the rest of your life!'

January 1975 came and still Susan was alive. She could hardly speak, she could hardly swallow and she had to be turned in bed; but having been given two months to live, she had survived for nearly three years. Once she surfaced and shook Nelson with her directness: 'I'm frightened,' she muttered. 'Tell me about death. Will it hurt? Don't let me suffer. Don't let me die alone.'

During the following weeks and months Susan slipped into

and out of consciousness. She talked lovingly with her sons and towards the end existed for ten days without food. On 14 March at 2 o'clock in the afternoon Nelson saw her tremble and her temperature soared. Although totally paralysed her whole body shook wildly. Nelson held her close and called the nurse. Her eyes opened and she turned to Nelson. 'How long will it take me to die?' she asked, adding with a typical hint of bitterness: 'But you said it wouldn't hurt.' Even as she spoke her head wrenched sharply, she gasped and her eyes turned upwards. Susan Hayward was dead at 56.

The doctors still say it was a miracle and there is nothing like it in medical history. 'It was amazing to live that long with that type of cancer. She was one of the truly great fighters.' Her twin sons estimate that she spent $350,000 staying alive but she still left some $750,000 to them in cash – as long as they didn't give a cent to their father.

When Susan placed her handprints in the forecourt of Grauman's Chinese Theatre (renamed Mann's in 1978), helped by Sid Grauman himself, she carefully sprinkled a handful of gold dust over the prints and still today hers are the only prints etched in gold.

Every year on 14 March, the anniversary of her death, a memorial notice appears in *Variety* anonymously: 'Susan Hayward, Academy Award Winning Actress. 30 June 1918–14 March 1975. A Star, Is a Star, Is a Star'.

John Wayne and Others

-

Cancer, The Conqueror

Starring with John Wayne in the epic Howard Hughes film *The Conqueror* were Susan Hayward, Agnes Moorhead and Pedro Armendariz, and the film's director was Dick Powell: every one of these five was to die of cancer and it could well be that the filming of *The Conqueror* (ironic name) was indirectly the cause.

The film was produced on location at St George, Utah, where across the Nevada border a couple of years earlier an atomic bomb had been exploded. This particular bomb, one of the 87 nuclear explosions that took place between 1951 and the 1963 Test Ban Treaty, was several times as powerful as the bomb that razed Hiroshima, and at Yucca Flat the bomb was fixed to the top of a 100 ft high concrete tower to provide the best possible photographic record of the event.

But on this occasion fate stepped in where man had dared to tread and at the same instant that the device exploded, according to plan, a sudden and unexpected wind blew up that swept the radiation-saturated cloud towards St George where within the next three hours a grey ash fell, coating the houses, the lawns, the fields and the schools and playgrounds, discolouring the clothes of everyone caught in the downpour and burning any unprotected skin. Over the next 25 years a distressingly high number of birth defects, leukaemia and other types of cancer occurred among the people of St George.

The explosion became known as Dirty Harry, America's worst nuclear accident but the Atomic Energy Commission always played down the incident, 'allowing the deadly fallout to silently take its toll in lives and suffering over the next three decades', as Christopher P. Andersen, an American editor has put it.

It was almost exactly a year after the explosion, which incidentally caused the deaths of scores of livestock, when John Wayne arrived in St George with the stars, directors and hundreds of cast and crew members to begin shooting *The Conqueror*, a film that was to be a $6 million disaster for Howard Hughes. It is unlikely that anyone associated with the film was aware of Dirty Harry or of the ten other later atomic tests there that had added layer upon layer of radiation to the already highly contaminated terrain.

Once the majority of the exterior scenes were completed in Utah the whole unit packed up and returned to Hollywood, but then a second and possibly fatal mistake was made. Unaware, of course, of the danger of the contaminated Utah soil, dozens of trucks were loaded with tons of red earth from the St George location and brought to Hollywood for further 'exterior' scenes actually shot inside the RKO studios. From beginning to end *The Conqueror* took two years to complete so for that length of time the cast and crew were exposed to the radioactive soil, spread over the floor of the indoor sound stage.

Dick Powell, actor, singer, director, was a close friend of Ronald Reagan and his then wife Jane Wyman, having known Ronnie Reagan from his earliest days in films. In 1944 he married June Allyson and invitations for the first dinner party given by the newly-weds went to the Reagans and George and Julie Murphy. George Murphy was to be elected a US Senator for California before Reagan trod the same path. When Ronnie and Jane split up Dick Powell was not surprised: 'They just seemed to pass each other going in different directions,' he said at the time.

Best remembered for such film appearances as those he made in *Forty Second Street* (1933) and *Gold Diggers of 1933*, both Busby Berkeley extravaganzas (Powell was Busby's most regularly used star) Dick also appeared in *A Midsummer Night's Dream* (1935), a work of remarkable film technique if not acting brilliance, a curio of a film in which form triumphs over content. Powell also appeared in *Right Cross* (1950) with Marilyn Monroe who played the wrong kind of woman and received no billing in the film as released.

Former child star Diana Serra Cary has revealed that on one occasion she encountered Dick Powell bemoaning the fact that he was tied to Warners who were paying him less than $100 a week while making millions from his musicals but in later years he became a shrewd businessman in the film and television world and for a while David Niven and Charles Boyer joined him as partners in a television production company. When he died, in 1963, he was running a company called Four Star which Reagan was anxious to join; Reagan introduced several of the Powell shows when the star was ailing.

Pedro Armendariz was the son of a Mexican father and an American mother who died when he was young and he was sent to live with her parents in San Antonio. When he grew up he first studied engineering but soon turned to acting and movies where he quickly became popular and was soon one of the top male actors in Mexico. He moved with his wife to Hollywood where he was to appear in more than forty films, mostly character parts that suited his appearance and delivery, which was everyone's idea of a Mexican. In 1952 he received the Mexican equivalent of the Oscar and then in 1955 he worked on *The Conqueror* with his close friend John Wayne.

John Wayne, born Marion Michael Morrison in 1907, grew up to be a tall man with an easy, swaying gait and a gravel voice. He worked at film studios shifting props and doing other menial tasks until one day director John Ford gave him a small part in *Mother Machree* (1927). Gradually Wayne obtained more and more work including a string of undistinguished Westerns where he was sometimes a singing cowboy (with dubbed voice) until Ford, casting *Stagecoach* (1939), gave Wayne the part of the Ringo Kid. After that 'The Duke' never looked back.

His familiar drawl was heard in more than 250 films and after having a lung removed, enduring open heart surgery, severe hepatitis and finally stomach cancer, he appeared in person to receive a special Oscar award in 1979. 'I'm mightily pleased I can amble down here tonight,' he said to a delighted audience. 'Oscar and I have something in common. Oscar first came to the Hollywood scene in 1928 and so did I. We're both a little weather-beaten but we're still here and we plan to be around for a whole lot longer.' Sadly he was dead within two months.

These three, Dick Powell, Pedro Armendariz and John

Wayne were among those who worked on *The Conqueror* and died from cancer. Within a few years the deadly soil began to claim its victims. Pedro Armendariz was diagnosed as having lymphatic cancer and when the pain became too bad he shot himself in hospital; five months later Dick Powell succumbed to lung cancer, as did actress Agnes Moorehead. Art director on the 'cursed' film, Carroll Clark developed prostate cancer; make-up chief Webb Overlander had a cancerous lung removed; character actress Jeanne Gearson developed skin cancer; and both John Wayne and Susan Hayward died from cancer. The Conqueror indeed.

4

'In faith, 'twas strange, 'twas passing strange'

-

UNUSUAL DEATHS

In Hollywood little is as one expects it to be and it has been described as a place stranger than paradise. Schwab's drugstore, where Lana Turner is supposed to have been discovered serving behind the counter, is still there, a gathering place for 'resting' actors and actresses where magnificent food at reasonable prices can be consumed and filmland gossip exchanged amid the sprinkling of pretty, young, aspiring actresses and the occasional and unmistakable rich and successful middle-aged film producer. But there are also pet perfumeries, bra museums, outdoor air-conditioning, a wedding place for dogs – and it all seems acceptable in the wonderful, crazy suburb that is Hollywood.

In a place where dreams can be bought and everyone feels they too can become a glittering star overnight if only fortune smiles on them just once, it is not surprising that there have been scores of unusual deaths like that of Clara Blandick, the woman who played Auntie Em in *The Wizard of Oz*. She ended her life by placing her head inside a plastic bag, closing the bag and pulling it tight.

The examples of unusual deaths included in this chapter are Jean Harlow, John Gilbert, Thelma Todd, Peter Lawford, Albert Dekker, James Whale and George Zucco.

Jean Harlow
who died aged 26

William Powell
at the time of his
affair with Jean Harlow

Jean Harlow

-

The Original Platinum Blonde

She deliberately cultivated a blatant sexuality while other female stars of the period strained to be ladies; her brash voice was overlooked and what she lacked in refinement she made up for in honesty. Her peroxided hair and high arcs of pencilled eyebrows set a pervasive fashion. She packed experience, good and bad, into her shockingly short life and she called herself 'the worst actress in Hollywood'.

Jean Harlow (1911–37) has been the subject of some highly coloured and probably inaccurate accounts of her life, for her real friends and close colleagues all have pleasant memories of one of the most popular stars of the Thirties. Some twenty years ago I shared the same publisher as Roy Fox, the famous band leader who lived in Los Angeles from a very early age where he grew up to develop his own soft, muted style of trumpet playing which attracted the celebrities of the new movie industry. One day, he and I met outside the publisher's London office and an hour later we met again, in a Georgian coffee house near by. It was the first of several meetings when we talked of books and publishing and then Roy Fox talked of his early days in Hollywood and in particular of his involvement with the girl who became famous as Jean Harlow.

In the days when he and his band would play at the film studios during the day and at nightclubs after dark, he arrived at the William Fox Studios early one morning and saw 'one of the most terrific girls' he had ever seen. He knew by sight a lot of film extras but he had never seen this girl before.

Fox introduced himself and began talking to this exciting girl

with remarkable blonde or silver hair; 45 years later he said he
had still never seen anything like it. She had an innocent, animal
quality, a tangy voice, a striking and unblemished skin and a
beautifully rounded body. She told him she had just arrived
from Chicago and wanted to break into pictures in Hollywood;
she had made her film debut in Chicago in 1926 when she was
15 – the year, she told Roy Fox, that she eloped with Charles
McGrew for a brief, passionless marriage that soon ended.
Louella Parsons quoted Jean Harlow in her *Jean Harlow's
Life Story* (1937):

> *It isn't true that Chuck and I ran off to marry without the
> consent of our parents. Of course, mother did not want me
> to marry so young. But we finally obtained her consent and
> that of Chuck's grandparents. We both thought we were
> madly in love. But we were too young to know the meaning
> of the word. We were in love with excitement and the swift-
> ness of our romance; then he pursued me to Kansas City
> with the biggest diamond engagement ring I ever saw ...
> We fell in love with night club music and the glamour of
> each other – for Chuck was the best-looking boy I had
> ever seen. Just to give you an idea of the solemnity of
> our wedding, a radio next door to the Justice's Office was
> blaring out St Louis Blues as we listened to the words that
> made us man and wife.*

The young couple took a house on Bedford Drive in Beverly
Hills, two doors away from where Clara Bow lived and for
a while they were happy, although in reality they were little
more than two spoiled children playing at marriage. Jean had
had French governesses as a child and at the age of nine she
attended the Hollywood School for Girls. Later she entered a
French convent and attended an exclusive and formal finishing
school. Her family was a solid and respectable family and she
had all the advantages of middle-class circumstances. Chuck
was in reality Charles Fremont McGrew III, the 20-year-old
scion of a wealthy family. In 1929, when she was still only 19,
she and Chuck were divorced.

Jean and Roy Fox met again the next day and the day after
that – in fact they met every day for over a year. A few weeks
after they first met Jean told Roy that she had been stopped on

Hollywood Boulevard by a man who asked her if she would like to call at the Hal Roach Studios to see about the possibility of getting a part in a film they were making and he had given her an introductory card.

Roy Fox drove her to the studio for the audition and she was successful. It was just a small part in an early Laurel and Hardy silent two-reeler called *Double Whoopee* (1929), a Hal Roach comedy. In later years Hal Roach was among many people who claimed they had discovered Jean Harlow. When the picture was previewed at a small picture house in Hollywood, Roy Fox and Jean Harlow went to see it together.

After that Jean worked fairly regularly in films in Hollywood but without any real recognition until she was again stopped in the street and asked to go to MGM Studios for a screen test for a picture they were planning. Fox told me he drove Jean to Culver City and waited for her for about three hours. When she eventually came out she was excited and said a very nice actor named Ben Lyon had been in the test with her. In later years Ben Lyon was to claim that he had discovered Jean Harlow.

She got her first strong part in *Hell's Angels* (1930). Actually the Norwegian star Greta Nissen had been cast in the role and had completed some scenes. But talkies were all the rage and when Hughes decided to make the film a talking picture and found Greta Nissen's imperfect English a problem, he was delighted when Jean Harlow suddenly appeared on the scene.

Shooting the film which rocketed Jean Harlow to fame was not easy. The part called for a sensational-looking girl, the only female in the picture, to exude sex appeal. Jean looked the part. She dressed the part too — with low-cut, slinky, clinging gowns — but a natural actress she was not. She found it difficult to remember her lines and during the first scenes in particular her movements were stilted and artificial. The set was closed for the day. She got through the first scene with Ben Lyon and James Hall in a London bar, by really getting a little drunk!

Gradually things improved and the shooting ran close to schedule. The other actors liked her and were pleasant and helpful; and the crew took to her because she was always considerate and cheerful; and she was beautiful in the stills.

Hughes sank well over a million dollars into *Hell's Angels* which he began as a silent in 1927, but finally released in 1930 as a talkie. There were many accidents and delays before the final result received acclaim. The flying sequences – and the aeroplanes have been said to be the real stars of the film – have seldom been surpassed. With the opening of *Hell's Angels* at Grauman's Chinese Theatre, Jean Harlow became headline news and thereafter she was never to be out of the spotlight until the day she died. Overnight she became the new sensation of Hollywood, but there was the other side of the coin. Enraged moralists tried to get the picture banned and the final result was that although the public wanted to see Harlow with her bedroom eyes and skin-tight dresses, producers were afraid to employ her because of the danger that her films might be banned in key cities.

While making *The Secret Six* Jean Harlow met Paul Bern, a German writer and director, an intellectual who was among those who doubted that talking films would last.

Paul Bern was considered by many people to be 'one of the sweetest human beings who ever lived' and so he appeared. Well-spoken and well-behaved, he joined MGM as adminis- trative assistant to Irving Thalberg, husband of Norma Shearer, and he had worked as writer, editor, stage manager and director at some of the top studios in Hollywood. He was a quiet little man with thinning hair and a wispy moustache, shorter than Jean Harlow and twice as old.

Bern, as emissary for MGM's production chief Irving Thalberg, visited Charles Boyer in 1929 when he was appearing on stage in France and invited him to Hollywood to make French-speaking versions of some MGM projects. Although he could converse in German, Italian, Spanish and Portuguese, Boyer knew no English whatever and he was reluctant to leave the country of his birth but he liked Bern and he went to Hollywood to become 'the great lover' and leading man to Dietrich, Bergman, Garbo and Hepburn; one of the most universally admired and respected stars in movie history.

Boyer was married to actress Pat Paterson for 44 years and they had one son, Michael, who was just making a name for himself as a television producer in 1965 when tragedy struck. In what appears to have been a bizarre Russian-roulette dare, Michael shot himself through the head. Neither Pat nor Charles Boyer ever really got over that and some years later, after devoted nursing by Charles, Pat died of cancer in Phoenix. Two days later Boyer killed himself with an overdose of Seconal.

Jean Harlow and Paul Bern were married on 2 July 1932 and they lived in Bern's charming hilltop, Bavarian-style home. John Gilbert was best man and the guests were modest but distinguished, including Mr and Mrs Louis B. Mayer, Irving Thalberg and Norma Shearer, Mr and Mrs David Selznick, Arthur Landau, Jean's agent, her beloved mother Mama Jean and her second husband Marino Bello. But things were not what they seemed. Early in the morning of 3 July 1932 Arthur Landau received an urgent telephone call from his client. Jean said she was outside the house. 'Come and get me,' she wept into the telephone. 'And hurry, he's liable to wake up!'

Arthur Landau found Jean Harlow sobbing outside the timbered house in Benedict Canyon. He took her to his home where he and his wife Beatrice found the actress's back striped by long and angry welts that had been delivered with a cane. The lowest one seemed dangerously near the kidneys. Dr Herman Sugarman examined her and told her she had no broken bones. He was concerned about the lowest welt where Jean said it hurt the worst and X-rays and urine analyses were carried out. No one knows the degradation and unhappiness that Jean experienced with Paul Bern while keeping up the appearance of being happily married to 'the man with the gentle eyes'.

Two months after their marriage Jean was working on the film *Red Dust* (1932) with Clark Gable. Before his marriage Bern had suggested the film as a vehicle for Jean and he had also signed Gable as her co-star but Jean seemed to be really enjoying the scantily clad scenes she enacted with he-man Gable and it was all beginning to get to Bern. Bern may also well have guessed, if he did not definitely know, that Jean and Gable were having an affair.

One night Paul wanted to talk. He said he wanted to insist that Jean had some time off after the picture was finished – then maybe they could go away together, Europe or somewhere. After a hard day Jean was in no mood to compromise on her determination to work hard and continuously on becoming a really big star. 'I told you no before on that,' she said. 'I'm getting used to putting on the act for us here but if we take a trip we'll have to be interviewed and all the rest of it and it will be harder for both of us.'

Paul looked at the vision of loveliness stretched out before him. 'Would you leave me if I had cancer or was dying of heart trouble?', he asked. 'Of course not,' she replied. 'Paul, I've had a long, rotten day on the set ... now get undressed and I'll fix you a drink. Then we'll go to sleep.'

Paul slipped out of the bedroom and returned a few moments later in a blue dressing gown. She noticed that his feet and legs were bare and then he untied the robe and stepped out of it. He was nude but strapped around his middle was a large artificial male member! He pranced round the room and then made to approach Jean who was helpless with laughter and the episode ended with Paul stealing away in embarrassment.

Early next morning Bern's body was found, still nude, doused with his wife's favourite perfume and facing a full-length mirror. There was a gun on the dressing table and another in his hand with one bullet fired. He had shot himself through the head. Louis B. Mayer, the head of MGM was on the scene before the police, anxious to protect the studio from scandal and to explain how one of the studio's chief executives could kill himself. Mayer found a suicide note which he attempted to keep from the police but which he finally surrendered to the detectives who hurried to the scene. The note read:

> Dearest Dear, Unfortunately this is the only way to make good the frightful wrong I have done you and to wipe out my abject humiliation, I love you. Paul. P.S. You understand that last night was only a comedy.

Gossip, as usual in Hollywood, was rife. It was suggested that Bern had been murdered, either on the instructions of Harlow's stepfather Marino Bello who was thought to have mobster friends; or by Dorothy Millette, one of Bern's former mistresses, or possibly wife, whose drowned body was soon discovered. Jean Harlow was closely questioned but her doting mother provided her with an unshakable alibi. All such rumours might have gradually ceased had not the coroner dropped a thunderbolt. It was stated that the hole in Bern's head was 'a typical suicide wound' with the tell-tale powder burns, but then came the announcement that Bern was free of any malignant ailment or disease that might have prompted his taking his own life, but the autopsy did reveal a physical ailment that 'might preclude marital happiness'. Paul Bern's genitals were frightfully underdeveloped but Jean, a very decent human being, would have cared no less for him because of that.

Years later it transpired that Bern had lived for five years with a lovely young actress, Dorothy Millette. It became a common-law marriage and she was known as Mrs Bern. Sadly she became unhinged and had to be confined in a mental hospital for several years, Bern paying the bills. When she was released and learned about Bern's marriage to Jean Harlow, she called him at the studio and said she was coming to visit him in Hollywood. On her arrival she rang Bern again and insisted on seeing him, saying she knew where he lived. To get Jean out of the house Bern manufactured a quarrel that was 'only a comedy'. Dorothy Millette arrived late that night, according to the evidence of neighbours; they talked and argued round the pool, again according to the evidence of neighbours. Presumably Bern was threatened that he would be charged with bigamy and after she left Bern shot himself and after his funeral Dorothy drowned herself.

For weeks after Bern's death Jean did not leave the house and she seemed badly shaken by the tragedy; afterwards she was a changed person. Even her closest friends could not get really close and her mother became desperately worried. Eventually Irving Thalberg, Bern's close friend, persuaded her to see some of her old friends and to get back to work. The good reviews of *Red Dust*, where she played the wise-cracking Vantine with the heart of gold, helped and soon she was making some of the best Hollywood comedies of the early Thirties, including *Reckless*, where the plot veered excruciatingly close to the Bern tragedy.

Eventually the likable, happy-go-lucky and fabulously successful star who always said she was the worst actress in Hollywood took it all in her stride and in film after film she revealed herself as a comedienne of the first rank.

Ben Hecht, the American writer who founded the *Chicago Literary Times*, wrote an article in 1960 that purported to reveal a number of unknown facts about Jean Harlow. Some were trivial such as, 'Jean took her fame seriously; she wore no bra beneath a white satin blouse and before making a public appearance she would rub ice on her nipples to improve her appearance', but other disclosures were quite sensational. He claimed the suicide note was a forgery; studio officials having decided it was better to have Bern a suicide than a murder victim — it was less of a shock for their superstar Jean Harlow — and Hecht said the 'weird' 'suicide whitewash' note was in keeping with director Henry Hathaway (who was to direct Marilyn Monroe in her first major film role), a man who once said: 'To be a good director you've got to be a bastard. I'm a bastard and I know it.'

Hathaway was ordered to make available to the District Attorney the 'weird' details and the director at once sought the advice of his attorney. In the event the District Attorney returned the records of the suicide to their files and closed the case. Whatever the truth of the matter everyone concerned seemed determined to keep the matter as quiet as possible.

As time passed and with the finding of Bern's third and final will, in which he left everything to Jean, problems with the estate built up and Jean gave up the house that was only a constant reminder of scandal and death. There was still virtually no money: although Bern had been earning in excess of $1500 a week for some years his cash assets, including his salary for the week he died, were less than $2000! There were whispers that he may have been a victim of blackmail; perhaps he tried to gain time or had an argument with his blackmailers and he had decided suicide was the only way out, if suicide it was. On top of everything else Jean began to have pain in her back, in the kidney region.

The next major figure in Harlow's life was the debonair actor, William Powell. At first Jean was not particularly attracted to Powell but she was intrigued by his suavity, his polish, his aristocratic and confident bearing, but most of all by his sense of humour. And Bill Powell quickly found in this vivid, laughing girl who was constantly joking and pulling his leg, the same qualities of frankness and lack of artificiality that had first attracted him to Carole Lombard with whom, he believed, he had been deeply in love.

So Jean Harlow and William Powell, two vital, intense and attractive film stars, laughed their way into a love story that was to end in heartbreak. Jean fell desperately in love and this time it was the real thing. She felt it as she had never felt anything quite like it before: she literally worshipped Bill Powell and it was apparent to everyone.

Louella Parsons says she talked to Jean Harlow in 1936

before a Hollywood Hotel radio broadcast and when Jean told Louella that Bill felt they shouldn't be married, Louella asked her how she felt about it. 'I love him,' Jean replied and went on. 'I have always wanted children and he is the only man I ever thought I would like to marry and settle down with and raise a family. But I suppose he is right. Marriage hasn't worked out for either of us and perhaps two movie people with careers shouldn't marry ... I have a feeling we will never be married.' However they did become engaged.

In 1936, as she began to work on *Saratoga*, Jean Harlow complained, 'Everything seems to tire me – I guess I'm just run down.' This was quite out of character for Jean who was usually one of the most cheerful people in Hollywood and throughout her short life she was hardly ever known to complain. She went down with a severe cold and while still suffering the effects, she had three impacted wisdom teeth extracted and found herself in hospital for several weeks.

After convalescence Jean returned to work on *Saratoga*, studying the lines and having wardrobe fittings. Jean still felt tired and, unusual for her, she was snappish and easily angered, but she was looking forward to working again with Clark Gable and with Lionel Barrymore, Frank Morgan, Walter Pidgeon and Una Merkel on what promised to be her most brilliant performance.

Jean's mother would accompany her to and from Beverly Hills and Culver City, ensuring that her beautiful daughter slept at night, even if it meant barbiturates or alcohol, and then shaking her awake next morning, assisting her to dress and forcing hot coffee down her throat and then off to the studio with Jean cursing every turning the car made, for she seemed to ache everywhere. And at the end of another day the worn-out actress would be helped to sit up in bed and study the script for the next day before nodding off to sleep after asking to be left alone. But her mother invariably ignored that request and sat in the corner of the white bedroom, praying aloud for most of the night.

Mayer was in a hurry to get the film completed before he left for an important European tour and to complete the picture on time more and more feet of film were shot daily and Jean began to feel worse and worse. The only sleep she seemed to get without her mother praying loudly was in her bungalow between scenes. She repeatedly told Bill Powell and her agent how rotten she felt but there was little they could do. They knew and she knew that her mother would never hear of orthodox medical attention; she was convinced that she had a direct line to God and all would be well.

Before the completion of the film Jean's illness became apparent to everyone. She had never been one to feel the cold but now she seemed never to be able to get warm and she was always asking to borrow someone's coat. She seems to have had flashes of intuition or prevision too. Once, on the set, she said to her hairdresser, Peggy MacDonald and to her make-up girl, Violet Denoyer: 'I'm always pleased to look after you kids when I'm here, but you must learn to fight your own battles because I may not always be with you.' And once she said to Violet: 'I have a feeling I am going away from here and not coming back.'

Louella Parsons spoke to Jean's mother at this time and Mrs Bello said: 'Jean is a very sick girl; much sicker than anyone realizes but she has great courage and with my prayers she will be all right.'

Six days before the film was due to be completed Jean Harlow collapsed on the set. It was a Friday so the director decided to close for the weekend. Jean was taken home from the studio, never to return. She told Red Golden, the assistant director: 'I feel so weak. I can't raise my hands to take off my make-up.' She insisted on looking in on Bill Powell on the set of *Double Wedding* where he was working with Myrna Loy, before leaving the studios. 'I feel terrible, Bill darling,' she told him and she seemed dazed and puzzled by what was happening to her.

Jean's mother welcomed her home and put her to bed. Mrs Bello felt that Jean's continuing poor health proved that the doctors, the dentists, the nurses and all their medicines were of no use; the truth of Christian Science was about to be made manifest and she believed that great revelations were imminent. The only outside advice she accepted was what she had already planned: keep Jean quiet and that meant no visitors. Two days were all that was necessary for Jean to understand the truth of Christian Science and its power over the mind and through this understanding the health of her body would be restored.

To exorcise the malicious influences and poisons from Jean's body, her mother decided she required absolute privacy so the staff were given the weekend off and to all telephone enquiries Mrs Bello said Jean was resting quietly and comfortably with no fever or other physical symptoms of illness; she explained that Christian Scientists knew that these things were merely delusions created through ignorance.

Sick with exhaustion Jean slept fitfully through the Saturday but by Sunday morning she was so weak she could not leave her bed and her mother had to half-carry and half-drag her to the bathroom. So many people called that the telephone seemed to be continuously ringing and when Jean said it gave her a headache, her mother took the telephone off the hook. With Jean unable to protest and with no disturbance from telephone-callers Mrs Bello felt able to administer to her daughter as she saw fit and she combed Jean's lovely blonde hair and assured the feverish girl that her hot forehead was not really even warm because Mama was concentrating on coolness and health and Jean should do likewise. She gave Jean a sponge bath, dressed her hair and massaged her cold feet. Towards evening Jean complained of pain in the stomach and back; then she vomited and lay for about an hour with her head pressed against the cold enamel of the commode before she was helped back to bed.

When she did not appear at the studio on the Monday morning a messenger was sent to the house by the director but he returned saying Mrs Bello would not admit him. She had promised to telephone later to say when Jean would return to work. Work of a kind on the picture continued with close-ups of Clark Gable and other actors in the film. In the late afternoon Mrs Bello telephoned the studio to say that Jean was feeling much better and would be at work again next day, Tuesday, immediately after lunch; another good rest would put the actress back on her feet.

When Jean did not appear for work on Tuesday afternoon Clark Gable decided to pay a personal visit to Jean but he returned about three o'clock to say he was very disturbed; Mrs Bello wouldn't let him in the house and she had been very cheerful and not in the least concerned, as a mother might be if her daughter was seriously ill. If all was well, Gable couldn't understand why he was not allowed to see Jean.

'She said Jean was sleeping,' Gable told the director. 'But if she's sleeping that much it means she's weak and ought to see a doctor.'

Gable returned to the house with Jean's agent, Frank Morgan and two of the studio staff. At length they managed to see Jean. She lay semi-conscious and moaning with pain that wrenched her stomach and radiated through her chest and back. She was continually sick and her cheeks were red with fever. She softly pleaded through dry lips for help and for Bill. Her pulse was erratic and the visitors instructed Mrs Bello to send at once for a doctor.

She laughed at them and said they were needlessly alarmed. She had ordered the evil to leave Jean's body and soon the girl would be better. Jean was her responsibility and she rambled on about Christian Science and how an hour's reading would make them see the truth as she had seen it. 'Evil is strong and stubborn,' she said. 'Right now evil is struggling to stay inside Jean but she's strong and I'm strong and together we're concentrating on good ... we'll win ... we'll win ...'

Dr E. C. Fishbaugh was hurriedly called and diagnosed Jean's illness as cholecystitis – inflammation of the gall bladder – and he recommended that she go to hospital immediately and he would make preparations for surgery. By this time Jean was so weak she could hardly speak and Mrs Bello refused to allow Jean to be moved.

Eventually she compromised and allowed the doctor to give a hypodermic to relieve pain on condition that she could continue with her medical healing. As soon as Jean was unconscious Mrs Bello wanted to begin but the doctors suggested another compromise: if Mrs Bellow would permit nurses to help to care for Jean they would also assist in mental therapy if they could.

Nurses arrived and did what they could in the difficult circumstances. The doctors asked permission to remove Jean to hospital where she could be given an intravenous lipiodol injection to prepare her for X-rays to facilitate a search for gallstones but Mrs Bellow was adamant that Jean must not go to hospital.

The medical people continued to do what they could. They sent blood samples and urine samples to an outside labora-tory and did their best to feed Jean intravenously since she was unable to take food in any form and her strength was ebbing away. Mrs Bello became hysterical and threatened to destroy any more medical equipment that was brought into the sickroom.

Everyone tried to reason with her but to no effect. Next morning she still refused to consider the idea and when another doctor was called in, she questioned everything that was done and demanded to be assured that everyone dealing with her daughter recognized the power and wisdom of Christian Science.

Next day Jean had an unusual pallor and there was a distinct ammoniac odour in her mouth, an odour like urine. An acute infection of the gall bladder was working through Jean's bloodstream because her kidneys were damaged and no longer capable of acting as filters for body waste. The dreaded uremic poison was critical for anyone in good health but Jean had been unwell for about a year. The doctors and medical staff made a combined stand against Mrs Bello. It was imperative that Jean was removed to hospital immediately where she could be operated upon. The gall bladder must be drained and the infections drained off. This was the only way to save Jean's life. For events to have occurred so quickly the doctors surmised that Jean must have had a kidney ailment that had troubled her for years — why had she not mentioned it? Almost five years earlier Paul Bern had beaten Jean with a cane across the back and had struck her over the kidneys. These blows must have caused damage, made the kidneys weak, and subsequent infections had increased the damage.

Still Mrs Bello refused to allow her daughter to be taken to hospital. They told her Jean might die. 'There is no death,' Mrs Bello replied. Someone thought of telephoning William Powell and he quickly got hold of Louis B. Mayer, the only person who had more authority over Jean than her mother. Within minutes Mayer had issued the necessary orders and the unconscious Jean Harlow was on her way from Beverly Hills to the Good Samaritan Hospital in Los Angeles.

A quick examination convinced the doctors that she was too weak for surgery. Throughout the night emergency blood transfusions were administered but by nine o'clock in the morning the onset of Cheyne-Stokes respiration — the heavy breathing and weak, shallow exhalation which is the harbinger of death — was unmistakable.

An intravenous injection of adrenalin was administered to help the breathing but she could not be roused from the coma into which she had lapsed. An oxygen mask was adjusted over her face and oxygen was pumped into her lungs. Mrs Bello was present and was talking and shaking Jean lightly, trying to rouse her. Jean talked incoherently during those last moments of her life. William Powell stepped forward to say something, but couldn't and he broke down and stepped back.

Jean Harlow was pronounced dead at 11.37 on 7 June 1937. Oxygen continued to be pumped for another three minutes. At the bedside when Jean died were her mother, William Powell and Dr Fishbaugh. As the doctor nodded that she was dead, William Powell sobbed and rushed from the room. He cancelled the film part he was currently working on and spent a month on Ronald Colman's ranch to get over the death of Jean Harlow.

As she realized that her daughter was indeed dead Mrs Bello became hysterical again and had to be sedated. In recent years there have been suggestions that in fact Jean died as a result of a clumsy abortion done by her mother with knitting needles. Others present in the corridor outside the room included Jean's agent, her chauffeur and friends; all of them wept silently and they were joined by many of the Los Angeles hospital staff.

At the funeral service 'None But the Lonely Heart' was played on the organ, Jeanette MacDonald sang 'The Indian Love Call' and Nelson Eddy sang 'Ah, Sweet Mystery of Life'. Jean Harlow was buried in a private crypt lined with marble in Forest Lawn's Sanctuary of Benediction, the most honoured place of rest in the park's Memorial Court of Honour. The massive casket with its silver nameplate reproducing Jean's signature and giving her dates of birth and death lies amid the remains of people like Irving Thalberg and Marie Dressler. Jean's coffin actually lies in a crypt named the Jean Harlow Room. The room was paid for by William Powell and cost more than $25,000. At first Mayer announced that all of *Saratoga* that had been shot would be discarded but in response to public demand the film was completed with Geraldine Dvorak doubling for Harlow in the few uncompleted scenes. *Variety* stated: 'Miss Harlow's performance is among her best in years.'

John Gilbert

-

He Glittered the Most

From the humblest possible beginnings he rose to be the highest paid star of 1928; he enjoyed the love and admiration of beautiful women and married four times but he fell foul of the studio bosses and he was one of the major casualties of the coming of sound to moving pictures.

John Gilbert (1897–1936) has been described as the greatest lover of the silver screen but American director King Vidor said that Gilbert often didn't bother to read the script of a film in which he was appearing! 'In the *Big Parade* (1925), enormously popular in both England and America, when Gilbert encounters a German soldier in a shell-hole, the whole thing was ad-libbed.' It was almost like hypnotism, the strange rapport that Gilbert had with his director.

> *Gilbert never read the script of* The Big Parade *and I can't describe it but it was almost like a love affair, we had a way of transferring emotion; I'd just have a sudden thought of the way something should be done, and Gilbert would immediately react, and do whatever it was he was doing, exactly as I had that instant visualised it.*

Dashing, daring, the role model for a generation, John Gilbert was the perfect screen lover. 'In Hollywood's glittering days', wrote Ben Hecht, 'he glittered the most.' Who could resist the piercing dark eyes and the dazzling smile, yet his life story has been blurred by gossip and distortion of the truth. It has been said time and time again that his career ended with his first talking film because his voice was high and effeminate. But there must be more to it than that. If his voice was so thin and squeaky and piping and unacceptable, why was it not noticed in the daily rushes during the 13 days when that last film was shot? Why was nothing done before the film was premièred? Had he perhaps offended important people? It may be pertinent to ask whether something happened to the sound-track prior to the première when the critics panned Gilbert's voice. At a time when there were 62 movie magazines and the public were hungry for any 'news' of the stars, Gilbert was one of those who resented intrusion into his past life and this attitude did not endear him to the studio bosses.

Louise Brooks was one who believed John Gilbert was the focus of deliberate sabotage. 'John was terribly unpopular with producers – he was such a ham, and he was always making a fuss.' Clarence Brown, Garbo's favourite director, was another who had no doubt about what happened to John Gilbert's voice. He told Gilbert's daughter, Leatrice, in 1973, 'I know what happened. I was there. The sound man on the film, Douglas Shearer, repeatedly requested retakes but they were denied by Lionel Barrymore who directed.' Shearer told Clarence Brown, 'We never turned up the bass when Gilbert spoke, all you heard was treble. Of course it was a "mistake".'

An objective assessment might well be that a combination of circumstances and events contributed to the fact that the career of John Gilbert suffered with the coming of the Talkies. It seems fair to say that, in part at least, he was a victim of the changing fashions that came to films with the Talkies. He simply did not seem able to adopt the low-key style of acting that was now required and his career suffered accordingly. From the glittering heights of being the hottest property among the male stars of the silent screen, earning $10,000 a week at one time, more highly paid than Rudolph Valentino, he plunged within a few short years to being practically penniless.

Those days may have seemed far ahead and impossible to contemplate in 1926, following *The Big Parade*, for John Gilbert was shot to stardom. Robert Sherwood described the film as 'among the few genuinely great achievements of the screen' and of *La Bohème*, his next picture, *Cinema Art* said, 'John Gilbert stands alone at the topmost pinnacle of film fame. There is no one who can approach him.' Gilbert became one of the best-known men in America, possibly in Europe too. Anything he wore became fashionable: John Gilbert shirts with long collars and John Gilbert blue ties with white spots. Everything he did, everything he ate, his home and his hobbies — they were all news and although the 'great lover' was by no means universally popular, it was known that he would discreetly perform many acts of kindness.

Born Cecil Pringle on 10 July 1899 at Logan, Utah, 70 miles north of Salt Lake City, his mother was a voluptuous, dark-eyed would-be actress married less than a year to John Pringle the producer of the show in which she was currently appearing. Within two weeks of the birth, Ida Adair (as she called herself) was back on the road. When he was six his mother left him in New York in the care of a fat and ugly seamstress whose daughter was a prostitute. The terrified child slept on a mat in the corner of the room where the daughter's clients were told to pretend he wasn't there. By the time he was seven, he used to say in later years, he knew more about the world than many people discover in a lifetime. He was rescued from this predicament by a friend and sent to his mother in Rochester where she was acting in a play with Bert Lytell; but Ida felt she had a career to follow, unencumbered by a child and within weeks she had packed the boy off to his grandfather, who farmed in Utah.

A year later Ida married Walter Gilbert, a cheerful comedian who later adopted the boy but, disliking the name Cecil, he changed his stepson's name to John Gilbert. John's mother died, not yet 40, in 1913 and after her funeral the teenager was somewhat taken aback when Walter Gilbert told him he could no longer take care of him or pay for his education. He was handed $10 and put on a train for San Francisco.

A couple of years later, while watching the William S. Hart movie, *On the Night Stage*, he recognized a member of his mother's stock company and decided then and there that he would become an actor. He discovered that his stepfather was now in films but Walter Gilbert couldn't risk employing an unknown and untried boy; however, he put in a good word with a friend who worked with Thomas Ince of the New York Picture Corporation and Ince took the boy on, paying him $15 a week.

John Gilbert began his screen career in a long-forgotten routine Western, as a half-naked Indian; the same afternoon he became a cavalryman; that night he was the victim of a mine disaster and in fact he almost died during the shooting when a fire got out of control. Years later John Gilbert wrote about those early days: 'I rode ponies for Ince and made no impression on the directors but I collected my wages at the end of the day ... I was happy ... for the first time in my life, I seemed to belong.'

After a bewildering variety of roles he was given a small part in a film called *Hell's Hinges*, directed by and starring William S. Hart, the first real Western star whose potential Thomas Ince had shrewdly perceived. In his autobiography Hart mentions the aspiring young actor, John Gilbert: 'He was one of the fifteen-dollars-a-week extras, "actor boys" we called them. I noticed his eagerness to please.'

The young John Gilbert was given a bigger part in Hart's next picture, *The Apostle of Vengeance*, against the judgement of Tom Ince, but Hart's faith was justified and Ince grudgingly admitted the worth of the young actor who was given a raise and found his name listed in the film credits.

John Gilbert's star seemed to be in the ascendant and he was ecstatic when, still under 17, he fell in love for the first time but not for the last time in his colourful life. Effie Stewart was a small, blonde actress a few years older than John. After a few drinks he went home with her and she gave him his first taste of sex. For three months the young lovers were deliriously happy and then they were both cast in what was to be the greatest cinematic achievement of director-producer Thomas Ince, the 2½ hour epic, *Civilization*. In one scene John was a cavalry soldier cursing the enemy while Effie and other ladies of the court watched from a balcony. Suddenly the flimsy balcony collapsed, pitching Effie and her fellow extras into the courtyard below among screaming men and frightened horses. Almost miraculously there was only one fatality; Effie Stewart was dead on arrival at Santa Monica Hospital. For a while John was inconsolable and his response (which he was to repeat many times during his life) was to bury himself in work, appearing in some 35 films during the next four years.

When he was invited to the wedding of King Vidor and Eleanor Boardman at Marion Davies's house in Beverly Hills, Greta Garbo seems to have agreed to making it a double wedding by marrying John Gilbert but at the last moment she backed out. It is all very strange. Gilbert is frequently described as the greatest love in the life of Garbo yet she was to say, according to Antoni Gronowicz, that John Gilbert was regarded in the film colony as intellectually primitive and crude in his acting as well as in his sexual behaviour and she frequently referred to his sexual escapades with Clara Bow, Mary Pickford, Beatrice Lillie and Dorothy Parker. His 'hilltop palace', overlooking most of Beverly Hills, was rumoured to be the setting for drinking and sex parties and she added that she had told Gilbert, 'Marriage with you would be a complete disaster. For you marriage is just one more publicity stunt.'

Gilbert had built himself a Spanish hacienda-type house near the top of Tower Road, a house he was to occupy for the rest of his life. The house had a secret panel in an alcove and a secret stairway that led to the basement, operated by a button in a bookcase. In the basement there was a bar that was much frequented in Prohibition days. Here Greta Garbo lived for a while in the guest room and almost every week guests would include people like Paul Bern, Irving Thalberg, King Vidor, Edmund Lowe, Anna May Wong, Ronald Colman, Herbert Marshall and David Selznick.

After Gilbert married Ina Claire, a major Broadway star, Garbo moved to the Santa Monica Beach Hotel and then to the Beverly Hills Hotel before buying a house at 1027 Chevy Chase Drive. Meanwhile Ina Claire had taken in hand the Tower Road house and virtually remodelled it.

Soon there was a parting of the ways between Ida and John Gilbert and he had a brief affair with Lupe Velez, the passionate Mexican actress. When attractive actresses were not at hand he availed himself of the services offered at Lee Frances's elegant brothel in Beverly Hills where his daughter says he was 'a frequent visitor', and at other times he entertained her girls at his house.

By 1932 John Gilbert could not hide the fact that he was ill. He had bleeding ulcers and alcohol made him sick; even a single scotch and soda, according to his daughter, had the effect of five. But still he drank and he only stopped when Irving Thalberg agreed to make a film of a story Gilbert had written years earlier. Reginald Owen and Paul Lukas were to be in the cast and the female lead was a delicate young blonde newcomer, Virginia Bruce; a girl who was to become

yet another Mrs John Gilbert. Their wedding was planned for
August, when Gilbert's divorce from Ina Claire would become
final.

John Gilbert, aged 33, married Virginia Bruce, aged 21, on
the set of *Red Dust* with Irving Thalberg and his wife Norma
Shearer as witnesses. Later Virginia Bruce said that her father
arranged a curious marriage contract. John Gilbert agreed to
write a will leaving everything to his new wife and her family if
Virginia was guaranteed to be a virgin. She was later to say:

> *Jack thought it was hilarious but I think he was also excited*
> *about it. I don't think he'd known many virgins in his life.*
> *My father allowed me to spend one night with Jack before*
> *we were married so that he could see for himself that I was*
> *a virgin; but he had to promise to return me to my father*
> *in the same pristine condition.*

For a time the couple were deliriously happy but then things
started to go wrong for John Gilbert and he began to suffer
from deep depression. Not only had he lost the important role
in *Red Dust* but the studio, to whom he owed one more picture,
were in no hurry to offer him anything. Then came the tragedy
involving his old friend Paul Bern. When the studio finally
put him in a movie, it did nothing for him, a second-rate
picture, *Fast Workers*, directed by Tod Browning, who was
being punished for his curio *Freaks*, made the year before.

There was a clause in Gilbert's contract that said he must
not be seen drunk in public so he drank at home, sometimes
all night. In the morning he would jump into his swimming
pool to clear his head. The shock did his body no good and
he began to vomit blood, sometimes over and over again until
he fainted.

His doctor Sam Hirshfield would go to the house and inject
sodium amytal into the actor's veins so that he could sleep;
otherwise the actor would sometimes stay awake for days on
end. Soon one of Gilbert's veins collapsed and became infected
and he had round-the-clock nursing.

He recovered and was offered the male lead in *Queen
Christina*, the story of the brilliant, eccentric seventeenth-century ruler of Sweden who dressed like a man, negotiated peace
for her country after years of war and who abdicated at the

age of 27. The film was to be a vehicle for Greta Garbo who, it has been said, had specifically requested John Gilbert as her co-star. The facts seem to be that Laurence Olivier had been cast opposite Garbo, as the Spanish ambassador and her lover, but the early love scenes between him and Garbo did not work and Olivier was told he lacked the necessary acting ability!

Pressure of various kinds assailed John Gilbert during the filming of *Queen Christina*. He suffered badly with his nerves at one stage; he needed time to 'dry out' and for his stomach to settle; Garbo was carrying on a romance with the film's director Rouben Mamoulian, who constructed the remarkable and most famous of all Garbo images: the final close-up as she stands at the ship's prow, her face, according to Mamoulian's instructions, a perfect blank into which the audience might read what it wished.

A sad event that added to the pressure on John Gilbert was the death of his former lover Renée Adorée, his co-star in *The Big Parade*, *La Bohème*, *The Cossacks* and *Redemption*. She died of tuberculosis at the age of 35 and Gilbert found it difficult to understand. 'God knows there are enough bullies and bastards around to fill the graveyards, but they just seem to go on and on while we lose people like Renée and Paul Bern.' And John Gilbert's marriage to Virginia Bruce was crumbling. Soon she filed for divorce after a marriage that had effectively lasted only 18 months. 'I am more sorry,' Gilbert was to say much later, 'about the loss of Virginia than I am about anything that has ever happened to me in my life before.' His disappointment at the generally unfavourable responses to his part in *Queen Christina* and his final separation from Virginia Bruce are often regarded as his reasons for becoming the depressed, unshaven, uncommunicative, unpopular, bleary eyed and hard-up drunkard that he was for most of the time that remained to him.

He was to make one more picture, *The Captain Hates the Sea*, this time for Harry Cohn (of infamous repute) who said to him: 'If you behave yourself, stay sober, and do your work, you'll be a star again. I'll bet my shirt on you. It's up to you.' John Gilbert did his best to stay dry, to be punctual and to work hard but everything seemed to be against him. A lot of the action took place on an old boat that was sailed around and around San Pedro Harbour. The weather was bad and people were sick and there was a lot of practical joking from a cast that included Walter Connolly, Leon Errol and Victor McLaglen. Before long, in spite of good intentions, John Gilbert was drinking heavily with the rest of the cast. There was one delay after another and director Lewis Milestone was to say in later years: 'Gilbert did a good job, despite being drunk most of the time and when he wasn't drunk, he was being sick; he had bleeding ulcers and fever; sometimes he had hallucinations. I've seen him raving out of his mind. When it was all over he knew Cohn would never hire him again. He was too much trouble.'

His daughter says her father's performance 'is remarkable. He suggests drunkenness only by an understated swaying and a sad smile that occasionally flickers across his face.' John Baxter in his *Hollywood in the Thirties* saw it rather differently: 'a sad picture of a declining John Gilbert, ulcer-ridden and alcoholic ... lurching through his last screen appearance'.

Yet it was after the completion of *The Captain Hates the Sea* that Marlene Dietrich came into John Gilbert's life. A remarkable woman who did many acts of kindness and was often quietly generous in helping those unable to help themselves (never admitting anything of the kind) she evidently decided that something ought to be done about John Gilbert. She knew what had to be done. Whatever he had done, whatever had happened to him, he needed help. The pitiful state he was now in was the result of drink, poor health and bad luck. She took him under her wing and soon he stopped drinking and she was able to take him out to Hollywood functions and parties, skilfully steering him away from arguments and generally setting him back on his feet.

Through Marlene Dietrich John Gilbert was tested for a role in her new picture, *Desire*. Gary Cooper was to co-star and the Gilbert part was that of a suave jewel thief. He got the part but just before filming was due to begin he suffered a mild heart attack while swimming in his pool with Marlene and was consequently replaced by Jack Halliday.

One day Garbo called at the house in Tower Road and she was seen by Marlene Dietrich. Thereafter the affair, if affair it was between Gilbert and Dietrich, cooled and was never really rekindled. Gilbert was in low spirits that autumn of 1935 and he had several more small heart attacks. A sad and lonely man he began to see more of his daughter, Leatrice, 'Tinker Bell' as he called her, before suffering another heart attack at the beginning of December. Marlene rushed to him and nursed him back to health.

On the morning of New Year's Day he sent a bouquet of roses to his daughter with a note that said he was sick and couldn't see her that day as they had arranged. 'Just as soon as I am strong enough I'll call you.'

During the night of 9 January, his daughter recounts in the biography of her father, he had trouble sleeping and a hired nurse gave him an injection. Next morning he was unconscious. The nurse notified the authorities and attempts were made to resuscitate the limp form. Marlene Dietrich sent her doctor, Leo Masden, who administered adrenaline but it was all to no effect. John Gilbert was certified dead at 9.05 in the morning of 10 January 1936 and the cause of death was listed as heart failure. His long-time friend, art director Cedric Gibbons, winner of eleven Oscars, rushed to his friend's house when he heard the news on the radio and he was just in time to prevent photographers from invading the star's bedroom and taking pictures of the distorted and anguished face in its last spasm.

Cedric Gibbons spoke to the nurse and returned home livid with rage. He told his wife that the nurse had given John Gilbert a shot to induce sleep the night before, but she had not stayed with him to check the effect of the drug. She left him alone and John Gilbert, the great lover of the silver screen, choked to death on his own tongue.

Details of the funeral were kept secret but even so Gilbert's final exit was crowded with people: Gary Cooper, Marlene Dietrich, John Barrymore, Irving Thalberg, Virginia Bruce, Sam Goldwyn, Robert Florey, King Vidor, Cedric Gibbons and Myrna Loy, among them. Eight months later Irving Thalberg was dead too, of pneumonia, at the age of 37. Garbo, in Stockholm, received the news in a stunned condition and did not leave her home for several days.

Apart from a few small bequests and $10,000 to his daughter, John Gilbert left his entire estate to Virginia Bruce who put up all his property for public auction: his clothes, books, records, household furniture and furnishings; even his toothbrush and the sheets he died on. When she heard about the sheets Marlene Dietrich, who was in England at the time of the sale, sent an agent who bought up all the bed linen; he had instructions to pay any price. John Gilbert's bed, massive and eight feet wide, was purchased for $1,250 by the Summit Hotel of Pennsylvania who announced that it would be installed in the 'John Gilbert Honeymoon Room' and rented out 24 hours at a time.

Gilbert's body was cremated and the ashes buried at Forest Lawn Memorial Park in the section known as Whispering Pines, marked by a bronze plaque engraved in a facsimile of his handwriting, 'John Gilbert'. His daughter ends her biography of her father: 'As long as there are movies, as long as people want to know how it all began – John Gilbert lives.'

Thelma Todd

-

The Ice-Cream Blonde

Born in 1905 at Lawrence, Massachusetts (she was to become a 'Miss Massachusetts'), delectable Thelma Todd, actress in countless comedies for Hal Roach, many with her friend Zasu Pitts, and a leading lady in Laurel and Hardy and Marx Brothers films, met her death in Hollywood in 1935, in a closed garage inside a car.

She was one of the supporting cast in *This is the Night* (1932), Cary Grant's first film which co-starred convent-educated and bisexual Lili Damita, the tempestuous French girl emotionally involved with the son-in-law of the Kaiser, Prince Louis Ferdinand, no less; and a girl who, a few years later, would marry Errol Flynn.

Thelma Todd starred in the curious and almost forgotten film, *Seven Footsteps to Satan*, a beautifully shot haunted-house comedy with a supporting cast of monsters that are 'disturbingly convincing', as Kevin Brownlow puts it. In the end the whole thing turns out to be a joke but the monsters, instead of removing their masks, sit down to a banquet, chatting happily.

Thelma had a bawdy sense of humour and while appearing as the leading lady in Laurel and Hardy's most successful film *Fra Diavolo* (1933) she went out of her way to draw Stan Laurel out of the depression he had slipped into at that time and they had many a laugh together. Two years later she was found dead one Monday morning in the garage loaned to her by her current lover Roland West. The garage was situated 500 yards from the restaurant they co-managed and where they both had apartments.

The ignition of the car was switched on and Thelma was slumped in the front seat. 'Death due to carbon monoxide poisoning' was the official but rather odd verdict that left a number of facts unexplained. She was not merely dead from asphyxiation for there was blood on her face. The police said she had died on the Sunday morning after returning from a party given for her by Stanley and Ida Lupino at the Trocadero on Sunset Boulevard where she had an argument with her ex-husband Pat DiCicco (who later married Gloria Vanderbilt). There were witnesses who said they had seen Thelma in a car with an unidentified man late on the Sunday morning.

After lengthy questioning West admitted there had been a violent quarrel between him and Thelma during the early hours of the Sunday morning at the popular Thelma Todd Roadside Restaurant and he had pushed her outside. Neighbours then asserted that they had heard Thelma shouting and screaming and pounding at the massive door which, it was discovered, showed recent kick marks.

Other puzzling facts were revealed at the inquest. Her friend Zasu Pitts had loaned Thelma thousands of dollars to finance the restaurant and had never been repaid. Ida Lupino said Thelma had seemed her usual cheerful self at the party that late December evening but she knew for a fact that Thelma was cheating on West and having an affair with a businessman in San Francisco. The lawyers for Thelma tried to have a second inquest, suggesting that the popular actress had been murdered by gangsters when she refused to co-operate with them in some crooked scheme; there were rumours too that West had a girlfriend who was persuaded to act as though she were Thelma and scream and kick the door while West was in the garage, knocking out Thelma, turning on the ignition key, and closing the garage door. West, it was also suggested, wanted to break off their relationship, against Thelma's wishes, and he attempted to commit the perfect crime – as screened in his successful film *Alibi*. Nothing was ever proved but Roland West never made another film and he died in obscurity in 1952.

Ruth Laurel, Stan's wife at the time of Thelma's death, was one person who always believed that the comedienne had been murdered. Why, she would ask, if she wanted to commit suicide, would Thelma go home in a hired car, climb dozens of steps up to the clifftop garage, get into her car and kill herself when she was known to have access to pills and drugs that would have done the job equally well? Also, why no suicide note? The morning that Thelma's body was found Stan and Ruth received a Christmas card from their friend.

The story of the full life and strange death of Thelma Todd filled the Hollywood papers for weeks with all sorts of ideas and suspicions being aired but the mystery was never solved.

Long queues of tearful fans and morbid curiosity seekers filed past the open casket at Thelma Todd's funeral at Forest Lawn. The undertakers had succeeded in restoring something of the Ice-Cream Blonde look to Thelma in death and Zasu Pitts remarked, in hushed tones, that 'Thelma looked as if she was going to sit up and talk at any moment.'

Instead the demise of Thelma Todd is one more strange and unsolved death in Hollywood.

Peter Lawford

-

Burnt-out Golden Boy

When Peter Lawford died in 1984 (he was born in Britain in 1923) he had been married four times, three times after his much publicized first wedding to Patricia Kennedy, sister of Jack, President of the United States of America and for the rest of his life Lawford surrounded himself with the Kennedys, either in person or with photographs.

He appeared as a child in the British film *Poor Old Bill* (1931) before moving to Hollywood where he started work parking cars for Jack's father Joseph Kennedy. His acting career took off when he was cast, mostly for his good looks, in the immense box-office success *Mrs Miniver* (1942), the Greer Garson patriotic pro-British weepie that won William Wyler a Best Director Oscar. Other films that Lawford appeared in included the successful Otto Preminger drama, *Advise and Consent* (1962), Charles Laughton's last film, but by that time Lawford was played out by drink and drugs, erratic habits and dangerous acquaintances.

He was offered the part of Blake Carrington on television and he turned it down but the long-running *Dynasty* role might have been his salvation. As with so much of his life a wrong decision made a great difference to the career and life of Peter Lawford who was never the easiest man to work with.

Samuel Marx, an MGM story editor, was given the job of executive producer of the Television Division and found it hard-going. When a pilot for a *Thin Man* series was finally sold with Lawford in the male lead, more problems arose. Lawford, as brother-in-law of the President, believed he could also call the tune at MGM and there were not too many people who were prepared to oppose him. Samuel Marx says he 'endured the situation' for two years and then moved to Associated British Television in London.

Ted Jordan, Marilyn Monroe's lover and friend for nearly twenty years, has related the circumstances in which Lawford, whom he describes as a 'beach bum' met Marilyn. It seems that Jordan and Marilyn would sometimes sit alongside the volley-ball courts at the State Beach and Lawford, a young actor with an eye for attractive females, soon noticed Marilyn. They struck up an acquaintanceship which was to become significant. Lawford, it seemed, regarded himself as a blue-blooded Englishman whose family could claim relationship with royalty and he always referred to his mother as a 'Lady'; Marilyn thought him snobbish, stuck-up and conceited, but at the same time found him a lot of fun.

Before long it was evident to Jordan if not to Marilyn that Lawford was a potentially dangerous man. Married to JFK's sister he was subservient to the Kennedy clan and he was a member of Sinatra's 'rat pack'. Sinatra had been a friend of Marilyn's for some years but other people in the pack sought to use her and Lawford was answerable to these people. Furthermore Lawford was a drunkard, addicted to narcotics and a man who used women; he kept a 'stable' of nubile lovelies for the amusement of himself and his friends.

One mistake that Lawford made and for which he never forgave himself was not going to Marilyn Monroe's bungalow on the night she died. She needed comfort and Lawford knew it but he always said his manager advised him not to go — 'it would be an odd thing for the President's brother-in-law to do,' and so on. It would have been far from the oddest thing Peter Lawford did in his life; nor was it the only thing he regretted. His continual self-pity was based as much on his reputation, as he saw it, as on any religious or moral scruples.

He reproved himself for having fallen out with all his old drinking partners, Frank Sinatra, Dean Martin and Sammy Davis Jr, but then he fell out with most of the people with whom he came in contact for any length of time. He worked hard to smooth the way, politically, publicly, privately and sexually for John F. Kennedy and when the President was coming to Palm Springs, Sinatra was so certain that Lawford would fix it for the President to stay with him that Sinatra had an annexe built to house the President's Secret Service guard; and he had a helipad built for the Presidential aircraft, defying the city ordinances! 'I'll land a 747 in the desert if I want,' Old Blue Eyes said at the time. But Lawford took the President to stay with Bing Crosby and Sinatra had nothing more to do with Lawford.

Soon Lawford was totally ostracized: cut off from his titled English background; from American politics, following his involvement with Marilyn Monroe and Jack and Bobby Kennedy; and show business in general where he had the habit of becoming annoying, embarrassing and unwelcome to just about all the stars, the directors, and the studios in Hollywood. He was his own worst enemy.

His fourth and final wife, Patricia Seaton Lawford was just 17 when she met Lawford at a club on Sunset Strip, not knowing who he was. She ran into him again three days after that first meeting at a party given by Henry Wynberg where, as Patricia herself tells it, a beautiful dark-haired woman asked who she was leaving with. Patricia pointed to Peter Lawford. 'But he's my husband,' the woman said. 'I didn't know you had a wife?' Patricia enquired of Lawford. 'Oh, that,' he replied, taking Patricia's arm, 'that's not important.'

That night Patricia moved in with Peter Lawford and found his flat saturated with pictures of the Kennedys. She thought he must be some kind of Kennedy freak, not knowing he was once related to them. Eventually she went into the bathroom and rang her mother and told her about all the photographs. 'Where are you and who are you with?' her mother asked and when Patricia told her: 'Oh! my God,' her mother exclaimed and told her daughter a little about Peter Lawford.

Not that it made any difference, nor did the 35-year age gap, but he was hardly a mother's dream man for her daughter and the relationship soon led to a rift between Patricia and her family. Her father, in particular, said it was obscene that she was sharing her bed with someone older than he was. Sharing his bed she may have been but Patricia insisted the marriage was never consummated. Peter's years of drink and drug abuse had left him unable to perform, she said, although he did have a lot of original ideas to help him recover his sexual ability and Patricia went along with his often ingenious suggestions but finally it all became too much for her when she discovered that he was using her money to buy drugs. She left him and went on a trip to Europe; where she soon felt sorry for him and went back.

When she first saw Lawford on her return he looked like the latter-day pictures of Howard Hughes: he had not had his hair cut for months and he had let himself go in just about every other way. Patricia worked hard to give him back some of his self-esteem but it was all too late and before long Lawford died from kidney failure and brain damage.

It was Peter Lawford who invited Marilyn Monroe to sing 'Happy Birthday' to President Kennedy at the massive birthday celebration held in Madison Square Garden, New York, with the knowledge and approval of both the President and his brother Bobby. Lawford was by no means sure she would be able to get there because of her filming commitments, although she immediately accepted; in the event her departure for the East Coast caused producer Henry Weinstein to make up his mind that Marilyn must be discharged from *Something's Got to Give*.

When Peter Lawford died Patricia spent all her savings on a simple funeral service which she had thought the wealthy Kennedy family might help to pay for. She didn't even have a suit to dress the corpse in and on Christmas Day 1984 she had to beg a suit for him from a tailor Lawford had patronized in better days. Even when he was dead there were still those who could not find it in their hearts to forgive Lawford for some of the things he did. For years after his death his widow was living in her stark apartment in Beverly Hills; alone with her memories of the last days of the one-time hell-raiser, Peter Lawford.

Albert Dekker

-

The Man with
the Twisted Mind

Born in Brooklyn, the always intense Albert Dekker appeared on Broadway with his friend Alfred Lunt in the title role of Eugene O'Neill's *Marco Millions* before arriving in Hollywood where he appeared in some strange roles in some strange films, but nothing could equal his bizarre end.

He appeared with Barbara Bates in her movie debut, *Salome, Where She Danced*, a curious, camped-up classic; she was to make several suicide attempts before she left Hollywood, got a job in a hospital, married a childhood sweetheart and, after he died, turned on the gas and finally died by her own hand.

Dekker also appeared in another very curious film, *Among the Living* with Frances Farmer who had one of the most unhappy lives of anyone who ever lived in Hollywood. He also appeared in such distinctly odd films as *Suspense, Slave Girl, Tarzan's Magic Fountain, Kiss Me Deadly, Seven Sinners* and the great but disturbingly odd period suspense melodrama with Hedy Lamarr, *Experiment Perilous*.

It has been said that Dekker's appearance was naturally somewhat strange and perhaps that is why he was chosen for so many strange roles in his film career. Strangest of all must be the remarkable, unique and distinctive *Dr Cyclops* (1940) with Dekker as the bald and bespectacled Dr Alexander Thorkel, a mad scientist working in the Amazon region who reduces a party of visiting scientists to doll-like proportions and, in a somewhat repellent scene, snuffs out the life of one of them with a wad of cotton-wool soaked in ether. Dekker's victims in the film struggle with seemingly gigantic insects, monstrous cats and so forth, giving the special effects department a field day. Thorkel, Dekker's most spectacular and best-remembered role, meets his doom when, deprived of his essential thick spectacles (hence the title of the film) he falls to his death down a well. The film was memorable on several counts, not least for being the first 'monster' movie filmed in full colour. It was directed by Ernest Scholdsack, one of the creators of the original *King Kong*.

The first film in a new seven-year contract that Marilyn Monroe signed with Fox saw her playing with Monty Woolley and Albert Dekker in *As Young as You Feel* (1951). Marilyn, as Dekker's secretary, affects a sexy voice and is called 'dear' by her besotted boss whom she is continually reminding to take his pills, and although the film was essentially a vehicle for Monty Woolley, the sexy voice and walk that Marilyn assumed in the film, whenever anyone needed to be impressed, mirrored the real-life Marilyn where she neatly separated the actress from the real person.

In 1967 Dekker's 16-year-old son, Jan, was found shot to death in New York; a death the authorities listed as suicide. The following year Albert Dekker was found dead in his Hollywood apartment and his death was certainly suicide, and a bizarre, unique and grotesque bondage suicide at that.

The 62-year-old actor was found in his locked bathroom, bound and handcuffed, hanging from the shower rod. For his last appearance he had chosen women's silk lingerie and before the final act he had written in red lipstick some of the unfavourable things that had been said about him and his performances on the naked parts of his anatomy.

He left no note or final message but perhaps he had said it all to a theatre critic a few years earlier. He told Ward Morehouse, as he reflected on his 40-odd years of acting on stage and screen: 'The theatre is a horrible place in which to make a living. They sit you on the shelf for years, then take you off the shelf for a little while and when your hopes rise, they put you back on that shelf.'

His real name was Albert van Dekker and for two years he served as Democratic assemblyman of the 57th District in the California legislature. He seems to have tried hard to live a normal life and perhaps he succeeded until the shattering

death of his son drove him over the edge, and then he must
have decided to indulge his fantasies to the limit, making a
Hollywood he found disappointing sit up for a moment and
notice him.

James Whale

-

Enigmatic Director
of Fantasy Films

Born in Dudley, England, in 1896 James Whale was captured by the Germans while serving in the First World War and he had his first taste of the theatre in a prisoner-of-war camp. After the war he found work as a cartoonist on *The Bystander* before deciding to make acting his career. Once having made the decision he worked hard and was soon touring the provinces and appearing on the London stage.

After a few years he turned his hand to stage design and directing and he was stage manager at the Savoy Theatre before enjoying considerable success in 1929 with R. C. Sherriff's play, *Journey's End*, about life in the trenches. After running in London the play went to New York and when it was decided to make a movie the logical choice of director was James Whale. He had already gained some experience of film-making as dialogue director on *The Love Doctor* (1929) and the Howard Hughes First World War flying epic *Hell's Angels* (1930).

Jean Harlow had her first real part in *Hell's Angels* and she remained eternally grateful to Whale for his help and understanding. On one occasion during the shooting of a difficult scene which demanded seductiveness on her part, she reportedly turned to the director and said, 'Tell me exactly how you want me to do it and I'll try,' to which Whale replied, quietly, 'My dear girl, I can tell you how to be an actress but I cannot tell you how to be a woman.'

In the end, so pleased was Whale with some of Harlow's later scenes that he reshot some of the earlier ones, thereby improving the over-all quality of her performance in the film.

Whale went on to make 20 films, most of them unusual in one way or another and he became closely identified with the classic horror film cycle at Universal during 1931–5, beginning with *Frankenstein* (1931), one of the finest of all horror films ever made – although today it appears somewhat crude, primitive-looking and lacking in humour. Whale chose his friend Colin Clive from *Journey's End* for the title role and when Bela Lugosi refused the part of the man-made monster because of the onerous make-up that the role demanded and because he would be unrecognizable, Whale chanced on the British actor Boris Karloff eating a meagre lunch in the commissary one day.

He called the tall, lean and hungry actor with the deep-set eyes over for a cup of coffee and Karloff agreed to test for the part of the monster. 'The part was what we call a "natural",' Karloff said to me when I was writing his biography. 'Any actor who played it was destined for success.' As ever he was being modest for he succeeded in portraying in masterly fashion the subhuman creature of little intelligence who talked with his eyes. The combination of sensitive Whale and talented Karloff made *Frankenstein* one of the most successful horror films of all time.

James Whale was a stylish director with a wicked sense of humour that showed to advantage in *The Old Dark House* (1932) where the waspishly effeminate Horace Femm (played by another Englishman, Ernest Thesiger), serenely observes the social niceties in a household that includes a mute, drunken, lecherous giant of a butler; a killer with a knife; a pyromaniac dwarf; a bedridden centenarian father (played by a woman) and a fanatically religious daughter!

It has been suggested that Whale, a working-class boy who made good, was perhaps compensating for his dubious upper-crust position in society; be that as it may the combination of malicious wit and terrifying characters and situations and locations in such horror films as *The Old Dark House*, written by J. B. Priestley, was quite irresistible to the film-going public of the day.

With the opportunity of returning to his native land to make *The Ghoul* (1933), his first visit to England in 24 years, Karloff turned down Whale's invitation to appear in *The Invisible Man* (1931) and the part in the H. G. Wells story was taken by Claude Rains; another great success for James Whale. Fortunately Karloff was able to accept Whale's offer of a repeat performance of his monster role in a film that turned out to be a masterpiece, *The Bride of Frankenstein* (1935).

Again Whale succeeded in assembling a remarkable collection of talented players: Colin Clive repeating his tortured scientist role; Karloff excelling himself as the pathetic monster, more humanized and sympathetic (although Karloff himself always thought it a mistake to have the monster speak); the wicked and eccentric Ernest Thesiger as the sinister Dr Praetorius who creates minute human forms; and Elsa Lanchester glancing at her intended mate and hissing in dismay. The bride's stunning make-up, modelled on Queen Nefertiti of the Ancient Egyptians, was entirely James Whale's conception.

Whale's later movies included a delightfully crazy black comedy, *Remember Last Night?* (1935), a large-budget musical, *Show Boat* (1936) and a stylish costume drama, *The Man in the Iron Mask* (1939) – which included Albert Dekker as the foppish King Louis XIII; but then, quite suddenly, James Whale left the world of films, took up painting in oils, and occasionally worked in the theatre as director.

James Whale was known to the world in general as a reserved man who had been associated with some memorable films, a gentle, talented director; to his closest friends he was known to be a homosexual with a devoted circle of brilliant friends of both sexes, a man who had invested well in land during his years of success and who was secure financially. But one way and another his world began to fall apart. His stylish anti-war film *The Road Back* (1937) had bought blunt threats of recriminations from Nazi Germany and to Whale's dismay the studio yielded and the film was cut beyond recognition; and then there was the unhappiness over David Lewis.

Shortly after coming to Hollywood Whale met David Lewis, a handsome young actor who became personal assistant to Irving Thalberg. James Whale lived at 788 Amalfi Drive, Pacific Palisades, between Beverly Hills and Malibu, and David Lewis moved in with him. They lived together until the early 1950s when Whale spent a year in Europe and took up with a young Frenchman, Pierre Foegel, whom he hired as chauffeur-cum-companion and whom he took back with him to Hollywood to share his home. David Lewis, of whom Whale

was very fond, refused to share Whale's home with the young
Frenchman whom Whale could hardly turn out in a strange
country and so David Lewis moved out. It was all very sad
and upsetting for the sensitive director.

In 1956 and 1957 James Whale suffered several strokes and
was partially paralysed. He became very depressed and the
following year he wrote a note:

> To all I love. Do not grieve for me. My nerves are all
> shot and for the last year I have been in agony day and
> night except when I sleep with the help of sleeping pills
> and any peace I have by day is when I am drugged by
> pills. I have had a wonderful life but it is over and my
> nerves get worse and I'm afraid they will have to take
> me away ... so please forgive me all those I love, and
> may God forgive me too. The future is just old age and
> pain. Goodbye all and thank you for all your love. I
> must have peace and this is the only way.

Having completed the note to his satisfaction James Whale
threw himself into the shallow end of his swimming pool,
striking his head against the bottom and dying instantly.

George Zucco

-

The Glassy-Eyed
High Priest

Born in 1886 in Manchester, George Zucco's family went to
Canada soon after he was born and he made his stage debut
in 1908. He had known from an early age that acting was what
he wanted to do. Although there were no professional actors
or actresses in the family and he encountered some opposition
in his chosen career, he persisted. Before long he was playing
leading men but his upright and authoritative bearing soon
marked him as ideal for military-officer roles and for a while
he found his niche.

Zucco returned to Britain in 1914 and served in the First
World War where he met James Whale when they were both
captured by the Germans and found themselves together in
prisoner-of-war camps. There they put together several shows
for their fellow-prisoners and after the war they kept in touch,
Zucco acting on Whale's advice to stay in England where stage
work was likely to be more rewarding than in Canada.

When *Journey's End* was being put together Whale had little
difficulty in persuading the play's author, R. C. Sherriff, to
cast Zucco as the kindly but doomed Lieutenant Osborne. The
play, with actors of the calibre of Colin Clive, Melville Cooper
and Maurice Evans, was an outstanding success; George Zucco
playing the steady, reliable officer, affectionately known to all
and sundry as 'Uncle', a solid man dropped into the Army from
the peaceful pursuit of schoolmastering, to perfection. In years
to come Zucco, a talented character actor with compelling eyes
who was much underrated, played mad scientists and sinister
high priests in a score of Hollywood films; and he would often

look back on his role in the play *Journey's End* as one of his happiest and most satisfying experiences.

Not that he was the only 'mad-scientist' type to catch the eye of Hollywood casting directors; Boris Karloff, Lionel Atwill and Bela Lugosi also suffered from being repeatedly employed in similar nefarious professions but whereas Karloff would invariably bring compassion to his portrayals, Atwill a chilly woodenness to his, and Lugosi a frightening passion to his, Zucco alone seemed completely plausible with an inner quiet and conviction that brought the character to life. His disturbingly glassy eyes, the even, purring voice and the quick, disconcerting gestures made him the perfect choice for many of the roles he played and he will always be remembered as a wonderful character actor.

In *The Mummy's Hand* (1940), one of the best Egyptian mummy pictures, Zucco had a typically villainous role. The High Priest, whose performance is almost more sinister than that of Tom Tyler as the mummy, gazes into smoking water and tells the tale of a curse, a 4,000 year-old half-mummified corpse of a prince buried alive, and a soulless demon who returns to life during the cycles of the full moon. *The Mummy's Hand* may not sound much but, as Leslie Halliwell puts it, 'innumerable audiences have breathed sighs of relief at the approach of the happy ending'. Zucco, deservedly, received second billing on the film, only Tom Tyler taking precedence.

A couple of years later Zucco repeated his performance in *The Mummy's Tomb* (1942), a film which made a surprising amount of money and so kept alive the Egyptian mummy theme for another half-a-dozen chillers — without George Zucco. Instead Universal, undoubtedly the leading fantasy-horror studio, carried on the Dracula-Frankenstein-Mummy tradition with cheaper degradations like the Wolf Man and Inner Sanctum mysteries, with ghouls, mad scientists and other creepy characters, often impersonated by the likes of Lon Chaney Jr and Lionel Atwill. George Zucco went on to excel himself in *The Mad Ghoul* (1943).

In his time Zucco worked with some of the best actors in Hollywood and *The Black Swan* (1942) is a case in point. A story of the seventeenth-century involving buccaneers and a villainous former governor of Jamaica (George Zucco), the cast of the beautifully depicted colour film included Tyrone

Power, Laird Cregar, Maureen O'Hara and George Sanders.

The following year the always sinister Zucco was back to *The Voodoo Man* as Bela Lugosi's dedicated assistant, capturing girls in an attempt to bring back to life the doctor's long-dead wife. A change of role came for Zucco when he appeared as the showman who owned the skeleton of Count Dracula, impaled with a wooden stake, together with earth from Transylvania in yet another Universal thriller, *House of Frankenstein* (1945).

Surely all these strange roles of mad and deranged people could not have unhinged the real George Zucco? He certainly began to believe that he was a kind of crazy high priest, like the characters he had so often portrayed on film and when fantasy eventually overtook reality he was taken to a mental institution.

His faithful wife and dutiful daughter, hoping against hope that their familiar presence would bring George back to reality, moved into the asylum to be with him. But for George Zucco the world of madness had become his whole world and one night, working himself into a paroxysm of fear, he screamed and clawed at the awful forms that filled his mind and then, from fright more than anything else, he died. The following night, in their grief and unhappiness and despair, and perhaps unable to live with the memories they had of their once loving husband and father, Mrs Zucco and their daughter joined him in death.

5

Mystery Is the Spice of Death

-

MYSTERIOUS DEATHS

Hollywood can be a mystery to those who enjoy mysteries. For a start, as the residents of Los Angeles will tell you, Hollywood does not exist. Film critic Alan Dent said to me after returning from a trip there nearly thirty years ago, 'Hollywood has nothing resembling Hollywood.'

It is not surprising that some of the film people who choose to live in such a mysterious, elusive, fascinating, enchanting, frustrating and impossible place should die mysteriously.

Hollywood still retains some of its glamour. There are still some luxurious houses in Beverly Hills although they are slowly disappearing: much to the disgust of Douglas Fairbanks Jr, the famous home of his parents, 'Pickfair', was purchased by a multi-millionaire in 1990 and promptly bulldozed to make way for a $5 million Renaissance-style palazzo.

And a recent attraction in Hollywood seeks to cater to the more jaded palates. Grave Line Tours visits the sites where some of Hollywood's brightest stars made their final exits. Greg Smith, dressed in funereal black, takes his customers around Hollywood in a silver and black hearse visiting some eighty appropriately gruesome areas.

Small wonder that in this curious environment there have been quite a number of people who have met mysterious deaths and those included in this chapter are the still puzzling demises of George 'Superman' Reeves; the curious death of Arthur Farnsworth (Mr Bette Davis); the unexplained deaths of prominent film directors Thomas Ince and William Desmond Taylor; and the unexpected death of Ray Raymond at the hands of actor Paul Kelly; entries in reference books for all these people often read something like 'died in mysterious circumstances ...'

George Reeves, the original Superman only weeks before his mysterious death

George Reeves

-

Was Superman Murdered?

George Reeves, whose real name was George Besselo, was the first man to portray Superman on television. He died in mysterious circumstances on 16 June 1959. It was a death that at first sight appeared to be suicide but the Beverly Hills police were never completely satisfied and the death has officially been classed as 'indicated suicide'.

Reeves appeared in several pictures before making the famous comic strip into even more famous screen adventures. His first film part was as one of the red-haired twins in *Gone With the Wind* (1939) and he also appeared in *So Proudly We Hail, From Here to Eternity* (1953), *Blood and Sand* (1941) and *Samson and Delilah* (1949).

Reeves's business manager, Arthur Weissman, has never accepted the suicide theory and 30 years after the event he talked of a bizarre plot which was brought about by the relationship which had existed between Reeves and Toni Mannix, wife of Eddie Mannix the vice-president of Loew's Theatre and one-time assistant to Louis B. Mayer at MGM.

Murder rather than suicide ended Reeves's life at his home in Benedict Canyon, according to Weissman and that is also the view of Milo Speriglio, a respected private investigator and criminologist who says that in his professional opinion it was definitely murder. John Austin, author and writer who covered the affairs of Hollywood for 30 years, also sees the death as murder; an event he explains fully in his recent book, *Hollywood's Unsolved Murders*. Helen Besselo, George Reeves's mother says she talked to George just a few hours before his death. 'He was in great spirits and not in the least depressed.' She went to her grave believing that her son had been murdered.

For several months prior to his death George Reeves – and also Toni Mannix – received numerous death threats by telephone. Toni, a brassy Broadway showgirl once known as 'the girl with the million-dollar legs' moved in with Eddie Mannix and soon became Mrs Mannix.

Reeves, in reporting the matter to the Beverly Hills Police Department (his telephone number was unlisted) even suggested a suspect: Eddie Mannix, Toni's jealous husband, and MGM studio manager, who might be instigating the threat, possibly through hired 'employees'. Aspiring actress and former model Toni was said to be 'deeply in love with Reeves' and their 'secret' romance continued for several years, an open secret in Hollywood, until Reeves announced his forthcoming marriage to Lenore Lemmon. Reeves is said to have sometimes received as many as twenty telephone threats in a single night and he certainly received a threat only two hours before his death.

Tough guy Eddie Mannix grew up to be a labourer and he helped to build apartments, supermarkets and amusement parks. He possessed the muscular physique and the profane vocabulary often associated with such men. When, with the help of the Metro boss, Louis B. Mayer, he reached the heady heights of studio manager, he was deeply grateful to Mayer and maintained unswerving loyalty to the man who had himself risen from his father's junk business to the very top of the film industry. Anything Mayer wanted done, he had only to ask Mannix. It is more than likely that Mayer used Mannix to help cover up evidence concerning the death of Paul Bern, Jean Harlow's husband. Mannix knew a lot about Jean's early life and about her step-father's underworld associates. Mannix was the type of man who managed things to his own advantage or arranged for things to happen to people who crossed him.

On the fatal day George Reeves had dinner at his home, prepared by his fiancée. Also present was journalist Robert Condon, staying at the house to write an article on Reeves (a former Golden Gloves boxing champion) and his planned exhibition bout with boxing champion Archie Moore, which was to be televised nationwide. After dinner the three sat around drinking and watching television until around midnight when they all retired to bed.

Between 1.00 and 1.30 in the morning a friend of Lenore, Caron Von Ronkel called at the house with a mutual friend, William Bliss. George and Lenore were not over-pleased at being disturbed at such an hour, but Lenore hurried down and let them in while George got up, grumbling, put on a bathrobe and started complaining in no uncertain manner at the lateness of the call.

Lenore calmed him down and they all had a drink together; George then said he was going to bed. It was at this point that Lenore said something like, 'Well, he's sulking; he'll probably go up to his room and shoot himself.' In fact, it would seem, that is exactly what George did. It later transpired that everyone in the house had consumed a considerable amount of intoxicating liquor and it was very difficult for the police to obtain a coherent account of the night's activities.

Those who subscribe to the suicide theory would of necessity have it that having entertained his fiancée and friends at his home, Reeves suddenly decided to commit suicide and he went to his bedroom, placed a pistol to his right ear and pulled the trigger. Interestingly enough, in the month preceding his death George Reeves had been involved in no less than three car accidents, any one of which could have killed him. First, his car was nearly crushed between two heavy lorries; second a speeding car nearly caused him to crash at speed and third, the brakes on his car failed on a narrow and twisting road – all the brake fluid having disappeared from the hydraulic system.

Many of the people in the studios who were close to Mannix and knew of his association with the underworld had no doubt that he had been responsible for the death of George Reeves. To dismiss the murder theory it is necessary to explain several curious circumstances regarding Reeves's death. There were no powder burns on his face as there should have been had the gun been held close to his head; this suggests that the gun must have been held at least 1 ½ ft away from the head which seems highly unlikely and practically impossible for a self-inflicted wound.

Reeves was allegedly found in bed, lying on his back, and the single empty cartridge case that had been fired from the gun was under his back; self-inflicted gunshot wounds usually propel the victim forward, in the path of the shot. The official police report listed the bullet wound as 'irregular', which seems odd for a bullet allegedly fired at close quarters.

The bullet itself was found imbedded in the ceiling and had seemingly been fired by Reeves's right hand (again according to the official report) but before his death Reeves had injured his right hand in yet another car accident, when his Jaguar skidded on an oil slick in the Hollywood Hills and he crashed into a brick wall. He was in the process of claiming half-a-million dollars in damages. And why were no fingerprints ever taken in the bedroom where the death took place?

After Eddie Mannix died Toni stayed on alone in their house in Schuyler Road, Beverly Hills, where she gained for herself the reputation of being argumentative and aggressive. During her marriage to the jumped-up studio manager she had been powerful behind the scenes and she obviously found it difficult to re-adjust after his death. Eddie Mannix died in 1974, still a studio manager; Toni survived him by ten years.

George Reeves left his entire estate, valued at $71,000 to Toni. (One might think that had he contemplated suicide he would have changed his will in favour of his fiancée.) Towards the end of her life Toni became something of a recluse, sitting hour after hour in her Beverly Hills home, watching Superman videos.

In common with other actors who find themselves continually associated with the roles they play, Reeves almost came to believe completely that he was the character that had brought him stardom: Clark Kent took over George Reeves. His death is likely to remain one of Hollywood's unsolved mysteries.

Arthur Farnsworth

Whatever Happened to Bette Davis's Husband?

On New Year's Eve, 1940 world-famous film actress Bette Davis (1908–89) was married privately in Arizona to young and handsome Arthur Farnsworth, the assistant manager of Peckett's Inn, Sugar Hill, New Hampshire. He was her second husband, the son of a Vermont doctor, and, according to Bette at the time, he would one day 'inherit a lot of money'. They had met a couple of months previously when the legendary actress had stayed at Peckett's Inn during a holiday. Dining alone one evening, the good-looking assistant manager got into conversation and they had become friends immediately. 'At last I've found the peace I have been searching for,' Bette sighed at the time. 'I have a career and the love of a man I respect.' Less than three years later Farnsworth was dead and the true cause of his death has never been established.

Outwardly the short marriage appeared to be serene and comparatively happy. When Bette was working, the couple lived in California; the rest of the time they spent on a farm they bought in New Hampshire. Farnsworth had interests in commercial flying and this work took him away from time to time. Rumours that all was not well with the marriage began to surface during the spring of 1943.

In the May of that year Bette had completed her work in *Old Acquaintance* (1943) in which she appeared with Gig Young. The making of *Old Acquaintance* was a traumatic experience, by all accounts. Bette's co-star was Miriam Hopkins; and Bette is credited with saying, on more than one occasion: 'Miriam

Hopkins was a wonderful actress – but a bitch; the most thorough-going bitch I've ever worked with.'

Talented Edmund Goulding was to direct but during the course of a loud and violent argument with Bette, Goulding had a heart attack and was replaced by Vincent Sherman. Jack Warner always maintained that 'Goulding faked his heart attack.' At all events, according to Sherman, there was very little peace on the set between Bette and Miriam, who both used every trick in the book to upstage each other and went out of their ways to have arguments, cause delays and generally disrupt the making of the picture.

When the film was eventually completed, in May 1943, Bette and her husband had made arrangements to set off for New York but now Bette made her excuses and travelled alone to Mexico where she had arranged to meet Vincent Sherman, the director, for an illicit holiday together; at the last moment, however, Vincent, perhaps remembering his wife and young baby, changed his mind and didn't meet Bette in Mexico. Instead Bette stayed for a while with the notorious Countess Dorothy Di Frasso whose lovers had included Gary Cooper, gangster Bugsy Spiegal and Benito Mussolini!

Bette extended her visit into June and then joined her husband at the farm. A couple of months later, in August, the couple returned to Hollywood where Bette had a new film lined up, *Mr Skeffington* (1944). She reportedly said at the time that she was anxious to get back to work as 'inactivity drives me mad.'

So we come to the afternoon of 23 August. Bette was to claim that she remained at home while Arthur Farnsworth had lunch with a lawyer, Dudley Furse, and afterwards they discussed the purchase of some property in Hollywood, among other things.

After lunch, walking to his car, Farnsworth suddenly screamed, fell backwards and hit his head on the pavement outside 6249 Hollywood Boulevard. He had in fact fractured his skull and he was rushed to Hollywood Receiving Hospital. Bette was to testify that she was called at 4.15 in the afternoon, and once she knew what had happened she telephoned her doctor, Dr Paul Moore, and asked for her husband to be transferred at once to Cedars of Lebanon Hospital, as it was then called. Bette visited the unconscious man but after conferring with the doctors, decided not to contact his parents.

All that Monday night and throughout the next day Bette sat at her husband's bedside. Mostly he was quite motionless but occasionally he stirred a little and moaned, when Bette would do her best to arouse him, but, still without regaining consciousness, Arthur Farnsworth died on Wednesday, 24 August 1943.

First accounts stated that death had been a result of a fractured skull following a fall on Hollywood Boulevard. 'A routine autopsy will be performed', it was stated, 'and a funeral service has been arranged for Saturday, at Forest Lawn.'

The evening after 'Farney' died Bette held a kind of party for her late husband's flying friends who called themselves The Quiet Birdmen; members included Charles Lindbergh. There Bette toasted Farney in champagne, 'because that's what he would have wanted'. During these somewhat curious festivities the party was joined by two more sombre mourners, Farney's mother and brother from Vermont, who had arrived too late to see Arthur Farnsworth before he died. They were accompanied by a lawyer and an investigator from the district attorney's office who informed Bette and her assembled company that foul play could not be ruled out in the matter of the death of Arthur Farnsworth. The autopsy had revealed that he had not died from the street fall but from a previous head injury.

Next day the *Los Angeles Times* carried the disturbing news: 'Farnsworth had a blood clot on the right side of his skull which apparently caused pressure that made him dizzy and precipitated the fall.' One of the doctors who took part in the autopsy added, 'The blow must have been caused by the butt of a gun or some other blunt instrument.'

Arthur's mother now insisted on a full inquest and inquiry into the whole matter because, according to her daughter, sister of the deceased, Arthur was involved in secret war work. The chief coroner for the area agreed that the case warranted a full investigation and he began to arrange things for the middle of the following week. Bette was very upset; but already there were whispers that her annoyance and distress were rooted in guilt. It transpired that far from being the devoted and loving wife, as presented to the world at large, the marriage was in trouble: Bette had requested a divorce and, more damaging still, it was said that she had been involved in her husband's fatal fall. 'I was never violently in love with Farney,' the actress admitted twenty years later.

A year before her husband died there were rumours of an affair between Bette Davis and an orchestra leader, a married man, and around the same time Bette tried to have an affair with her film director, Vincent Sherman (as we have seen) telling him that her physical relationship with Farney was over; Farney, she said, was a drinker and that made him impotent. When she did not succeed with Sherman, although he confessed that he was strongly attracted to her, Bette set out to ensure that they were thrown together by seeking to arrange for him to direct *Mr Skeffington*, scheduled to begin in July 1943. When she discovered that Sherman was tied up with another film, she said *Mr Skeffington* could wait. She decided to take the opportunity of the delay by joining her husband on the farm in New Hampshire. Bette later maintained that by this time the relationship between her and Farney was like that of brother and sister, although it seems clear that this platonic arrangement was not to the liking of her husband.

At all events it was during this period, while Bette and Farney were at the farm, that Farney suffered a fall which probably precipitated his fatal fall. According to his wife he was hurrying downstairs one afternoon to answer the telephone when he slipped and fell.

Farnsworth's sister, Mrs Roger Briggs, later explained that there was a loft at the farmhouse with a stairway leading to it. Both Bette and Farney were up there when the telephone rang. Farney fell and hit the back of his head but he seemed all right. Farnsworth was not worried about the fall although he did complain of a stiff neck and he seemed to find himself a little off-balance on occasions. It could well have been her husband's shakiness and occasional loss of balance that led Bette to think he was drinking heavily.

On the train back to Hollywood Bette and Farney argued about the ending of their marriage (according to Vincent Sherman, quoted by Shaun Considine) and during a fight Bette either hit him or he fell, sustaining a second injury to the head.

Writer Hector Arce told the author of *Bette and Joan − The Divine Feud* (the story of the long-running battles between Bette Davis and Joan Crawford) that the lunch Farnsworth had on the day he died had nothing to do with the purchase of any property – Farnsworth did not have any money. The purpose of the lunch was to help Bette in her tax returns by having her husband file a joint return with her. The returns had to go in the following week so the forms were signed in the lawyer's office on Hollywood Boulevard and afterwards, walking back to their car, Farnsworth became unsteady; Bette accused him of drinking too much and she gave him a push. He fell sideways and hit his head on the curb.

On Saturday, 28 August 1943 a funeral service was held for Arthur Farnsworth at the Church of the Recessional in Forest Lawn. The burial would not be in Forest Lawn but in New Hampshire. The body could not be moved there for several days, until the official hearing into the death was held.

Bette Davis duly put in an appearance at the inquest and made quite an impression by all accounts. The *Los Angeles Times* reported:

> *No role of tragedy Bette Davis has portrayed before the camera ever equalled her appearance before the six-man Coroner's Jury when she testified ... she left glamour behind her when she entered. Her face was devoid of make-up and she looked drawn and tired. She took the witness stand and answered all questions briefly, in a monotone.*

Asked about any accident previous to the fatal one, Bette told of the incident in New Hampshire the previous June when Farnsworth fell downstairs. 'He was kind of wiggly there for a few minutes and very limp,' she said, but he never consulted a physician; nor did he complain. Bette made no mention of the alleged subsequent fall on the train two weeks before his death nor of any arguments about the marriage or anything else.

The autopsy surgeon, Dr Homer R. Keyes, maintained that any injury sustained two months before would have healed and would not be the cause of death; likewise he maintained that the fall on Hollywood Boulevard was not responsible for Farnsworth's death. 'A basal skull injury probably caused the man's death,' Dr Keyes said. He thought the fracture that resulted in death was inflicted about 14 days previously.

Reversing the examining surgeon's conclusion the six-man

inquest jury decided that Farnsworth's death was caused by
the accident in New Hampshire, two months earlier and
they did not recommend any further investigation. Bette and
Farnsworth's family took the body to Vermont, Farnsworth's
home town, and then it was taken to New Hampshire and
buried on the farm.

A couple of years later the body was exhumed and reburied
in the family vault in Vermont. By that time Bette Davis had
remarried but she would never talk about the death of Arthur
Farnsworth, his many funerals and their last weeks together. It
has to be said that there was talk of his being an epileptic, of
being a heavy drinker, even of his seeing another woman who
was married and whose husband murdered Farnsworth. 'No
one ever found out the true story,' Vincent Sherman says today;
and Sheilah Graham, a knowledgeable writer on Hollywood
said: 'The subject of Farnsworth's death was off-limits and
remained a mystery, because that was what Warners wanted.
You must remember that studios were enormously powerful in
those days.' Bette's daughter says: 'There were certain topics
Mother would not go into details about and that was one of
them.'

Six months after Arthur Farnsworth's death Fredda Dudley
wrote in *Photoplay* (November 1943) that Bette Davis had
indeed been with her husband at that last lunch, on the day
he died. Three years later William Grant Sherry, whom Bette
had by that time married, said that he and Bette were walking
along Hollywood Boulevard one day when they reached the
spot outside her lawyer's office. 'Bette turned white,' he said.
'I asked her what was wrong and she said, "This is where Farney
fell that day, after I pushed him."'

The death in Hollywood of Arthur Farnsworth, husband
of Bette Davis, seems to have been far from completely or
satisfactorily explained. 'What a fool I was ever to go to
Hollywood,' Bette once said. 'Where they only understood
platinum blondes, and where legs are more important than
talent.'

Thomas H. Ince

-

'Movie Producer Shot on Hearst Yacht'

One of the truly mysterious deaths in Hollywood concerns the demise of Thomas Harper Ince (1882–1924), a film director who graduated from the Broadway theatre, working first with Carl Laemmle and then moving to the old Kessel and Baumann's Bison-Life Motion Picture Company where he was to direct more than a hundred films, mostly Westerns, in 1911 and 1912. He renewed his friendship from theatrical days with William S. Hart, one of the best-known early cowboy actors and later a director himself. Ince built up his reputation by concentrating on the characterization of the hero and heroine and he directed a number of Mary Pickford films before concentrating to a large extent on faithful reconstruction of films of the Old West.

Ince involved himself totally in the business of making films. He often wrote the script from a story outline and he would then plot in detail every action and emotion in each scene, thereby eliminating wastage, since there was little film that was shot that was not used. It was not so much that he wanted to stifle creativity, rather his aim was to 'create' at the earliest possible time and so economically and advantageously affect the film from its inception. In fact Ince can claim to have innovated some movie-making techniques, such as smearing petroleum jelly on camera lens before filming a dream sequence or filming such a sequence through a layer of gauze. Ince was also the first director to place cameras actually in an aeroplane or under horses' hooves as they careered over the dusty ground in scores of Westerns.

In 1915 Ince, with Mack Sennett and D. W. Griffith, became the core of the newly formed Triangle Distributing (and later production) Company that, working from new studios in Culver City, saw Douglas Fairbanks achieve stardom and became known for its Westerns and comic films. Ince had great influence during the early days of film-making but he personally directed only three films, of which *Civilization* (1916) is generally considered to be his finest achievement.

During his later years, when his influence and film-making genius waned, there were persistent stories of a romantic link between him and Marion Davies, the girl whom newspaper tycoon William Randolph Hearst had 'discovered' and regarded as his personal property. Hearst could not marry her because his own wife was Roman Catholic and would not consider divorce but Hearst lived openly with Marion Davies, whom he obviously adored, at his famous San Simeon 'castle'.

Whether or not there was any truth in the stories of a romantic liaison with Tom Ince, it seems certain that Marion Davies and Charles Chaplin were seeing each other. Hearst read in the *New York Times* that the famous, important and well-off comedian was 'paying ardent attention' to the beautiful, blonde young actress in such Hollywood nightspots as the Montmartre; Hearst was furious and may well have decided to do something about it. He was a man of considerable power, few scruples and enormous wealth. Chaplin himself told me he never knew a person throw his wealth around in such a manner as did Hearst. He gave Marion a 'beach house' at Santa Monica which was in fact a palace with 70 rooms and it was the scene of many extravagant parties. At a party which Hearst gave there to welcome Marion back from a European trip, one guest, more than a little the worse for drink, was hurt in a shooting accident. The police arrived and reporters made much of the story but it is indicative of Hearst's power that not a word of the event appeared in any of Hearst's newspapers; he also instructed Marion's lawyer to inform all the other newspapers that she was not even at the party — given in her honour!

In 1924 Hearst was negotiating with Tom Ince the possible use of his Culver City studio for filming when he read the press report about Marion and Chaplin. Not that this was the first Hearst knew about the affair: in fact, he had private investigators watching her. Once he telephoned her and read

out a report from one of the detectives concerning her meetings
with Charles Chaplin, but she insisted they were only friends.
Hearst was not happy about the affair and he left New York
for California without delay, sending an invitation to Chaplin
to join him and a number of other guests, including Marion,
on board his yacht *Oneida* for a short cruise. He also sent a
similar invitation to Tom Ince who accepted but said he would
join the boat a day late as he had to attend a film première.

Louella Parsons also received an invitation. She was a
New York journalist who was about to become one of the
most powerful of all gossip columnists, virtually making and
destroying careers through exposure of stars' private lives as
she chose to see them. She was popular with Hearst because
she went out of her way to support the popularity of Marion
Davies. I am indebted to James Mason for showing me another
side of Louella Parsons; she was of enormous value to the
masters of the big Hollywood studios for not only did she
loudly advertise their products but she could also be relied upon
to bring to heel recalcitrant actors and actresses. James Mason
told me that Louella Parsons ended up 'losing her coherence'
and she was taken to a home in Hollywood where she survived
for several years. 'They gave her a disconnected telephone to
play with so that she could imagine that she was conducting
endless conversations with the stars.'

The excited guests, ominously 13 of them according to
Marion Davies's own account, boarded the *Oneida* and next
day awaited the arrival of Tom Ince. He duly arrived and was
somewhat upset that he could not drink a toast to his son's
birthday but Hearst would never serve intoxicating liquor to
his guests. Elinor Glyn, the English writer of wildly romantic
novels, some of which were filmed, was another guest and
she interjected to say, 'Whatever you do, don't drink a toast
in water, it's very bad luck,' but, again according to Marion
Davies, 'I think we did.'

Marion's version of the events that followed says that next
morning there was no sign of Tom Ince and she was told that
after an attack of indigestion, he had vomited most of the night
and said he would like to go home. Tom was set ashore and
went home. Marion Davies continues, 'a member of his family
was a Christian Scientist and didn't want a doctor. Tom was
sick for two days and then died.'

Another version of events on that fretful night has it that Hearst became aware that Marion and Charles Chaplin were missing from the party. He went in search of them and found them together on a lower deck in a position that left nothing to the imagination. Marion suddenly saw her jealous older lover standing over them and she screamed. Guests came running from all parts of the boat and some were in time to see Hearst aim a pistol at Chaplin. During the confusion that followed a gun was fired and a man dropped to the deck but it was not Chaplin, it was Tom Ince.

Yet another version of events has it that when Hearst went looking for Marion he found her on a lower galley, sitting at a table facing a man whose back was towards Hearst. It looked like Chaplin and in a jealous rage Hearst took the revolver he kept on board to shoot troublesome seagulls and shot the man – but it was Tom Ince not Chaplin.

The following day Toriachi Kono, Chaplin's Japanese driver and friend, was summoned to fetch Chaplin from the yacht. While waiting for his master he saw Ince carried unconscious from the yacht and he saw what looked like a bullet hole in his head.

Without delay Hearst addressed the shocked guests and sought to convince them that the wisest course was to say nothing about the events of the previous 24 hours. Some of those present went as far as to insist that they were never there! Louella Parsons was taken to one side and promised that her column would be syndicated throughout Hearst's newspaper chain and she would be the most powerful gossip columnist in Hollywood – if she forgot all that had happened.

Charles Chaplin, Marion Davies, Douglas Fairbanks, Mary Pickford and Harold Lloyd attended Ince's funeral in Hollywood on 21 November 1924; Hearst was conspicuous by his absence. The body was cremated without an inquest. Two days after the funeral Chaplin hurriedly journeyed south, his affair with Marion Davies over for good.

In his autobiography Chaplin says he was not present on the trip when Ince died and Marion Davies does not mention him among the guests who made up the unlucky 13. Chaplin says Elinor Glyn told him Ince was struck with paralysing pains during lunch on the first day and he was taken off the boat. In hospital they said he had suffered a heart attack. 'He was sent to his home in Beverly Hills, where three weeks later he had a second attack and died' was the official story.

Chaplin pours scorn on the 'ugly rumours' that were spread about Ince being shot and Hearst being implicated and he says, 'Those rumours were completely untrue. I know this because Hearst, Marion and I went to see Ince at his home two weeks before he died; he was very happy to see the three of us and believed that he would soon be well.'

The authorities looked into the matter and found that Hearst was in New York before the fateful cruise, was suspicious of Marion's relationship with Charles Chaplin and had employed private detectives to keep watch on her. But, the authorities decided, there was no 'affair', the couple really were 'just good friends'. Ince had delayed his joining the party for a day and Chaplin had not been able to go because of his involvement in filming *The Gold Rush* (1925); it does not seem to have been established whether or not Chaplin actually declined the invitation. In spite of his suspicions Hearst liked Chaplin and probably thought that if he and Marion were both on the cruise he could see for himself how they behaved.

With Ince on board the party enjoyed a meal but the following morning Dr Daniel Goodman (Hearst's head of production) left with Ince who seemed unwell with acute indigestion. Before they reached the train that was to take them back to Hollywood Ince felt a pain in his chest. On the train he suffered a heart attack and Dr Goodman arranged for him to leave the train and they went to the nearest hotel where Goodman rang Tom Ince's wife. He then called a doctor and waited for him to arrive before continuing his own journey to Los Angeles. Some time after he left, Ince died and Dr Goodman diagnosed 'acute indigestion'.

The *Los Angeles Times* of 19 November 1924 announced the death of Tom Ince and the headline read: 'Movie Producer Shot on Hearst Yacht'. Later editions of the same day omitted the story without explanation. Meanwhile Hearst's newspapers carried a different story. 'Special Car Rushes Stricken Man Home from Ranch' and the item stated that Ince, with his wife and two young sons, had been visiting Hearst at his ranch for several days before the attack and when the 'film magnate' suddenly became unconscious he was assigned a special car and, attended by two specialists and three nurses, he was hurriedly conveyed to his own home. In this version of events there was no hint that Ince ever as much as set foot on the *Oneida* but the story is a blatant fabrication. Ince was seen on the yacht by witnesses and when Hearst was faced with this evidence he changed the story and said that Ince was on board the yacht but had died from acute indigestion, as stated by Dr Goodman.

Still the rumours that Ince had been shot continued. Marion Davies said she 'was shocked' when she read the story that Tom had been shot. 'Who would shoot him? And why? The whole thing was preposterous. There were no weapons aboard the *Oneida*, ever.' And he didn't die until late Monday. 'How long can one keep a bullet in his system?' Marion Davies also denied that Louella Parsons was on board the yacht. Whatever the truth of the matter it seems indisputable that Hearst *did* keep a gun on board for shooting gulls.

If Ince really died an innocent death from acute indigestion, why are there so many inconsistent stories associated with the affair? Why should Hearst seek to deny that Ince had ever been on the yacht? Why had Hearst not attended the funeral of a friend who had died on his yacht? Why should Marion Davies go to great lengths to seek to perpetuate obvious untruths: that Louella Parsons was not aboard and that there was no gun aboard? Certainly word went around Hollywood that every member of Hearst's yacht party on that occasion had received a gift of one million dollars just to keep quiet about how Ince really died.

Journalist and author Michael Munn suggests that the centre of the controversy is Charles Chaplin's implication in the whole affair. The murder theory would only appear to ring true if Chaplin was in fact on board the *Oneida* at the time of the shooting. Hearst had to have thought he had found Marion with Chaplin to have contemplated murder.

Chaplin would have found himself in an impossible position. If he had been on board and admitted it, he would become implicated in an alleged case of attempted murder that would also have involved Marion. It might be thought that even if he were on board, he would have to deny it. His account of the incident in his somewhat unreliable autobiography refers to Ince's surviving for three weeks, which hardly squares with the offical version where Ince is cremated on 21 November, four days after he became ill.

And if Chaplin was not on board when Ince left the boat and never had been, what was his chauffeur Toriachi Kono doing anywhere in the vicinity? It has to be said that Kono, who was in Chaplin's employ for some 18 years, never said or did anything, as far as we know, to compromise his master. He was always a trusted employee and certainly knew a few secrets which he never talked about. In 1933, when Chaplin married Paulette Goddard, Kono felt his unique association with Chaplin had come to an end and he decided to return to his native Japan. Chaplin was very reluctant to see him go and gave him and his wife a thousand dollars each; Chaplin also put in a good word for Kono at the United Artists Corporation in Tokyo. It was only before he knew the implications of his story of seeing Ince with a bullet hole in his head, that Kono told numerous people what he had seen.

And then there is the evidence of Marion's stand-in, Vera Burnett, who said she saw Marion and Chaplin at the studio as they were leaving to join the yacht. She also said she saw Louella Parsons at the studio with Marion and Chaplin but the columnist claimed she was in New York and nowhere near Hollywood at that time!

A subsequent inquiry heard the evidence *only* of Dr Goodman and a nurse who had attended to Ince in his final hours. Their stories corresponded with Hearst's account of the affair and, inconceivably, having heard the evidence from just these two people, the District Attorney said he was satisfied that Thomas Ince died from natural causes and the inquiry came to an end.

Could Marion have been having affairs with both Chaplin and Ince? Could Chaplin have been the one who killed Ince and Hearst covered up the whole affair for the sake of Marion Davies? He certainly covered things up – but why?

Whatever the whole truth of the matter William Randolph Hearst would never discuss it with anyone and Marion used to warn first-time visitors to San Simeon never to mention the name of Tom Ince in Hearst's presence. D. W. Griffith once stated: 'All you have to do to make Hearst turn white as a ghost is to mention Tom Ince's name.'

John Gilbert, according to his daughter Leatrice Gilbert Fountain, was one of many people who knew Ince and were upset by his death under mysterious circumstances. Gilbert had been devoted to Ince and always gave the 'first prophet of modern cinema' credit for starting his career. Gilbert also said, 'Everyone that touches me seems to die young.'

William Desmond Taylor

-

Hollywood Murder Mystery

In 1922 the man known as William Desmond Taylor was a leading director at Famous Players – Lasky studios, a subsidiary of Paramount and, in the wake of the 'Fatty' Arbuckle scandal that had all but ruined the film industry, he had been elected president of the Motion Picture Directors Association with clear instructions to clean up the industry and make sure everything about it was acceptable to the general public.

Taylor liked to pass himself off as having been an officer in the British Army and he kept an officer's uniform at his bungalow apartment on Alvarado Street in the suburb of Westlake, Los Angeles. A somewhat mysterious, unbending and unfriendly man, he fancied that he cut a dashing figure in the jodhpurs and riding boots that he frequently wore both on and off film sets. In fact his real name was William Deane Tanner, he was born in Ireland on 26 April 1877 and had come to America with his family and settled in New York where he had operated an antique business with his brother Dennis.

William had met and married a girl he saw in a vaudeville act and their union was blessed by the arrival of a little daughter. One day William Deane Tanner disappeared, deserting his wife and child, and shortly afterwards a man calling himself William Desmond Taylor surfaced in California, saying he was a stage actor; he seemed a gentlemanly and charming person who boasted of having served in the British Army.

It was an appropriate time for actors with directing ambitions to arrive in Hollywood and after a few appearances as an actor William Taylor followed men like D. W. Griffith and

Cecil B. De Mille in expressing their talents *behind* the cameras. Taylor's first directorial job was a serial starring Lottie Pickford, younger sister of Mary, who in 1915 was already the biggest money-making actress in the film industry. For William Taylor it was the beginning of a long working association with the Pickford family who, it has to be said, were not quite as snow-white as their studios presented them to be. To preserve her teenage image Mary Pickford, for example, was presented as an unmarried virgin although in fact she was married to Owen Moore and committing adultery with Douglas Fairbanks Sr at the time. Furthermore all the Pickfords drank heavily and innumerable instances of embarrassing behaviour were hushed up by the studios; Mary's brother Jack in particular was a hopeless alcoholic and drug addict.

People like the Pickford family, so well-known by sight, had to be carefully shielded from the public gaze but William Desmond Taylor was a different matter. His face was not known to the average person and he could go just about anywhere more or less as he pleased. It is known that he was fond of frequenting some of the more seedy dives in the environs of Hollywood where effeminate men and masculine women were to be found and where narcotics were freely available. The rumour was that Taylor was a homosexual and that he had in his employ a homosexual negro butler.

In 1920 Mary Pickford joined Douglas Fairbanks, Charles Chaplin and D. W. Griffith to form an independent company, United Artists, and Paramount signed up Mary Miles Minter, one of Hollywood's leading child performers before she blossomed into a charming romantic leading player, to replace Mary Pickford. Taylor directed her first real success, *Anne of Green Gables*, and other successes followed. During the evenings and nights before filming, the seemingly respectable and dignified William Taylor spent a lot of time at his quiet bungalow with the seemingly innocent Mary Miles Minter.

Not that she was the first or the last of Taylor's conquests; in fact he went through a string of screen beauties who were willing to gratify the whims of the powerful and influential film director. Sometimes he arranged for his 'butler' to take photographs of himself and his complaisant starlets.

During the course of investigations carried out after his death it transpired that some of the screen's best-known actresses took part in activities with Taylor at his bungalow and allowed themselves to be photographed in compromising attitudes and positions with the director. The discovery of such pictures could well end their film careers so the reason for their taking such risks must have been powerful; possibly drugs or blackmail of some kind.

The night of 1 February 1922 saw Taylor alone in his study and the trim, handsome, middle-aged man was probably contemplating his next film project. He was answerable to Charles Eyton, general manager of the studio, who was in turn answerable to the powerful head of Paramount, Adolph Zukor – to whom the recent scandals in the film industry had become a nightmare.

Suddenly Taylor must have realized that he was not alone and, turning, he caught sight of a muffled figure in a long coat standing in the open doorway, pointing a gun at him. The director hurled himself out of his chair towards his desk where he kept a pistol but in so doing he presented his back as a target for the intruder. The gun fired twice, both bullets finding their mark in Taylor's back. He fell in front of the desk and was probably dead before he hit the ground; at all events his eyes were open when his body was eventually found.

The deed accomplished, the killer retreated from the bungalow, the face still hidden by a muffler and cap, seen only by a Mrs Faith Cole MacLean who had been startled by the sound of the shots and went to the window in time to see someone leave Taylor's bungalow and disappear from sight. She knew many of Taylor's visitors by sight but did not recognize this one.

The body was found early the following morning by Taylor's negro manservant, Henry Peavey, who ran out into the courtyard and away down Alvarado Street, sobbing and crying, 'Dey've kilt massa ... dey've kilt massa ...' over and over again. One of those he awakened was Edna Purviance, the pretty young leading lady in many of Chaplin's films. She hurriedly put on some clothes and ran over to Taylor's bungalow where she too saw the lifeless body.

She ran back to her own apartment and reached for the telephone; then hesitated. She sensed another film scandal and instead of contacting the police she telephoned instead her friend Mabel Normand, the beautiful, clever and vivacious actress who appeared for Mack Sennett, Charles Chaplin and Sam Goldwyn in a string of successful films. Normand's fabulous wardrobe was to set a standard which was to be imitated by other beautiful girls who followed her to become stars of Hollywood. Mabel said she would come over at once but first she too made a telephone call, again not to the police, but to Charles Eyton. He in turn wasted no time in making a telephone call, also not to the police but to Adolph Zukor who said he would meet Eyton at Taylor's bungalow as soon as he could get there.

Meanwhile Edna Purviance made another call, this time to Mary Miles Minter, Paramount's demure answer to Mary Pickford, a ringletted embodiment of innocent maidenhood although she was actually 22 years of age. When there was no reply from her, Edna rang Mary's mother, Mrs Charlotte Shelby. She said she didn't know where Mary was but she would break the news about Taylor's death as soon as she found her daughter.

Eventually the police were called by an irate neighbour complaining about being awakened by 'a crazy negro' screaming through the neighbourhood. The police soon picked up Peavey who led them back to the Taylor bungalow. The door stood open and a number of cars were parked outside.

Inside the bungalow the police found a hive of activity. Still lying where he had fallen, with two bullets through the heart, was the body of William Desmond Taylor but also in the room were Adolph Zukor, Charles Eyton, Mabel Normand and Edna Purviance. According to later police evidence Zukor was hurriedly burning papers in the fireplace, Eyton was scooping up bottles of bootleg liquor into a sack, Normand was poking about in nooks and crannies in Taylor's desk, while Purviance stood silently watching, seemingly in a state of shock.

The police took charge and quickly ruled out robbery. Among other valuables the director's flashy diamond ring was still on his finger. He had worn that ring for luck ever since his first film, *The Diamond From the Sky*, although it seemed his luck had now run out. Although it was obvious that a lot of evidence had been destroyed, the police soon found a wealth of incriminating material that sparked off a Hollywood murder mystery and a scandal that was exactly what Zukor and Eyton had hoped to prevent. Chief among the finds was a pile of photographs, hidden at the bottom of a drawer, that depicted the dead man and a variety of identifiable young ladies engaged in unusual activities. Stories of Taylor's being a homosexual seemed to be very wide of the mark.

When she was questioned Mabel Normand admitted she had been searching for a letter in Taylor's bungalow when the police arrived, 'but only to prevent the terms of affection being misconstrued'. The letter was eventually found in one of Taylor's riding boots.

Another find by the police was a book of erotica by Aleister Crowley entitled *White Stains,* and when the book was shaken, out fell a scented note that read:

Dearest – I love you – I love you – I love you x x x x x x x x x Yours Always! Mary.

The pink stationery was monogrammed 'M.M.M.' and there could be no doubt that the author of the note was the beautiful Mary Miles Minter. She admitted to the police that she had indeed loved Taylor, 'deeply and tenderly, with all the admiration a young girl gives to a man with the poise and position of Mr Taylor'. Further finds by the police at Taylor's bungalow included a closet full of ladies' underwear, each item marked with initials and a date. One item was embroidered 'M.M.M.' and it set the seal on Mary Miles Minter's sweet and innocent image. There was a clause in Mary Minter's contract that forbade marriage, yet she was undoubtedly contemplating 'marriage' to Taylor, not knowing, presumably, that he was already married. But the police were only interested in investigating a murder.

The only witness, Mrs Faith MacLean, was of some help. She said she had heard an explosion and when she looked out of her window she saw a man leaving the house – 'Well, I suppose it was a man,' she added. 'It was dressed like a man ... but it walked like a woman with quick, short steps.'

And Mrs MacLean had an additional piece of information for the police. About ten minutes before the explosion she had seen someone leave Taylor's bungalow in a car: it was Mabel Normand. Furthermore Mary Miles Minter had been to visit Taylor that evening. On being questioned both actresses admitted that they had indeed been to see Taylor on the fatal night, and it seemed he was having affairs with both young stars simultaneously. The police were more or less satisfied that the young actresses were not involved in the actual murder. The police then learned that Taylor was also having an affair at the same time with Zelda Crosby, a writer at the studio that employed Taylor, but they were unable to question her − she had commited suicide a few days after Taylor's death.

Finally one other suspect has come to the attention of those interested in this still officially unsolved crime: Mrs Charlotte Shelby, mother of Mary Miles Minter. Mrs Shelby, it was discovered, was on what might be termed friendly terms with William Desmond Taylor and she was a very jealous person; furthermore she owned a .38 calibre revolver (Taylor was shot with a .38 pistol) and she was known to have been practising shooting shortly before the murder. 'Everyone knew who shot Taylor,' writer Adela Rogers St John said in 1977. 'There was never any doubt about it. We were in America's wild west and California had several unwritten laws: one was that a father or mother had a perfect right to kill a man who had debauched their little girl. It really was accepted.'

Soon after the Taylor murder Mrs Shelby was allowed to slip away from Hollywood and she spent some time in Europe. Apparently she was never seriously questioned by the police, although admittedly the police had plenty to do; within six weeks of Taylor's death over 300 people confessed to the murder. In fact no charges were ever brought against anyone and the case was classified as 'unsolved'. Film director King Vidor spent a year investigating the case and believed that there was a massive cover-up, probably organized by Will Hays, the official Hollywood watchdog who was determined to go to any lengths to stop another big scandal. King Vidor felt certain that the police had been bribed to drop the case. Stranger things have happened, especially in Hollywood.

Paul Kelly

-

Should He Have Been
Called Killer Kelly?

The tough, lean, red-blooded Irish actor who usually ended up losing the girl in a score of Thirties and Forties gangster films was Brooklyn-born Paul Kelly who appeared, often briefly, in something like 200 films, and some of his most successful appearances were after he had been imprisoned for murder.

Paul Kelly's first appearance in the movies was at the age of seven and he was still working in pictures when he died. Kelly's father owned a saloon near the old Vitagraph Film Studios where actors, crews and production teams often dropped in for a drink, and, from time to time, they would borrow pieces of furniture and articles for films currently in production from the always helpful Mrs Kelly. One day she suggested that in return they might find an acting job for her little boy Paul, and they did.

A few years later Paul Kelly was on Broadway, opposite Helen Hayes in Booth Tarkington's *Penrod*; in 1926 he set out for Hollywood where he was to live, sometimes dangerously, and where he would be involved in a death that sent him to prison. Soon after arriving in Hollywood he became friendly with Ray Raymond, a wiry song-and-dance man, and his wife Dorothy MacKaye, a dancer and actress who received good notices for her role in *Peg O' My Heart*, a play that ran for two years. She also appeared successfully in *Head Over Heels* and *Rose Marie*. The Raymonds had not been long in Hollywood themselves and Paul Kelly soon became one of their fast-living and hard-drinking friends. Often they would meet at Kelly's place but sometimes at the Raymonds' flat, and sometimes at the house of director Lewis Milestone, who knew where to obtain liquor in those Prohibition days.

For a while everyone was happy and then Paul Kelly and Dorothy MacKaye began to see a lot of each other. Soon there were rumours that they were lovers and Ray Raymond, especially when he was in his cups, complained loudly and to all, and sundry that the Irish actor was stealing his wife. After one boisterous evening in April 1927, when Raymond's loud mouth upset everyone within distance, someone called Paul Kelly later that night and told him to 'lay off Ray's wife.'

Kelly, more than a little drunk at the time, immediately rang Ray to talk about the rumours and to hear what Ray had to say, but the discussion quickly became a slanging match. Ray too, as usual, had had more drink than was good for him and told Kelly to come and tell him to his face what was going on. Kelly hurried over to the Raymonds' apartment where, unfortunately as it turned out, Dorothy was out shopping for Easter eggs.

The door was opened by Ethel Lee, the Raymonds' black maid, and when she saw how things were, she hurriedly took Valerie, the couple's four-year-old daughter, into another room. Within minutes words became blows between Paul and Ray, while the terrified maid tried to comfort the child and the Raymonds' little dog. Paul Kelly, taller and heavier than Ray Raymond, really began to pound the song-and-dance man who showed his bravery, persistence and tenacity by repeatedly coming back for more.

Eventually Kelly grabbed Raymond by the throat and slapped him hard over and over again. As the smaller man slumped to the floor Paul Kelly stooped and began banging Raymond's head against the wall. When he realized that there was no fight left in the crumpled, quiet and bloody heap at his feet, Kelly took one last look at his rival and left the apartment.

Completely unaware of what had taken place Dorothy returned with her purchases to find the flat practically wrecked, her daughter and the maid hysterical and her husband bleary-eyed, covered in blood and very battered. She helped him to his feet and guided him to the bedroom where she helped him to bed. By this time he had regained his usual good humour and made some joke about the fight, but he soon fell into a deep sleep. Next morning when he didn't wake up Dorothy sent for a doctor who said Ray's heavy drinking had aggravated his kidney trouble and a rest would do the trick. Two days later Ray was dead and the doctor certified the cause of death as due to complications from past illnesses.

It might have all ended there had not the police talked to Ethel Lee who showed them dozens of love letters from Kelly to Dorothy and told them about the fight and how Ray's head had been repeatedly thumped against the wall. It seemed that Dorothy had failed to mention any of this in her statement. When the police decided they might well be investigating a murder, they lost no time in arresting Paul Kelly.

Kelly immediately confessed that he was in love with Dorothy Raymond but he said his love had never been returned. Dorothy now said that after the fight Paul had apologized to Ray who accepted the apology and all was forgiven. She also said her husband had begged her not to drag Paul's name into the affair. She said she did not love Kelly but looked on him as a good friend to both herself and her husband. All this was rather spoiled when Kelly's Japanese houseboy gave evidence to the effect that he had 'often' served breakfast in bed to Dorothy and Paul.

The verdict was manslaughter. Paul Kelly was sentenced to serve from one to ten years in the state prison, San Quentin, and soon afterwards Dorothy was charged with compounding a felony and was also found guilty and sentenced to serve one to three years, also at San Quentin Penitentiary. Before she had served one year Dorothy was paroled for good behaviour and Kelly, hoping to reconstruct his film career after leaving jail, took elocution lessons and studied the technique of movie-making in some detail. After two years he too was paroled for good behaviour. Paul and Dorothy were married in 1931 and by 1932 Paul Kelly was back in the movies. In the years that followed he played in scores of films, many of them B-pictures and often inferior gangster stories; but they had a good marriage. Nine years later Dorothy was driving home to their ranch in the San Fernando Valley when the car skidded, spun out of control and turned over three times. Dorothy, pinned behind the wheel, died aged 37.

Paul Kelly continued to work in films and in the theatre, winning several awards for acting, and he appeared in some good films in his later life. One remarkable film that revolved around anti-Semitism, Edward Dmytryk's *Crossfire* (1947) was one of the finest films of its time. With a superb script (by John Paxton), imaginative camerawork, direction and acting, it is unquestionably the best film that Paul Kelly appeared in. Opening with an interior shot, we see in shadow a man being beaten and left for dead. The remainder of the film seeks to discover the identity of the killer and the reason for the crime; the settings are hauntingly atmospheric: an all-night movie theatre, a seedy bar, a hotel, a tawdry apartment; and among the inhabitants of this midnight-to-dawn drama we meet a sardonic and bedraggled character whose 'boyfriend' is a pathological liar, played by Paul Kelly. The scenes where he is involved have a bitter edge and well illustrate the exceptional writing. Charles Higham and Joel Greenberg in *Hollywood in the Forties* say: 'As a beautifully organised and proportioned melodrama, written, directed and acted with unostentatious excellence, and creating its own poetically heightened "reality", *Crossfire* has few rivals.'

Paul Kelly died of a heart attack in his Hollywood home in 1956, aged 57.

6

Death Shall Have Dominion

-

SUDDEN DEATHS

'I n the midst of life ...' It happens everywhere but when it happens in Hollywood to household names and familiar faces, it is a reminder of the uncertainty of life and the inevitability of the parting of the ways between the seeming permanency of life and the abruptness and finality of death.

When this happens to people we feel we know the shock is all the greater; after all movies, as one anthropologist has pointed out, are successful largely because they meet, wisely or unwisely, some of modern man's deepest needs. Like drama or literature, movies extend the experiences of audiences; all entertainment is education in some way and when those who participate in or form part of these influences depart, suddenly and for ever, from the world we have come to accept as theirs, our feelings cannot but be affected.

Those who have met sudden death in Hollywood are many and varied; this chapter looks at the lives and deaths of Edgar Wallace, James Dean, Ramon Novarro and Lionel Atwill.

Edgar Wallace

Edgar Wallace

-

Fiction Writer Extraordinaire

Edgar Wallace was born in Ashburnham Grove, Greenwich, England on 1 April 1875 and he died in Hollywood on 10 February 1932. He was the most prolific writer of his time, possibly of all time. He produced some 170 books, some really excellent plays, hundreds of articles and an autobiography, *People* (1926).

The illegitimate son of an actor, he was entered in the parish register as Richard Horatio Edgar. When he was nine days old he was adopted by George Freeman, a Billingsgate fish porter and his wife and after attending an elementary school at Peckham, he left at the age of twelve and, as newsboy, errand boy, milk roundsman and labourer, he roamed the streets of Greenwich and Deptford, absorbing the atmosphere. Indeed his rare gift of immediately assimilating atmosphere served him in good stead all his life. His daughter says that within 24 hours he would become familiar with the topography of a place and, more important, with the feelings of the people in it.

One morning in 1929 Wallace arrived for the first time in Chicago and he left the following evening. On his way home he had the idea for a gangster play and on arrival in England he completed the play, down to the final stage directions, over one weekend. At the première in New York the audience, which included notorious gunmen and racketeers from Chicago, were amazed at the authenticity of the plot, the place and the characters.

When he was 18 Edgar Wallace, as he now called himself, borrowed sixpence for the bus fare, said goodbye to his adopted parents, and enlisted in the Royal West Kent Regiment at Woolwich. Later he transferred to the Medical Staff Corps and was sent to South Africa. Rudyard Kipling arrived soon afterwards and Wallace, who admired him greatly, wrote a poem in Kipling's honour. As a result some of Wallace's poems were accepted for publication and he soon began writing articles for South African newspapers.

In 1899 Wallace bought himself out of the army and became a correspondent for Reuters. During the Boer War he sent a cable to the *Daily Mail* reporting that the Boers were returning to the battlefield and shooting injured British soldiers. Lord Kitchener censored the cable but Wallace had also sent a written report and that was published. Questions were asked in the House of Commons and the incidents were denied but finally Kitchener had to admit that the reports were true. Wallace however was eventually sacked by the *Daily Mail* for involving them in a libel suit.

In 1904 Edgar Wallace became editor of London's *Evening News* and in 1905 he founded the Tallis Press to publish his own books which established publishers had repeatedly rejected. This imprint saw the first publication of *The Four Just Men* in which the author offered £500 if readers could guess correctly how the murder was committed. The book had an enormous sale but Wallace lost heavily on it. Later he sold the copyright to George Newnes for £72 and promptly gave the money to a colleague who he knew was heavily in debt.

Wallace's visits to South Africa resulted in some of the best books he ever wrote including *Sanders of the River* (1911) and *Bones* (1915). He became interested in horse-racing, an interest that was to last for the rest of his life, and he became racing editor to several periodicals and newspapers. He also founded two racing papers.

After the First World War Edgar Wallace began to write sketches and lyrics for reviews at the Palace and Hippodrome theatres and after producing a wealth of articles on diverse subjects for various magazines and newspapers he began writing thrillers and detective stories seriously; stories that were to bring him fame, if not fortune. He became Chairman of the Press Club, a member of the Savage Club, and he inaugurated the Derby Lunch.

Meanwhile his first marriage had ended in divorce and he

had married a girl who had come to him as his secretary —
admitting that she had never heard of Edgar Wallace. It was
a happy and successful marriage that strengthened and encouraged his writing work. He succeeded in negotiating a contract
with the publishers Hodder & Stoughton and this marked the
turning point of Edgar Wallace's financial career. He proceeded
to write best-selling books and successful plays, *The Squeaker*,
The Ringer, and *On The Spot*, to mention only three.

As fast as he made money Edgar Wallace spent it; on a house
in the country at Bourne End in Buckinghamshire; holidaying
abroad with family and friends; large sums to bookmakers time
after time; and the upkeep of a large maisonette in Portland
Place, later the Chinese Embassy.

Wallace became Chairman of British Lion Film Corporation
and during his first year eight silent films of his plays were
produced. In 1931 he stood as Liberal candidate at Blackpool
but his admission that he preferred racing to going to church did
not endear him to the. Nevertheless, although he was not elected,
he polled a substantial number of votes.

He accepted an offer from RKO for a three-month script-
writing contract in Hollywood and as *The Empress of Britain*
left the quayside he scribbled on a streamer, 'Goodbye — Edgar
Wallace' and threw it overboard. It was a prophetic gesture.

Before reaching America at the end of 1931 Wallace had
developed a 'husky throat' for which he had 'a small throat
syringe and a bottle of dope'. A week later he was writing to his
wife that he had 'developed a sore throat, a catarrhal condition'
although he did not seem to have a cold. On landing in New
York he saw his friends Nigel Bruce, Leslie Banks and Charles
Laughton and then he was off to Hollywood.

Wallace stayed first at the Beverly-Wilshire Hotel in Los
Angeles and then he found a house at 716 North Maple Drive,
Beverly Hills. He planned to move on Sunday 13 December (he
regarded 13 as his lucky number) but in fact he moved on the
11th. The owner Mrs Cook had a very bad cold and a few days
later Edgar Wallace was coughing and complaining of 'a little
chest', due he thought, 'to going out in the cold' when he was
hot and he spent 'a very uncomfortable night's sleep'. He rather
fancied it might be something he had eaten, although he had no
pain.

On 19 December he reports: 'I dreamed last night that Steve

Donoghue was dead. Is this a sign that Michael Beary [a jockey friend of Wallace's] is coming out here?' On 24 December he wrote home: 'I have had a wire from Michael Beary on the *Majestic*; he'll be here in a fortnight. I never dreamed he would come at all.' On 29 December he said he was feeling 'a bit tired' although he had written three film scenarios and nearly finished another that was to become one of the most successful films of all time, *King Kong*.

He said he was now eating well − more than he should, he thought − and without thinking he began to put on weight. Later he says: 'I have put on about five pounds since I have been in Hollywood, from which you will gather I am not dieting really strictly, but I really am "going to" one of these days!'

Shortly afterwards he decided to go on a diet and he did his best to skip dinner parties but it was difficult to do so without giving offence, especially when he was meeting people like William Powell, Ann Harding and Constance Bennett. He also mentions having coffee with, among others, 'a budding star', Sari Maritza, 'who had a horrible cold'. Wallace gave her a nasal douche but he seems to have been surrounded by people with heavy colds during these weeks around Christmas. He was working very hard too and getting only about three hours of sleep at night.

On 18 January 1932 Wallace was writing home about 'a slight chest' and a couple of days later, at a party at the home of Walter Huston, he met Bobbie Jones, the scenery designer and director of some of Eugene O'Neill's plays, including *Desire under the Elms*, and Dr Ellis Owen Jones, a 'big bone specialist'. They talked about ghosts throughout the meal and also premonitions − 'a very interesting evening'. Soon, however, Wallace was describing his sojourn in Hollywood as 'like living in a madhouse.'

On 28 January he wrote of 'feeling rather tired' and going to bed early. Soon the weather turned bad: 'It poured all day yesterday and today ... and I have an ingrowing toe-nail.' On 3 February he wrote home: 'I woke at five, coughing, due to the very strong east wind that blew in on me; then I dozed most of the morning.' In the afternoon he 'had a good sleep'. Next day he was complaining again of his throat: 'my throat isn't even sore, it only feels as if it's going to be sore'. He had arranged for his wife to join him in Hollywood in mid-February but his daughter, Penelope Wallace, says he wrote to her on 4 February: 'I've an odd feeling that you won't come.'

He 'nursed' his cold all the next day and said his throat was 'not very sore' and he had 'no temperature'. His friend 'Coop' had exactly the same kind of throat and he blamed the drinking water. Wallace was inclined to trace his ailment to the sudden change of weather, the dropping of the temperature and the heavy rain, in spite of which he slept with his windows open. Next day he was still 'nursing this suppressed cold' but he said he was sleeping well. He asked for an osteopath to call to treat his cold and he reported afterwards: 'He gave me a real tossing about – broke my neck twice, broke my feet four times, gave me belly treatment and back treatment, used a vibrator and alcohol and generally left me feeling a better man!'

His last letter from Hollywood, dated Sunday 7 February 1932, tells of Wallace's giving a dinner party when the guests included Genevieve Tobin, Evelyn Brent, Jesse Lasky and Ricardo Cortez. At the next table was 'Fatty' Arbuckle – 'he is a most amusing devil' – and at another table Lily Damita and Thelma Todd. It was 2.30 before anyone made a move to go and Wallace got home at three o'clock in the morning. There is no word in that last letter of his physical condition but within three days he was dead, for the sore throat had turned to double pneumonia.

The body of Edgar Wallace was brought back to England and he lies buried in the country churchyard which he could see from his study window when he lived at Chalklands, Bourne End.

Ivor Novello spent some nine months in Hollywood, basking in the glorious weather and living in a beach suit. Writing in spurts between having a sun bathe and then a swim, he produced eight different versions of his successful play, *The Truth Game* and such uncharacteristic work as the dialogue for the film *Tarzan the Ape Man* (1932), the first and arguably the best of all the Tarzan films; he then obtained a release from his MGM contract and headed home to his beloved London.

Novello's biographer Peter Noble takes up the story:

> *On the journey back to New York Ivor had a rather macabre experience. Three days before he left Santa Monica, where he had a beach house, he gave a party*

to all the people who had been so charming to him in Hollywood. Edgar Wallace was coming, with Ramon Novarro, Ruth Chatterton and Billie Burke, but on the morning of the party Wallace rang up to say he had a slight cold and was afraid he would not be able to come along to say goodbye. Three days later Ivor left California for good. With him he took the dog Jim. Jim's quarters were in the guard's van, and three times a day, on that long, tiring journey, Ivor took him his meals. At Chicago they changed trains. As soon as they were off again he took along Jim's mid-day food. In the guard's van was a Negro porter sitting on an enormous packing case, making out his list of passengers. Ivor asked him if he would be nice to Jim during the journey, and added: 'What an enormous case. I hope there is no one inside.' 'Sure there is', the porter replied casually. 'It's a film writer who died in Hollywood.' At that he turned the label over and showed it to Ivor. He glanced at the name and received a terrible shock. In the case was the dead body of Edgar Wallace!

Edgar Wallace left an estate encumbered with £150,000 in debts which royalties from his works paid off in less than two years and today a flourishing Edgar Wallace Society exists, founded by his daughter Penelope Wallace, now President, and organized by the helpful John A. Hogan from Amersham in Buckinghamshire, Wallace's favourite county.

Soldier, foreign correspondent, reporter, author and playwright, Edgar Wallace is a monument to the success that can come with hard work, tenacity and persistence, not to mention a remarkable and sincere popularity that shows no sign of waning 60 years after his sudden death in Hollywood.

James Dean

-

The Cult of
the Restless Youth

James Dean (1931–55) made only three films but in one of his best, *Rebel Without a Cause*, released in 1955, the year he died, he made a prophetic statement to Natalie Wood (who was to suffer a mysterious death herself 26 years later). Dean said, 'I see you and I thought to myself this is going to be one terrific day so you better live it up, boy, 'cause tomorrow you'll be nothing.'

This dynamic young man appeared on television and in a few off-Broadway plays before he attracted any real attention and then it was as an Arab boy in the 1954 dramatization of *The Immoralist* by the French Nobel prize-winning novelist André Paul Gide (1869–1951). Dean won a Tony award for most promising newcomer, and director, producer, actor and film writer Elia Kazan was so impressed that he somewhat impulsively offered Dean a part in the screen adaptation of the John Steinbeck novel, *East of Eden* (1955). The rest, as they say, is history.

The bravado appearance of James Dean with his much-copied casual style of dress that has never really dated, hid a troubled and insecure inner self. He was born in Marion, Indiana, and when he was eight his mother died of cancer; an event that affected him deeply. Thereafter he was raised by an aunt and uncle on a farm, growing into a sombre and often sad boy who was inclined to be aggressive, especially later when under the influence of drink.

He obtained a part in a Pepsi Cola television commercial and this led to more work of a similar nature, but he found the repetitive rehearsal work irritating and taxing and he became depressed and moody, feeling that he was getting nowhere. Sometimes bouts of extreme depression came over him suddenly and without warning; something he was to suffer throughout his short working life.

He never learned to 'switch off' after work and sometimes seemed to live out the roles he played on film, even to the extent of carrying a flick-knife and not being afraid to threaten to use it.

He was accepted by Lee Strasberg's Actors' Studio and Strasberg said after Dean's death that he had always had a strange feeling that in Jimmy there was a sort of doomed quality. Dean moved to New York in 1952, a place he found suited him with its uninhibited lifestyle. Before long the Louis Schurr agency obtained a few bit parts for him.

One young male friend, a fellow student at the acting school, has revealed that Dean spent hours talking about death and 'the end'. Once, in the middle of eulogizing about 'the beauty, the joy of death', Dean suddenly ran to the window of the skyscraper apartment and tried to throw himself out. His friend grabbed him and after a struggle managed to pull him back. 'I knew then that Jimmy didn't have long to live,' he said. 'He was determined to end it one way or another.'

James Dean became friendly with Ursula Andress, the Swiss actress who was to become the sex symbol of the Sixties in such typically nubile roles as her appearance in *Dr No* (1962) and *She* (1965). She stopped seeing Dean because she found herself becoming depressed and distressed by his constant harping on the inevitability – almost desirability – of death. 'He was sick, very sick,' she said after his death. 'And the complete opposite of myself. I was all for life, for greeting each new day with confidence and hope. Jimmy dreaded waking up each morning and felt he had nothing, and no one, to live for.'

A particular female friend of Dean's was the beautiful young actress Pier Angeli. The couple fell in love and wanted to marry but Pier Angeli's mother did not approve of Dean and when the boy began to make arrangements to convert to Catholicism in an effort to overcome her disapproval, she persuaded Pier to marry singer Vic Damone. James Dean sat on his motorcycle outside the church while the wedding ceremony took place and then disappeared for ten days, distrustful, depressed and withdrawn as he had never been before. The marriage did not work out and Pier was to tell many of her friends: 'I was only in love once in my life and that was with Jimmy Dean.' After his tragic death she began to go to pieces and wrote to a friend: 'I'm so afraid of growing old – for me, being forty is the beginning of old age and that would be the end of everything. Love is now behind me, love died in a Porsche.' In 1971 Pier Angeli took a fatal dose of barbiturates in her Beverly Hills apartment and became one more death by suicide in Hollywood.

Elia Kazan was used to handling actors and he tried hard with James Dean but in the end he could no longer stand the young actor's self-indulgence, his unpredictability, his unreliability, his temper tantrums and his habit of falling asleep without warning (Dean suffered from chronic inability to sleep at night) and there were many ugly scenes between the two men. However the film itself, *East of Eden*, embodied vulnerable adolescent uncertainty and social destructiveness and generated an overwhelming and enthusiastic response.

During the making of the film Dean walked into the studio canteen and saw that a photograph of himself had been pasted on to the wall. He immediately tore it down saying, 'I told them I didn't want this kind of stuff. I told them no pictures on the walls. No pictures of me anyplace. Can't they understand? I don't want it, I won't have it.' The thing was of course that such behaviour attracted publicity and then Dean had to deal with gossip columnists and magazine writers; journalists said they found him dirty, rude, unhelpful and bad-tempered but some at least of this criticism could well be the result of his refusing to accommodate them in their fantasy-building and having little respect for what they were doing and telling them so.

Dean enjoyed working with Elizabeth Taylor on *Giant* and she was to say afterwards: 'He was the real thing and would have contributed a great deal to the film industry had he lived.' In that autumn of 1945 Sir Alec Guinness was in Hollywood to make *The Swan* (1955), his first Hollywood film, with Grace Kelly. He arrived in Los Angeles somewhat exhausted after a long flight from Copenhagen, and Thelma Moss, who had written the script of his next film, *Father Brown* (1956) said she would take him out to dinner. They tried three restaurants but at each they were refused admission because Thelma was

wearing slacks. Then she remembered a little Italian bistro —
but when they arrived there was no table available.

As they were walking away they heard footsteps behind them
and turning, they found a fair-haired young man wearing a
sweat-shirt and jeans. 'I overheard,' he said. 'You want my
table?' 'Join me, my name is James Dean.' Turning back,
their new-found friend beckoned them towards the restaurant
car-park. 'I'd like to show you something,' he said and led them
to a brand new powerful Porsche 550 Spyder car. 'It's just been
delivered,' Dean told them proudly. 'I can't wait to drive it —
she'll do a hundred and fifty.' He had become obsessed with
speed and was planning to take part in a race meeting in a few
days' time.

Sir Alec Guinness was really exhausted and hungry by this
time and, he freely admits, perhaps a little ill-tempered but he
was still surprised to find himself saying to Dean, in a voice he
hardly recognized as his own: 'Please, never get in that car.' He
looked at his watch and went on,' 'It's now ten o'clock, Friday
23 September 1955. If you get in that car you will be dead by
this time next week.'

James Dean laughed and Guinness later apologized for his
remarks which he was at a total loss to explain, but which he
said he put down to lack of sleep and need for food.

They had a meal together and both Alec Guinness and
Thelma Moss found Dean an agreeable and generous host
with lots of humorous stories about Strasberg and the Method
School of Acting. An hour or so later they parted, full of
humour and the car was not mentioned again. In spite of his
apparent good humour on this occasion Dean did almost seem
to have a death wish. Once he was asked what he respected
most. 'That's easy,' he replied. 'Death. It's the only thing left
to respect. It's the one inevitable, undeniable truth.'

The following Friday James Dean was on his way in the new
car with his friend and mechanic Rolf Weutherich to take part
in a race meeting. At a speed approaching 100 mph Dean col-
lided head-on while attempting to overtake. The Porsche was
completely wrecked and Dean was killed instantly. Rolf was
seriously injured but the driver of the other car was unhurt. It
was 30 September, a week after the prophecy made by Sir Alec
Guinness. Dean's last film, *Giant*, had been completed on 22
September and he died a month before the film was released.

Some macabre stories quickly arose surrounding James Dean's death: that it was the result of a black magic curse; that he had deliberately committed suicide; that, vain to the end, he had refused to wear his spectacles and had, in fact, 'driven blind'. The most likely explanation is that a speed-mad youngster made an error of judgement and at the speed he was travelling, he had no chance of survival.

The critics and public were unanimous in their praise for James Dean's final film performance and the irony was that in death Dean became even more famous than he had been in life; and he received an Oscar nomination for his performance in *Giant*.

Four days after the crash Dean's body, miraculously uncrushed and even the face unmutilated, was flown to his home state of Indiana for burial but thousands of Dean's fans refused to believe that he was dead or that anyone could have been taken from the crushed car without being mangled; no, they said, another body had been buried in his grave and James Dean, horribly disfigured, lived on in seclusion, too sensitive to show the scarred travesty of his once-handsome face.

Pieces of the wrecked Porsche were sold as souvenirs and life-size models of Dean's head were fashioned out of plastic and sold throughout America at $5 each. A cult quickly grew up around the name of James Dean, a cult that exists to this day and in the year after his death fan letters addressed to him outnumbered those of any living film star.

James Dean in *Giant* (1956)

Ramon
Novarro
Successor to
the Immortal
Rudolph Valentino

Ramon Novarro was to endure a ghastly death in 1968. He
had come to Hollywood with his family in 1913, fleeing from
the Huesto Mexican revolution, when the young Ramon Gil
Samaniegoes was 14 years of age. His father had been a dentist
in Durango, Mexico but he died in 1915 and Ramon, at the age
of 16 took on the role of providing for his widowed mother and
making a living for himself.

His first job was helping in a restaurant where he soon
graduated to becoming a waiter. After a while he became
something of an attraction as a waiter who doubled as a
singer at the restaurant. He could see the possiblities of the
rapidly growing film industry, even in the Hollywood of those
days, and he sought and obtained work as a singer and bit
player in vaudeville, always with an eye to the films. More or
less by chance when he was 18 he obtained work as an extra
in *The Hostage* and he appeared briefly in more movies, some
directed by Rex Ingram, including the fabulously successful
Four Horsemen of the Apocalypse (1921) and then Mack
Sennett hired him to perform a novelty dance routine in a
full-length comedy, *A Small Town Idol*, starring the cross-eyed
comedian Ben Turpin. Novarro wore a turban and loin-cloth in
the single sequence but one of Sam Goldwyn's scouts spotted
Novarro's talent and he was put into *Mrs Barnes of New York*
in 1922. A small but starring part followed in *The Rubaiyat
of Omar Khayyam* directed by Ferdinand Binney Earle whose
friend and associate Mary O'Hara was preparing the scenario
for MGM's *The Prisoner of Zenda* (the 1922 version). The

director was again Rex Ingram. Film historian Paul Rotha refers to Ramon Novarro's 'clever acting as the dashing Rupert' and says that his playing in this film 'against the reserved dignity of Lewis Stone, was beyond reproach'.

It was at Mary O'Hara's express suggestion that Ferdinand Binney Earle persuaded Rex Ingram to view the *Omar Khayyam* film which had little or nothing to commend it, but Ingram was again impressed by the extra, Ramon Samaniegoes, whom he recalled working with on his *Four Horsemen*. He saw the ambitious but struggling young actor and offered Novarro a good role in *The Prisoner of Zenda* – on condition that he changed his name to something easier to remember. Ramon Novarro was mutually agreed and the Mexican extra obtained a personal film contract and a regular wage of $125 a week.

Novarro was hard-working and his striking appearance helped in the aftermath of Valentino's striking success which put Latin lovers very much in vogue. Parts followed in such films as *Ben Hur* (1927), where he played the title role, *The Student Prince* (1927) with Norma Shearer and *Mata Hari* (1932) with Greta Garbo. By this time Novarro had attracted an enormous public following although he never really became one of the great Hollywood stars of his era. Garbo is credited, in her unauthorized life, *Garbo – Her Story*, as referring to 'the handsome but untalented Ramon Novarro'.

Ben Hur, which P. B. Schulberg used to say added 'super-colossal' to Hollywood's list of exaggerated hyperbole, was begun by the original Goldwyn Film Company; it was inherited by MGM and Louis B. Mayer and Irving Thalberg somewhat reluctantly authorized the continued shooting of the film in Italy. When production costs doubled and then trebled, a new script was ordered, Ramon Novarro replaced the original star George Walsh, and the multi-million dollar production was brought back to Hollywood.

In 1926, Rudolph Valentino, the unrivalled 'Latin lover' whose passionate films fired the imaginations of female audiences, died suddenly and unromantically, probably of a ruptured ulcer, in New York. Blatantly bi-sexual he had enjoyed a homosexual relationship with Ramon Novarro and the latter always cherished a large black Art Deco phallic emblem adorned with Valentino's signature in silver, which Novarro kept in the bedroom of his home high up in the Hollywood Hills.

It was a present frum Rudy and was to figure in Novarro's appalling death.

With the passing of Valentino there was an immediate search for Latin lookalike lovers and Ramon Novarro came as near as anyone to duplicating Valentino's success, although, it has to be said, 'his less virile beauty tended to inspire maternal rather than erotic responses'. Be that as it may Ramon Novarro enjoyed considerable motion-picture success and his voice was highly praised when he sang the 'Pagan Love Song' in *The Pagan* (1930); he also sang in the Napoleonic drama *Devil May Care* which included Technicolor sequences, but while his singing was universally praised his voice, as he moved into talking pictures, was less admired. One leading magazine of the period went as far as to say, 'Frankly, Ramon Novarro is one of the disappointments of the Talkies.' In fact Ramon Novarro had an enormous and faithful following and an enthusiastic fan club that outlasted his death.

As he paused in his career, facing the fact that he was not the overwhelming success he had been led to expect he would be, he began to drink to excess. For the rest of his life Ramon Novarro had to be on his guard against drinking too much but he tried hard to control the habit when he saw what it might do to him. At one stage he took refuge in (or as he put it 'retired to') a monastery, re-embracing the Roman Catholic faith of his youth and losing himself in prayer and contemplation. For a while he considered becoming a monk and living permanently in a monastery. He also considered the possibility of leaving Hollywood and turning to opera-singing, but MGM still considered him one of their stars (they were the studios who claimed to have 'more stars than there are in heaven') and in 1932 they offered him a new seven-year contract.

Sadly his career did not take off a second time and two years later MGM cancelled his contract. Still considering the possibility of leaving Hollywood and its memories behind him, Ramon Novarro journeyed to England and starred in a musical at the Palladium called *A Royal Exchange*. While in England he spoke bitterly in several press interviews about Hollywood and its star system and he announced that he had plans to write, produce and direct a Spanish-speaking picture.

Back in Hollywood and installed again in his home in the

Hollywood Hills where he was to die, Ramon Novarro did direct some Spanish language remakes of John Barrymore's Warner Brothers successes. He also wrote, produced and directed the Spanish film *Contra la Corriente* and, returning to acting, he made *The Sheik Steps Out* for the recently formed Republic Pictures in 1937, a spoof on his old, already outdated movie image. Ramon Novarro found it all rather distasteful and his heart was not in it, but the studio that was to become more associated with light weight Westerns was delighted and signed him to do four more pictures. Novarro controlled himself sufficiently to do one, aptly entitled *A Desperate Adventure* and then he asked to be released from the contract.

There seemed no doubt whatever but that his heady days as an immensely popular romantic star, in spite of or perhaps because of his thick Mexican accent, were indeed over, never to return and in his despair and loneliness he turned again to drink in an effort to drown his sorrows. At least four of Hollywood's newspapers of the day are liberally sprinkled with reports of Ramon Novarro being picked up by the police for conduct unbecoming a Hollywood star and for driving while under the influence of drink.

In 1940 Ramon Novarro pulled himself together sufficiently to go to Europe and direct and star in a French movie, *La Comédie de Bonheur*. Back in Hollywood it was nine years before he worked again; character parts in four films in a little over a year and then the reformed, subdued and reticent 'new Valentino' disappeared into the shadows of Hollywood once again. He re-emerged briefly for a small part, a cameo appearance really, in George Cukor's *Heller in Pink Tights* (1960) and then told friends that he was resigned to permanent retirement at the age of 61.

It might be thought that gentle, thoughtful and kind Ramon Novarro hadn't an enemy in the world, and neither had he, but in the uncertain Sixties death stalked him to his comfortable Hollywood home on Hallowe'en night, 1968.

Teenagers Paul and Tom Ferguson came to Hollywood from Chicago and once in Tinseltown they existed as best they could, keeping their eyes and ears open; mugging the infirm and the elderly, breaking into empty houses and helping themselves to whatever they could find. As long as they could help themselves to a few dollars they didn't care who might be hurt in the process.

One day they heard that an old-time movie star called Ramon Novarro lived all alone in the Hollywood Hills and had thousands of dollars hidden away in his house. He was nearly 70 and, having had a look at the house, they decided it would be easy money.

Not wishing to risk being identified by anyone who might see them, since they were already well-known to the police, the brothers adopted grotesque Hallowe'en costumes and masks, quietly approached the silent house and loudly broke in. Ramon Novarro was alone as they had heard he would be but he wouldn't tell them where the money was. They could have tied him up and ransacked the place until they found what they had come for but they were vicious young thugs bent on violence.

They roughly stripped the idol of so many silent pictures and they mercilessly and relentlessly beat him almost to a pulp, the blood from his bruised and tortured body splattered the souvenirs and pictures of his glorious days in movies. Even when he collapsed and lay unconscious and more dead than alive they continued to beat him and as they began to search for the money they came across Valentino's gift to his friend, the black phallus, and they forced it into the mouth of Ramon Novarro and down his throat until he finally choked on his own blood and died. Then they ransacked the place and left with $5,000 for their trouble. But they left a multitude of clues and the police soon picked them up. Both were convicted of murder and sent to prison for life.

Ramon Novarro was one of Hollywood's gentlest gentlemen and he is still remembered with affection by those who knew him and by just about everyone who crossed his path when he was a romantic hero in the heyday of Hollywood films.

Lionel Atwill

-

The Two-Faced Man

Born in Croydon to wealthy parents in 1885, Lionel Atwill was educated, he used to say, at Mercers' School, London – actually St Paul's School, Hammersmith, governed by the Mercers' Company, one of the twelve great livery companies of the City of London. He never lost the dulcet, cultured and essentially English voice. After leaving school he studied architecture for three years before deciding to submit to his long-time ambition to become an actor. He made his stage debut in *The Walls of Jericho* at the Garrick Theatre in 1904. Several other London productions followed, including *Milestones* (1912) which ran for a year and a half. He played in several touring companies and then signed with Charles Frohman to appear in *Years of Discretion* and revivals of other successful plays.

With the good grounding of acting behind him Atwill went on an extensive theatrical tour of Australia and then he went to America in 1916 as leading man for Lillie Langtry. There he played in *The Silent Witness*, first on stage and then on film, and under his own management in *The Lodger*, with Billie Burke, which played in New York for over a year. His enthusiastic reception encouraged him to stay in the United States where he went on to achieve considerable and varied stage and screen experience and success. He was able to claim to have worked for David Belasco and to have played opposite Helen Hayes in *Caesar and Cleopatra*. In the play *Another Man's Shoes* he probably enacted the perfect role for him – playing a man with a dual personality.

Lionel Atwill began making talkies in 1927 with *The Whitefaced Fool* and among his later, better-known films are *Mystery of the Wax Museum* (1933), *Dr X* (1932) with Fay Wray of *King Kong* fame, and *Son of Frankenstein* (1939) – who can forget the police chief with an artifical arm, facing the enraged monster? 'One does not forget an arm torn out by the roots.'

Some of these appearances were individual and first-class characterizations. His Police Inspector Krogh for instance (*Son of Frankenstein*) became a much-parodied performance which is generally accepted as having been the origin of Kubrick's Dr Strangelove and Atwill's sympathetic portrayal and the smashing of the false face in *Mystery of the Wax Museum* can still bring a gasp from the viewer.

Lionel Atwill was two-faced in more ways than one. He really did have two different faces, or so he thought, for he once told an interviewer:

> *Look for yourself: one side of my face is gentle and kind, seemingly incapable of anything but love of my fellowman while the other side, the other profile, is cruel and predatory and evil, incapable of anything but lust and dark passion. It all depends on which side of my face is turned towards you or which side faces the camera.*

To the outside world Lionel Atwill was a cultivated host who prided himself on having played Ibsen, Shaw and Shakespeare on the London stage, who had been a contract player in films since the early Thirties, a man who treasured the paintings of old masters and usually acquired a new one to add to his considerable art collection with practically every film he made. He was perhaps most convincing in 'mad doctor' roles: *Dr X*, *The Vampire Bat*, *The Sun Never Sets*, *Man Made Monster*, *The Mad Doctor of Market Street* and his last film, *Genius at Work* (1946).

Many of his film roles may look shallow and stereotyped in retrospect but they were good for his bank balance and when sincere acting was called for he was capable of giving a superb performance, as when he appeared with Marlene Dietrich in Josef von Sternberg's *The Devil is a Woman* (1935). The film was based on an erotic novel and was the story of a Spanish siren who enslaves a young political refugee and an older grandee, but it was a commercial failure after the Fascist Spanish government demanded its withdrawal and Adolph Zukor gave in to Franco; it even provided Paramount with an excuse to end the contract of the uncompromising perfectionist director, Sternberg. Atwill, however, came out of the film with nothing but honours, having played to perfection an army officer who has been emotionally crushed and ruined by his affair with Concha (Marlene Dietrich); a masochistic part which Atwill made extremely sympathetic – and incidentally he bore an uncanny physical resemblance to Sternberg, Dietrich's real-life close friend and adviser for over five years.

Lionel Atwill's first marriage to Phyllis Rolph was dissolved; his second to Elsie Mackay ended when Atwill and detectives raided an apartment in New York and surprised Mrs Atwill and his friend Max Montesole together. After the divorce Atwill married Louise Cromwell, an heiress who had recently divorced the General-to-be, Douglas MacArthur.

She was a direct descendant of Oliver Cromwell through her father, Oliver Eaton Cromwell, and her brother was soon to be named Ambassador to Canada. The Atwills were frequent guests at splendid San Simeon where Marion Davies and William Randolph Hearst held lavish parties. The posthumously published autobiography of Marion Davies contains a photograph of Lionel Atwill in the company of Cary Grant, Leslie Howard, Ernst Lubitsch and Mary Carlisle, among others.

Lionel Atwill had exotic tastes and unusual pastimes. He enjoyed attending murder trials and he was attracted to snakes. During the making of *Murders at the Zoo* in 1933 he became very friendly with 'Elsie', a 15ft python, but when he took Elsie home, his wife threatened to move out! Atwill took the snake away and for a time the Atwills continued to live a seemingly happy life with their dogs, and their two yachts, and living part of their lives on their farm.

Fellow Englishman, dapper James Whale, found a splendid home for the Atwills on d'Este Drive, Brentwood Heights, a spacious and secluded Spanish-style property in an affluent community north of Santa Monica; a property that was sufficiently spacious and sufficiently secluded to be ideal for libidinous weekend parties after Louise had moved out. Lionel took great care in selecting his guests and in choosing the girls for his special blend of ritual, role playing and erotic imagination; he even went as far as to insist on everyone having medical examinations to avoid the possibility of any unwelcome disease pervading his gatherings.

Louise Atwill finally left Lionel in 1939, blaming his 'surly character' as the final straw. She moved to Washington, D.C., and hosted a popular radio programme of political satire called *Mrs Atwill's Dinner Party*. Lionel settled down to life in his spacious house which he shared with a python, six Dobermans and a talking macaw, but before long his other side began to surface and he began to indulge his erotic imagination and fantasies, for in reality Atwill's principal and abiding interest and hobby was sex. His weekend parties were highly individual although they involved some well-known names in the film world, actor Victor Jory and directors Edmund Goulding and Josef von Sternberg, to mention only three. For a time the wild orgies continued without anyone outside the Atwill circle being aware of the strange goings-on at the secluded house but then, after a memorable 1940 Christmas Party, everything fell apart.

Apparently these Christmas parties were jolly and decorous to start with. Everyone was dressed-up for the occasion and nothing untoward happened until after dinner, coffee and brandy. But then, at a sign from Atwill, the orgy would begin. To the strains of 'The Blue Danube' masks and evening gowns would be shed, shorts and lingerie would follow, although the rules allowed jewellery to be worn, but nothing else. No wonder the Lionel Atwill parties were strictly for invited guests only and well-paid, efficient and discreet servants carefully screened everyone before they entered the wrought-iron gates to the oaken fortress.

One of the 16-year-old girls at the party discovered that she was pregnant and wrote to her parents for money. They became suspicious of her companions and the company she was keeping in Hollywood and they went to the police. The law quickly traced one of her daughter's friends who had been to the Atwill party and everything came out, including the 'blue' movies that the girls claimed Lionel Atwill had shown before and during the orgy that had taken place. In the end the evidence of an acquaintance of Atwill's who was present and the, as ever, dignified demeanour of Lionel Atwill himself registered with the jury and the actor was cleared. He must have heaved a sigh of relief but a year later he was back in court.

Atwill's acquaintance who had helped to clear him turned vindictive; he felt Lionel Atwill had not 'helped' him when he had 'saved' Atwill and he wrote to the grand jury and told the real story of that Atwill Christmas Party. Atwill was recalled and, on the advice of his lawyer, pleaded the right to refuse to testify for fear of incriminating himself. By now thoroughly frightened of the possible consequences, he went to see an experienced judge and attorney who strongly advised him to tell the truth, the whole truth.

Back in court Atwill suddenly remembered that he did have a few 'blue' films at his house: they had been rented to entertain a friend, a Royal Canadian Mounted Policeman, no less, who had been a house guest and the films had been shown at a stag night party for the policeman.

Atwill insisted he had never even seen the films himself and if someone had exhibited them at his house he had been unaware of it. He further denied that any improper conduct had taken place at the Christmas Party and said he was being blackmailed. This time the jury was unconvinced and, as a start, he was charged with having perjured himself to the previous jury. Later he was charged with a second perjury, accused of having lied twice, two years in succession. This time Atwill admitted he had 'lied like a gentleman' to spare the reputation of others. He was permitted to change his plea to 'guilty' on the perjury indictment and he admitted having shown 'blue' movies to his friends.

With a possible sentence of up to 14 years on the perjury charge alone, Lionel Atwill was lucky to obtain probation and to be released, mainly because the district attorney pointed out in arguing to have the orgy charge dropped, that if it went ahead the prosecution witnesses would consist solely of persons with criminal records.

In 1942 Lionel Atwill was given a five-year probationary sentence and he was to present himself to the police weekly. What worried him more than anything at this time was that the film studios refused to employ persons on probation. After seven months without any work Atwill applied for termination of his sentence.

Judge McKay, the same man who had sentenced Atwill, now reheard the case and decided that in all the circumstances, including the fact that the person who caused the complaint to be made in the first place was not activated 'by a sincere desire to bring about justice' and being 'convinced that the ends of justice have been met at this time', the judge completely exonerated Atwill of all charges, saying, 'You are now in the position Mr Atwill where you can truthfully say you have not been convicted of a felony.'

Lionel Atwill was finally divorced from Louise in 1943 and, no longer feeling at home in Hollywood, he went to New York to look for work. Finding none he returned to Hollywood but was never again offered a major role by a major studio. After a few small parts and 'quickie' features he worked on the forgettable and forgotten *Lost City of the Jungle*. He contracted pneumonia and died very suddenly, his remaining scenes in the film being completed by a double.

In spite of his odd opinions and odder practices Atwill's chilling baritone voice added nuances of apparent depravity that never occurred to scriptwriters. 'All women love the men they fear,' he once said enigmatically, or perhaps he was indulging in wishful thinking, since he went on:

> *All women kiss the hand that rules them ... I do not treat women in a soft fashion. Women are like cats: their preference is for a soft fireside cushion, for delicate bowls of cream, for perfumed leisure — and for a Master!*

7

Age Shall Wither and the Years Decay

-

DEATH FROM OLD AGE

We all want to live into old age – at least all but the very young do – although some of those who reach it wonder whether it was worth while. Somerset Maugham once said, 'There are many advantages to growing old ...' Here he paused and then after a full minute went on, ' ... I have been trying to think what they are.' Charles Chaplin complained that: 'The trouble with growing old is that there is always something wrong with you.' Groucho Marx said, 'Anyone can grow old, he only has to live long enough ... any old man is aware of his limitations and he realizes that the creaking he hears is not the sound of the rocking chair, it is the sound of his withered carcass, groaning in despair ... he is not dead but he might as well be.' And Joan Crawford used to say: 'There is *nothing* good about growing old.'

And yet, and yet, with age, sometimes, comes wisdom, contentment, a peace of mind and tranquillity before the last great journey. Some achieve great age softly; the silver hair, the quiet voice, the gentle touch, the kind eyes and the ready smile greeting everyone each day, only too happy that there is another day. For others age seems to descend suddenly and cruelly with impaired hearing, poor eyesight, a short temper and a rasping voice. Most cruel perhaps are the marks that old age sometimes foists upon the unsuspecting beauty of yesteryear: the bent spine, the thinning hair, the lined face, the spotted hands, the scrawny neck and the brittle bones. So old age may be a blessing or it may come as a curse and no one knows how it will affect one person or another if one is lucky enough or unlucky enough to reach it.

Among those who have reached old age in Hollywood, Mary Pickford, C. Aubrey Smith, Groucho Marx, Norma Shearer and Alfred Hitchcock are included in this chapter.

Mary Pickford. She died alone amid the crumbling glory of her home, *Pickfair*

Mary Pickford

-

The Most Popular Girl in the World

They called her 'America's Sweetheart' and 'the World's Sweetheart'. She was the first real movie star. By 1913 she had become the best-known and highest paid woman in the world. She appeared in 143 silent films between 1909 and 1912 and then featured in more than 50 films between 1913 and 1933. She rose from working for $5 a day to making a million dollars a year. She was married to Douglas Fairbanks and they entertained the cream of Hollywood and of the world at their famous home, Pickfair, on Summit Drive off Benedict Canyon in Beverly Hills, where neighbouring estates were owned by Harold Lloyd, Ronald Colman, David O. Selznick and Charles Chaplin. She was a business woman who rose to be a founder and head of United Artists and she survived two scandal-ridden divorces and the death in rapid succession of her brother, her sister and her mother. Her name was Mary Pickford.

She lived at Pickfair from 1920 when Douglas Fairbanks gave it to her as a wedding present, until her death in 1979 at the age of 86, in the large bedroom which had been hers for all that period.

Canadian-born and wealthy, Mary Pickford, whose real name was Gladys Mary Smith, was for years a convinced spiritualist who went to extraordinary lengths to keep such convictions to herself, but those of her friends who knew, like Merle Oberon and Norma Shearer, never doubted her sincere and comforting beliefs. Mary Pickford regarded the English medium Lilian Bailey OBE as a personal friend who had convinced her of the reality of spiritualistic phenomena.

Lilian Bailey purportedly gave sittings to Queen Elizabeth the Queen Mother and other members of the British Royal Family, Canadian Premier Mackenzie King, Air Chief Marshall Lord Dowding and other people of quality and standing.

A professional actress from the age of five, Mary Pickford had established a niche for herself on Broadway by the time she was 16 and it was only when she was faced with a few weeks out of work that she turned to see what the films might offer. D. W. Griffith saw the potential value of her delightful and appealing 'little-girl' quality and took her on. She made 78 films under his direction, all with Biograph, the first studio she had approached. By the time she divorced Owen Moore (who had appeared with her in several films) to marry Douglas Fairbanks in 1919, when she was 26, she was still playing innocent adolescents in her films.

Owen Moore was eventually found dead on the floor of his kitchen at his home in Beverly Hills, Hollywood, on 12 June 1939. He had suffered a cerebral haemorrhage. On hearing the news Mary recalled having been told by a medium when she was last in London that 'death hovered around ... someone close to you and yet not close to you ... the death won't cause you to cry'. Strangely enough Douglas Fairbanks, whom Mary had by this time divorced, after he was named co-respondent in Lord Ashley's divorce in 1935 after 14 years of marriage, died exactly six months later, on 12 December 1939, Owen's birthday.

The day before his death Douglas Fairbanks had pains which he took to be indigestion at his house in Santa Monica, where he had been doing strenuous exercises to which he was obsessively addicted (possibly trying to keep fit enough to keep up with the busy social activities of his wife Sylvia Ashley). A heart specialist diagnosed a coronary thrombosis and advised several weeks, possibly months, in bed. That same night Douglas Fairbanks died alone in bed.

Mary Pickford's mother Charlotte always hovered about the set when Mary was filming her early, fantastically successful films. She used to occupy a chair beside the director and she was not averse to suggesting ideas for dialogue and production as the shooting progressed. The showgirl wife of Jack, Mary's brother, committed suicide by drinking mercury and Jack became dependent on drink and drugs. Before long he too was dead, destroyed perhaps by an overwhelming mother and a formidably talented sister. Mary's sister Lottie also drank heavily through four unsuccessful marriages.

As Mary became a millionairess several times over her mother had nothing to fight for and she began to feel unnecessary and superfluous to her famous daughter and in her own palatial Beverly Hills house, full of valuable furniture and priceless silver, Charlotte too turned to drink for consolation.

But still Mary depended on her mother occasionally. When she needed a mourning dress for her part in *Little Annie Rooney*, her mother remembered a piece of black material that she had tucked away in an old trunk. Unfortunately the heavy trunk lid fell with considerable force on one of Charlotte's breasts and a growth developed. Although she was told that she must undergo surgery or risk death Charlotte refused to suffer the indignity of having a breast removed. When she became increasingly ill, Mary stopped work and moved into Charlotte's house to do what she could. When death eventually came Mary became hysterical and refused to accept the inevitable for by then Mary had become a Christian Scientist, a sect that regards death as an illusion.

Among the best-remembered films of Mary Pickford are *The Little American* (1917), *Rebecca of Sunnybrook Farm* (1917), *Daddy-Long-Legs* (1919), *Pollyanna* (1920) and *Little Lord Fauntleroy* (1921), in which she played both the boy hero and his mother. Mary's work in talking pictures was less successful and she returned briefly to the stage and worked in radio during the 1930s.

After the divorce from Douglas Fairbanks she married Charles 'Buddy' Rogers. In 1955 she wrote an autobiography, *Sunshine and Shadow* but by then she was beginning to become something of a recluse. There is a story that when the time came for her to think about having a facelift, she arranged for her studio stand-in to have one first. Some weeks later, when the bandages were removed, the stand-in looked wonderful and Mary decided to go ahead with the operation. But history did not repeat itself; when Mary's bandages came off the surgeons discovered that a nerve had been severed on one side of her face, causing the world's sweetheart to have half a permanent smile! Was that why Mary Pickford turned her back on films and became a recluse?

On 1 April 1956 Mary Pickford held a party at Pickfair for

more than 200 stars of the silent films. The fading stars of the silent screen were all present including William Boyd ('Hopalong Cassidy'), Harold Lloyd, Zasu Pitts, Marion Davies, Buster Keaton, Francis X. Bushman and Ramon Novarro. Sadly it turned out to be April Fool's weather with hail, thunder and lightning. Everyone moved indoors and circulated through the hall, living room and dining room where in the old days the table was always set for 15 people, just in case a few friends called unexpectedly. That 1956 party was one of the last times that Mary Pickford, by this time all but an alcoholic, welcomed her colleagues and the press to Pickfair, allowing photographers the run of her famous home (with its name a combination of the names of herself and Douglas Fairbanks) and even permitting pictures to be taken of her with her feet up after all the guests had gone.

Mary Pickford made her last public appearance in Paris in 1965 for the French government's 'Mary Pickford Retrospective' and next morning she said: 'The French never forget an artist who pleases them. I have received many honours in my life and have had audiences with kings and queens and the world's greatest; but this tribute touches me most of all. Last night my heart sang.'

Five years later she gave 51 early silent Biograph films to the American Film Institute but, although in the few years remaining to her, she read about Mary Pickford Festivals in Los Angeles, New York and London, the uncrowned queen of Hollywood attended none of them. Soon she rarely talked to anyone, even on the telephone and more and more she refused to leave her bed. And fonder and fonder she became of the bottle. Gavin Lambert has described the great star lying in bed, drinking; 'while cracks widened in the walls and ceilings' and weeds grew unchecked in the great estate that was Pickfair.

Mary Pickford, during her last years, became excessively religious and embraced various aspects of the occult. She had long been a devotee of astrology; now she accepted without reservation anything that might have a supernatural origin: extra-sensory-perception, extra-terrestrial activity, unidentified flying objects, paranormal activity.

She became a total recluse as she became depressed, not only by the Vietnam war and the Sharon Tate murders, but also by the ever more frequent, it seemed, deaths of her contemporaries – Harold Lloyd, Bebe Daniels, Zasu Pitts and other friends and film people she knew and loved.

At one of her last parties, in 1971, given in honour of her son Douglas Fairbanks Jr, Pearl Bailey asked whether she could go up and see Mary and, to everyone's surprise, the reclusive star agreed to see the singer, whom she had long admired.

Pearl went up alone and on entering the bedroom asked Mary, 'How is the doll?' 'What doll?' Mary demanded. 'The one I dreamed about, with the broken head,' responded Pearl. Mary was astonished and silently pointed to the doll playwright and producer David Belasco – he who had renamed Gladys Smith, Mary Pickford – had given her when she appeared in her first Broadway role, at the age of 13 in 1906, in *The Warrens of Virginia*. It was the last doll she played with and she had kept it all those years – but how could Pearl Bailey have known about the doll, its head broken long ago?

Soon Mary Pickford hardly left her bed at Pickfair. She saw very few people, her voice became incoherent and she lost the use of her legs through disuse. In 1979, her 87th year, the queen of Hollywood passed away. A very remarkable lady, Pickford was one of the very few in the history of the movies who managed to combine superstardom with perfect artistry.

C. Aubrey Smith

-

Character Actor
Par Excellence

A theatrical knight before there were many of them, apart from actor-managers, Sir Charles Aubrey Smith (CBE, 1938) the celebrated actor born in Brighton (1863) was the son of a doctor, Dr Charles John Smith. Educated at Charterhouse and Cambridge he married in 1896 and had one daughter Honor – now a grandmother herself – with whom I have corresponded and talked at some length.

C. Aubrey Smith's daughter tells me that her father trained to be a schoolmaster and then, while between jobs, started giving private theatrical shows with his two sisters. A London actor saw him and recommended him to Sir George Alexander who was also impressed and offered him a job on the stage.

C. Aubrey Smith was knighted by King George VI. The King was not very tall and the actor, a tall man then in his 70s, was a little worried when he saw the low stool beside the ceremonial sword in front of the settee in the small room at Buckingham Palace into which he was shown. He was the only person honoured at that particular investiture but he need not have worried. His daughter tells me that after he had been touched on both shoulders by the royal sword and as he struggled to regain his feet, he felt the king's arm under his shoulder and the next thing he knew they were sitting side by side on the settee.

After an extensive stage career in England where he had made his stage debut in 1892 at Hastings, he acquired a life-long love of cricket and in fact he captained Sussex soon after leaving Cambridge and later captained an English team that toured

Australia and South Africa. He made one or two films in England, including *The Face at the Window* but he felt he was not
being fully exploited and he went to America to play in his own
stage success of *The Bachelor Father* (1931) in which he scored
a personal triumph. He decided to settle in Hollywood and he
spent almost half a century there at 2881 Coldwater Canyon
and he was to die there, although he always longed to return
to England and the South coast which he remembered fondly
at all times. During his many visits to England for filming he
always tried to rent a house in Sussex and he usually succeeded.

C. Aubrey Smith had always been psychic and he and his wife
once looked over a house near the South coast when they were
going to be in Britain for some months, but while his wife loved
the place, which did seem utterly charming, Aubrey would not
think of taking it on any account. He said he had encountered
'something' in the garden and he took his little daughter there
without saying anything and she too said she felt an 'invisible
presence' at the same spot.

Aubrey Smith thought there had been a bad haunting associated with the house, and he also felt that several exorcisms
had taken place there; exorcisms that had been only partially
successful for 'something' was still left behind that could be
detected by sensitive people. If such a property was lived in by
people who were aware of such things and alive to the possibility
of such happenings, Aubrey felt that 'things might easily start
up again'. Curiously enough, it subsequently transpired that
the house had indeed been badly haunted at one time; there
had been more than one murder in either the house or garden;
and a series of exorcisms had almost cleared the place. The
house, they learned, was 'very much better' but 'something
still lingered' in the garden.

With men like Reginald Denny, Boris Karloff (a special
friend) and Alan Mowbray, Aubrey Smith became one of
America's favourite Englishmen, making star-status appearances in a score of films before settling for individual character
appearances which he continued to make in literally hundreds
of films for the rest of his life.

In 1925 C. Aubrey Smith went to San Francisco to play in
the silent film, *Never the Twain Shall Meet* (1925) directed
by the outstanding French film-maker, Maurice Tourneur
and produced by William Randolph Hearst; C. Aubrey Smith

playing the father of Marion Davies, Hearst's real-life long-time mistress. It was a story set in the South Seas, starring popular Bert Lytell, and while making that film Aubrey Smith struck up an immediate friendship with another cricket-mad Englishman, who was predictably playing one of the villains, Boris Karloff.

In 1932 when 'that magnificent old man, C. Aubrey Smith' (as one biographer of Karloff puts it) came to organize the famous Hollywood Cricket Club, Karloff was one of its most eager and loyal members. The Club came to be an important part of what was in those days a very distinguished British Colony in Hollywood and each and every one of them made their mark as being British in one way or another. Aubrey Smith invariably flew the Union Jack over his croquet lawn; Boris Karloff always had the New Year piped in with real bagpipes and throughout the Colony the King was loyally and enthusiastically toasted on every possible occasion.

Celebrated members of the Hollywood Cricket Club included Ronald Colman (born at Richmond in Surrey), Clive Brook (born in London), Nigel Bruce (born in London), Basil Rathbone (who was actually born in South Africa), H. B. Warner (born in London), Frank Lawton (born in London), and later Cary Grant (born in Bristol), David Niven (who was born in Scotland), and Errol Flynn (born in Antrim, Northern Ireland). Each and every member of the HCC was inordinately proud of being a member and sported the boldly striped Club blazer whenever possible. Actor Peter Cushing has revealed that when he was in Hollywood in 1939

> *that grand old stalwart of the British theatre, Empire and cricket, C. Aubrey Smith, invited me to play in his Eleven, which included Basil Rathbone, David Niven and Boris Karloff . . . I was out first ball and missed several easy catches while fielding at mid-on, being so distracted by all those luminaries surrounding me, and my services were not called on again!*

C. Aubrey Smith was instrumental with Boris Karloff and a few other members of the HCC in founding and running the Screen Actors Guild (where for years the office secretaries referred to the latter as 'Dear Boris' as if that were his name). Both actors

were among the twelve founder-members of the Guild that was
to do so much to improve the lot of the film actor in the early
days and to grow in strength and repute with the years. But
in the very early days it was a question of secret meetings in
secret places and in a copy of the *Screen Actors Guild Bulletin*
in which he wrote of the early days of the Guild, Boris Karloff
said:

> *I carry today in my heart the picture of Sir Aubrey
> Smith in impeccable snowy flannels, swooping about on
> the dance floor at the Hollywood Cricket Club, pausing,
> stage whispering through bristling white moustache to a
> fellow dancer ... My house tonight — not a word — park
> on another street — come in the back door ... One, two,
> three, dip — and away!*

One of C. Aubrey Smith's best-remembered appearances was
his totally believable Colonel Sapt in the classic Ruritanian story
of intrigue and adventure, *The Prisoner of Zenda* (1937), and
David Niven has left a vivid picture of the veteran actor (whom
he calls 'that splendid old gentleman') at that time in his book
of reminiscences, *Bring on the Empty Horses* (1975):

> *C. Aubrey Smith was over seventy when* Zenda *was made.
> Six foot four, ramrod straight, alert and vigorous, never
> did he forget a line or misunderstand a piece of direction:
> unfailingly courteous, kind and helpful, he was beloved by
> all.*
>
> *Every Sunday, he ordered me to turn out for the
> Hollywood Cricket Club; I always called him 'Sir', and,
> though dreading long hot afternoons in the field — I
> obeyed. His great craggy face was frequently creased by
> worry because he loved England very deeply and as it
> was early in 1937, he had little faith in the way Neville
> Chamberlain was coping with the Rome-Berlin Axis and
> Germany's anti-Comintern Pact with Japan. Refusing to
> read the 'local rags',* the Los Angeles Times *or the* Exam-
> iner, *trusting only* The Times *of London to keep him
> up to date, and with air mail across the Atlantic almost
> non-existent, Aubrey was usually eight to ten days behind
> a crisis. Nobody spoiled his fun by telling him the news*

so it was almost two weeks after it happened that the old man flung down his morning paper and boomed across the set: 'The bloody feller's done it!' 'Who, Sir? What, Sir?' we chorused. 'That whippersnapper Hitler! He's marched into Austria!'

Over 70 he may have been but C. Aubrey Smith's diction was as clear and perfect as ever and there is no doubt that theatre training stood him in excellent stead in this respect as it did for Ronald Colman, Leslie Howard, Nigel Bruce, George Arliss and other English actors who enjoyed the sun, the sea and the sand of southern California in the 1920s and 1930s.

This much-loved star was, as we have seen, psychically sensitive and his daughter has told me of many instances that reveal this side of his nature. He was a natural water diviner or dowser; he took part in many table-turning sessions when that method of apparent communication with the afterlife was in vogue — and once he found himself to be the last person round the table with only his hands touching it, and it was still moving! He experienced several striking instances of precognition and foreknowledge and his daughter tells me, 'Dad and I had many odd happenings together ...'

On the late afternoon that his daughter heard that her father had died in 1948 in his 86th year, her husband, a rear-admiral, came home to comfort her and gave her a glass of sherry. She was sitting on the floor, leaning against her husband's knees with their two teenage children when there sounded two very loud knocks and the glass of sherry went for six! Later, back in his office at Lee on the Solent, her husband found his hand suddenly and quite inexplicably writing automatically in his father-in-law's hand; a message about family matters that was known only to C. Aubrey Smith.

After her father died Honor went over to Hollywood to try to comfort her mother and it had been arranged for a few people they all knew to look in: the Boris Karloffs, Edmund Gwenn and others, and while Honor and her mother were tidying themselves in their bedrooms beforehand, Honor saw a large puff of blue smoke, 'just as when Dad was puffing at his pipe' in her room. She thought the smoke must be the result of someone having arrived rather early so she called out to her mother who came into the bedroom; she also saw the cloud of smoke and almost wept, saying softly, 'It's Aubrey.' She said afterwards she felt so comforted to have seen it and it made her determined to stay on in the house in Coldwater Canyon, which she had always loved.

C. Aubrey Smith wanted his ashes buried in England so they now rest in the tomb with his mother and two sisters not far from the sea in his beloved Sussex. Sir C. Aubrey Smith lived a long and happy life in Hollywood. In his old age he was still hale and hearty but one day he had arranged to go out and he had quite a heavy cold. His wife tried to dissuade him but he went anyway. The cold got worse and within a day or so he was dead; more from old age than anything else. Every single person who knew him remembers him with the greatest affection.

Veteran actor C. Aubrey Smith

Groucho Marx

-

Hallo, I Must Be Going ...

Groucho Marx, the zany comedian with the sparkling eyes, levitating eyebrows and unruly moustache, the master of devastating one-liners who was rarely seen without a cigar in his mouth, was in fact an intelligent man of great sensitivity. His real name was Julius Marx and he was born in 1890 on East 93rd Street, New York. Charlotte Chandler, who knew Groucho well for the last five years of his life, comments in Groucho idiom: 'He wasn't at all embarrassed to find himself in bed with a woman.'

The famous comedy team, consisting of his brothers Chico (real name Leonard), Harpo (real name Adolph), Zeppo (real name Herbert) and originally a fifth brother Gummo (real name Milton, who later became Groucho's business manager) was built up by their mother Minnie Marx, a strong and determined lady who struggled to make the boys successful. On the night, many years ahead, when Groucho collected his Oscar, he paid tribute to his mother, saying that without her the boys would have been nothing. She died in 1929 of a heart attack after a family party and sadly did not live to see her sons become Hollywood stars but she saw them on Broadway and in their first film. Groucho always treasured his mother's reply when he asked her how she thought the audience liked their first film *The Coconuts* (1929). Minnie said, simply, 'They laughed a lot!' As a tribute to her all the daughters of the Marx brothers were given names beginning with the letter M.

A neighbour remembers the Marx family in New York City during the early 1900s:

They were wild youngsters with a talent for having fun. The place would be a shambles, especially if Mrs Minnie Marx left them alone. They would think nothing of tearing down the draperies or jumping through a window. There used to be a woman who lived opposite, a doctor's wife, and she used to send notes to Mrs Marx, saying she was going to call the police; but threats only seemed to make the boys worse. They never had to create the zany characters they played so convincingly on stage and screen; they already were those characters.

After successful work in vaudeville, two musical films virtually established the boys' lasting reputation: *The Coconuts* (1929) and *Animal Crackers* (1930) (in which Groucho proudly showed his son Arthur to audiences in the opening scene of the latter); both were filmed almost exactly as they had been presented on stage.

After the Marx family moved to California in 1931 they were fortunate in that their first three Hollywood films were produced for Paramount by Herman J. Mankiewicz (the younger brother of Joseph, the accomplished and charming writer, producer and director of Hollywood films for over twenty years). Mankiewic's Marx Brothers pictures: *Monkey Business* (1931), *Horse Feathers* (1932) and *Duck Soup* (1933) are regarded as vintage Marx films, embodying their typically anarchic humour and bearing the unmistakable imprint of their iconoclastic producer.

Duck Soup in particular showed the indomitable Margaret Dumont at her most statuesque. She was the perfect comic foil as a pillar of rectitude responding to Groucho's mixture of amorous advances and insults. She appeared in 7 of the 13 Marx Brothers films and in 36 other films, working with W. C. Fields, Laurel and Hardy, Danny Kaye and Jack Benny. Groucho often said how much he enjoyed his romantic scenes with Margaret Dumont. 'She was a wonderful woman,' he'd say. 'Just the same off-stage as she was on it; always the stuffy, dignified matron. She took everything so seriously. She used to say to me, time and time again: "Julie, why are they laughing?".'

Morrie Ryskind, co-author of three Marx Brothers films said that Margaret Dumont really was the character she played so successfully. 'She'd been a lady in society but when her husband died she found herself in reduced circumstances and she needed a job.' She had truly believed that *A Day at the Races* (1937) was a serious film and she told Margaret O'Sullivan before they started filming: 'You know, this isn't going to be one of *those* things. I'm having a very *serious* part this time.' Perhaps George Cukor summed up Margaret Dumont best: 'Her elegance was so perfectly bogus.' She died in Hollywood in 1965 of a heart attack at the age of 76.

Each of the Marx Brothers had a distinctive persona in the Marx Brothers films: Chico (so-called because of his enduring passion for young ladies) was the traditional Italian piano-playing street vendor; Harpo (so-called for obvious reasons) played the harp but never spoke: Zeppo (no one knows why he was so-called) was the awkward romantic straight man before he retired after the first five films; and Groucho (so-called on account of his serious demeanour) with his villainous moustache, huge twitching eyebrows, and ever-present cigar, wore an ill-fitting suit which was a parody of the uniform of the society he attacked with wisecracks, often shatteringly irreverent, delivered in a dry, sardonic tone as he walked with knees bent and the whole body inclined in a caricature of some peculiar feline creature. Long before they were established stars Groucho discovered his walk. 'I was just kidding around one day,' he would explain. 'And I started to walk funny. The audience liked it and I kept it in.'

The boys' uncle Al Shean, their mother's brother, helped to establish the brothers' individuality: Groucho would talk incessantly, Harpo wouldn't talk at all, while Chico would play the straight man to both.

Groucho's antics in Hollywood are legion. One day, according to this story, Groucho saw the well-known figure of Garbo in slacks and floppy hat and, approaching her, he bent down in his famous crouch and peeked under the brim of her hat. Two ice-cold blue and unsmiling eyes stared down on him and he backed away, muttering, 'Pardon me, ma'am, I thought you were a guy I knew in Pittsburg.'

Groucho married three times but he often said that women baffled him, and all three of his wives left him. This never stopped him liking women and pursuing them from when he was about 14 until the last few days of his life. His early life was a succession of romantic episodes, many of them with chambermaids in the hotels the boys used to stay in. Once, when W. C. Fields was on the same bill, there were twenty girls in the show and 'they were all white and they were all friendly. I knew them by number rather than by name.' Ruth, Groucho's first wife, was 19 and Groucho was 30 when they married. His second wife Kay was born the same year as his first child, 1921, and his third wife Eden was born in 1934, making her 44 years younger than Groucho.

Dilys Powell has reminded us that when one thinks of the Marx Brothers, one thinks first and most devoutly of Groucho. From the start Groucho mastered a timing that was peculiar to himself but which worked impeccably in the movies. The history of the cinema, says Dilys Powell, is crowded with kings and Groucho was the King of Insult and it is true that his insulting remarks were always memorable: 'They say I never forget a face but I'll make an exception in your case'; 'I wouldn't join a club that would have me as a member'; 'One day I shot an elephant in my pyjamas. How he got into my pyjamas I'll never know'; 'Hallo, I must be going ...'

Hollywood's wonder boy, Irving Thalberg, probably made more impact on films and filming than any other man. He produced a welter of wonderful and lasting films and even revived the faltering Marx Brothers with their greatest hit, *A Night at the Opera* (1935) but then Thalberg died in his 30s in 1936.

Without Irving Thalberg, who had taken the Marx Brothers under his wing at the biggest studios in Hollywood (Groucho always said that Thalberg saved their careers after *Duck Soup* did poorly at the box office) the future of the Brothers could well have been bleak. Zeppo had left the act after *Duck Soup* and started a talent agency; Gummo, who had not returned to show business after he came back from the army in 1919, now joined his brother and together they built up one of the biggest agencies in Hollywood. Groucho, Chico and Harpo made three more pictures, *At the Circus* (1939), *Go West* (1940) and *The Big Store* (1941), all on a production-line basis for MGM. The following year they were ready to retire as a team and each brother went his own way professionally.

Groucho, who had always aspired to be an author and had published *Beds* in 1930, turned to writing and eventually wrote five books, and he worked from time to time in radio. Harpo and Chico made personal appearances, sometimes alone and sometimes together, and occasionally Chico joined Groucho on the radio but Chico, apart from his other virtues, was an inveterate gambler and by 1945 he was completely broke.

To help him Groucho and Harpo came out of retirement and the three brothers made *A Night in Casablanca* (1946), satirizing the famous Humphrey Bogart and Ingrid Bergman classic thriller *Casablanca* (1943). In spite of this successful reunion the team disbanded immediately afterwards and when they rejoined forces for a later film, *Love Happy* (1949) it was with less success, and Groucho made little more than a cameo appearance. He had found his feet with meaty little roles in major motion pictures and with his successful television quiz show, *You Bet Your Life.* He was happy with his life.

'Groucho did not grow old gracefully,' says his biographer Charlotte Chandler. 'Growing old is what you do if you are lucky,' he once said and on another occasion: 'I'm as young as the day is long, and this has been a very short day.' 'Age isn't very interesting to talk about,' he was especially fond of saying in his last years when all sorts of people asked him all sorts of questions about growing old. 'Anyone can get old,' he'd say. 'Everybody gets older, if you live long enough.'

As the years passed he became slow in walking and slow in talking but put him in front of an audience and he would still come up with funny ad lib remarks. When he was in Cannes, France, to receive a decoration (the French Commandeur des Arts et Lettres) from the French President, he was invited to appear at a Royal Command Performance in England. He said that he was honoured to be asked and was about to accept when he learned that by tradition all proceeds of such performances go to charity. The palace emissary was told: 'Tell the Queen that Groucho doesn't work for nothing.'

Before his 82nd birthday he was found unconscious on his bedroom floor, having suffered a slight stroke, and he was in hospital for nearly three months. He was taken to hospital again in August 1973 after another stroke. His condition was diagnosed as 'probably pneumonitus, acute anteroseptal myocardial infarction, arteriosclerotic cerebrovascular disease and chronic urinary tract infection secondary to bladder retention.' In short, as his son Arthur puts it, 'Old age was catching up with him.'

Groucho now lived more or less alone until, after his condition steadily worsened and at the age of 83, he had to have nursing round the clock. Each morning the day nurse would drive Groucho up into Beverly Hills and walk with him, at a snail's pace, past Beverly Hills Hotel or down Rodeo Drive and call and see his old friend Sidney Sheldon. In 1974 Groucho was awarded an 'honorary' Oscar; he looked old and frail as he shuffled on stage to collect the award but he received a standing ovation.

Towards the end of his life Groucho spent a lot of time in bed. His house in Beverly Hills had a bar, just off the dining room, filled with Marx Brothers memorabilia. Once, when his daughter-in-law came to see him, he pointed towards the bar and said, 'Name your poison, but you'll have to fix it yourself. I don't drink any more. In fact, I don't do anything that's fun any more.' He was a great boxing fan and always watched fights whenever he could. At the beginning of the Foreman–Norton fight he was heard to say loudly: 'I remember when there were white fighters.' Foreman knocked Norton out in the second round. 'I guess Foreman had an early date,' commented Groucho. The strokes he had suffered had sobered him but Groucho composed his own epitaph: 'Here lies Groucho Marx and lies and lies and lies. He never kissed an ugly girl.' Whether he was serious or not is something you never knew with Groucho.

His first wife and the mother of two of his three children was Ruth Johnson to whom he was married for 21 years; his second wife Kay was the ex-wife of one-time Dead End Kid Leo Gorcey; the marriage lasted six years and produced Groucho's third child Melinda. His third wife was the beautiful Eden Hartford and that marriage lasted 15 years, but he remained friendly with all his wives. Later young Erin Fleming came into Groucho's life. A Canadian who had acted in New York, she came to answer his fan mail and, as Groucho used to say, 'To answer my prayers.' There was a half-a-century's age difference but she became Groucho's secretary and personal manager, trusted confidante and treasured companion.

Even in his middle 80s Groucho came up with a lot of new stories and new material almost every day. Towards the end of his life he was asked his style of humour. He replied simply: 'I'm a funny-looking jerk.'

After a spectacular 85th birthday party at his home, 1083 Hillcrest Road, on Sunday, 5 October 1975, 'from 4 'til 8 pm' the public hardly saw Groucho. He had a hip operation and then another stroke and, no longer able to take the walks through Beverly Hills that he had so enjoyed, senility began to take over. Even the little things in life became an increasing struggle. His only son Arthur felt that Groucho was no longer able to decide things for himself. For a few hours he would seem to be in good spirits although he had difficulty speaking because of respiratory problems, then he would rapidly tire and lose interest in even staying awake. Now deaf and finding it increasingly difficult to keep in touch with reality, he was never told that his brother Gummo had died on 21 April 1977. As Groucho grew increasingly frail he was moved to the Cedar Sinai Medical Centre where he died on 19 August 1977, holding his son's hand.

Shortly before his death Erin told the press: 'Groucho's having a nice little dream right now. Soon he's going to have a deeper nap and rest his eyes for several centuries.'

After Groucho's death there were furious court battles between Arthur and Erin and in the acrimonious disputes the surviving Marx Brother, Zeppo, took Erin's part. He defended her role in Groucho's life and said, 'She kept Groucho alive.' It is difficult to argue with that observation but as Groucho's son Arthur has pointed out, there are no winners in cases like this, other than the lawyers. Legal fees ate up most of Groucho's estate by the time it was eventually distributed to his family, in 1988, eleven years after Groucho's death.

Zeppo was not invited to either the Bel Air service or to the burial itself. He had only learned of Groucho's death from press reports. But none of this really mattered. Groucho wasn't impressed by funeral services. 'It doesn't do any good,' he once said. 'When you're dead, you're dead. I don't want a lot of people at my funeral. I want them to go out and find a Marx Brothers film and laugh a lot.'

All through his life Groucho hated the word 'Goodbye'. 'Never say goodbye,' he used to say and in a way he has not said goodbye because the legacy of his humour will always be with us. 'Say Auf Wiedersehen,' Groucho would say. 'Say Hasta la vista, say Au revoir, say anything; but never say Goodbye.' All right then, we'll just say, 'Thanks, Groucho.'

Norma Shearer and Irving Thalberg

-

The Queen of MGM and Hollywood's Boy Wonder

A brilliant and shrewd young man who was known in Hollywood as 'the boy wonder' before he was twenty years of age, Irving Thalberg was born in Brooklyn in 1899. Even as a child he suffered from a rheumatic heart condition and he was confined to his bed for weeks at a time; all his life he was frail and had to guard against taking any risks with his health.

When Thalberg was only 19, Carl Laemmle, president of Universal, made him executive producer, and he soon earned considerable respect for his handling of difficult directors such as Erich von Stroheim and for the fine quality of the films he produced, although he never allowed his name to appear on the list of credits. His last film to be released, *The Good Earth*, was unfinished at the time of his death and a tribute to him was attached to the film; it was the only screen credit he ever had.

When Thalberg was led to think that Laemmle had plans for him to marry his daughter, Thalberg decided it was time to move and he went to the Mayer Company (to be absorbed into MGM in 1924) where Louis B. Mayer offered him a vice-presidency. Thalberg had a commendable attitude to films and film-making and once told King Vidor, who was worried about the possible public reaction to a film about social conditions: 'Well, I think MGM is making enough money that they can afford an experimental film every once in a while. It will do something for the studio and it may do something for the whole industry.'

Thalberg was instrumental in the successful careers enjoyed by Greta Garbo, Clark Gable, Joan Crawford, Jean Harlow, Spencer Tracy, Robert Taylor and many others, including Norma Shearer whom Thalberg married in 1927. Always careful to select the right story, the right co-stars and the right directors for his leading actors, Thalberg believed that good movies meant good entertainment and the films made under his guidance are outstanding for their polish, glamour and style. One has only to think of *The Champ* (1931), *Trader Horn* (1931), *Grand Hotel* (1932), *Tarzan the Ape Man* (1932), the lavish and expensive *Rasputin and the Empress* (1932), *Mutiny on the Bounty* (1935) and *The Good Earth* (1937) to realize the remarkable talent and flair that Thalberg brought to the movies.

Marion Davies is the perfect example of a Thalberg manufactured star. Newspaper tycoon William Randolph Hearst spent enormous sums of money on her pictures, the sets and the glittering casts that astounded even Hollywood, and his frequently ridiculous publicity did her more harm than good, but Marion pressed on and it was Irving Thalberg who recognized her true talent as a comedienne. He starred her in a series of popular pictures and after the gloss and froth of Hearst's efforts, she was rewarded towards the end of her film career with some brilliant characterizations and some real appreciation from the public.

Irving Thalberg made the Marx Brothers' films, *A Night at the Opera* and *A Day at the Races* in particular, romantic comedies set amid lavish production numbers that MGM could afford, but Thalberg died suddenly during the filming of *A Day at the Races* and things were never the same again for the Marx Brothers. When Groucho and his brothers attended the funeral of Irving Thalberg at the Wilshire Boulevard Temple in 1936, together with Greta Garbo, Jean Harlow, Charles Chaplin, Mary Pickford, Louis B. Mayer, Erich von Stroheim and just about every other MGM employee, the ushers were Clark Gable, Fredric March and Douglas Fairbanks Sr.

All his life Thalberg had a weak heart and he always feared an early death; to his wife Norma Shearer and a few close friend he would say he felt he was living on borrowed time and a year before his death he said he would be happy to settle for another ten years but would not be surprised if he joined 'the great majority' in ten *days*.

Norma was aware that the ever-handy nitroglycerin pills and other medicines scattered about her husband's desk, the muffler and the topcoat he wore in winter, even on the mildest days, the lessening of his working hours which he found himself forced to accept and, more frightening perhaps, the gradual depletion of his energy, were all serious signs of exhaustion and strain. He had suffered a heart attack in 1925. Now Norma cut down their social appearances, arranged script and production conferences at their home, 707 Ocean Front, and sought to relieve her husband of fatiguing social activity by making herself a conspicuous centre of attention.

The tragic death of the wife of Norma's brother, Douglas Shearer, a few years earlier, had upset Irving too. As the Hollywood *Citizen News* reported it:

> *Before horrified pleasure seekers at the Venice amusement pier yesterday afternoon, Mrs Douglas Shearer, wife of the brother of Norma Shearer, motion-picture actress, killed herself with a target pistol in front of a shooting gallery by firing a shot between her eyes.*

In August 1936 Irving Thalberg felt too weary and tired to attend the première of *Romeo and Juliet* but he did attend, with Norma, the première of *The Great Ziegfeld* later the same month. Two days later Norma and Irving drove to Del Monte Lodge, where they had spent their honeymoon; the air was unseasonably cool but Irving, uncharacteristically, ignored Norma's advice to stay indoors or put on a sweater. A few days later, at the Hollywood Bowl, it was noticed that he seemed to have a very heavy cold.

Next morning he woke up with a fever, alternatively shivering and perspiring. Norma sent for a doctor who diagnosed an infected throat. Twenty-four hours later the throat had not responded to treatment and Norma called in another doctor who diagnosed lobar pneumonia but said Irving's weak heart was not affected. Nevertheless Irving was depressed and seemed convinced that he was going to die. He told one visitor: 'This time I'm not going to make it.' There was talk of flying Irving to a clinic in Rochester, Minnesota, where recently discovered drugs were available but Irving's condition deteriorated and he was in no shape to be moved anywhere.

Sunday 13 August saw the annual MGM boisterous picnic party at the ranch of Clarence Brown, the rich and popular film-maker and Garbo's favourite director. Norma sent a telegram in Irving's name that was read over the loudspeaker system: 'Only illness keeps me from being with you.'

That night Irving's condition became critical. He coughed blood and had fits of shivering with hot sweats. Norma and a nurse were at his bedside and were relieved to see him grow calmer. After a while he seemed to breathe more easily and they left him sleeping calmly. But next morning his fever was noticeably higher. Members of the family were summoned and filed quietly past Irving's bed but he hardly seemed to recognize anyone, even Norma. At 10.15 that morning he died in the presence of Norma. Stories of his last words have varied from, 'Don't let the children forget me,' to advising Norma not to choose an actor if she remarried or that he attempted to recite the Lord's Prayer while holding Norma's hand. According to Norma Shearer's biographer, Gavin Lambert, Irving did none of these things; he died after being in a coma for over two hours. Before losing consciousness he did mutter a few unintelligible words but in fact his death was a slow, silent fade-out.

Born in Montreal, Canada, in 1902 gentle and reserved Norma Shearer decided in her teens to become an actress. In 1919 she and her sister went with Mrs Shearer when she walked out on the girls' father and in 1920, armed with a letter of introduction to Florenz Ziegfeld which had been inveigled from a local theatre manager, the three moved to New York where Norma soon found work as an extra in several films and did some modelling for newspaper advertisements.

In 1923 Hal Roach was in New York looking for an actress to play in a forthcoming serial. Norma was interviewed and got the contract. It was the beginning of a long and successful film career with parts that varied from a circus rider to Marie Antoinette.

Norma successfully negotiated the all-important changeover from silent to sound pictures and her future was assured when, in 1927, she married Irving Thalberg, then head of production at MGM. As Joan Crawford, one of the studio's leading actresses (there were those who called *her* the Queen of MGM) was heard to comment somewhat bitterly at the time: 'What chance do I have now. Norma's sleeping with the boss.' The marriage of Norma Shearer, whose lack of striking beauty was offset by strong acting skills, was one of the few romantic stories of a successful union in Hollywood between film people, lasting as it did from 1927 until Thalberg's death. After Irving died Norma worked out her existing contract with MGM and then, in 1942, she retired.

By 1967 Norma had suffered several severe attacks of anxiety and she underwent a series of electric shock treatment at a sanatorium. At first there was some improvement, but she was still subject to depression and she talked about euthanasia with her son but when she was told that the legal risks for an accomplice were extremely serious, she gave up the idea.

In June 1970 she attempted suicide. While in a dentist's waiting room, on the top floor of a high-rise building, she suddenly stood up, ran to the windows and tried to throw herself out. As she was restrained, she had a blackout. After another course of shock therapy she became calmer but found her memory affected and she gradually retreated into a private exile.

In 1977 Norma Shearer's sight began to fail; at first she would go for walks in the Beverly Hills, wearing dark glasses, and accompanied by her second husband Marti Arrougé, but finally she stopped going out at all. Her face became covered with fine, weblike wrinkles and her memory again became blurred. At times she would recognize Marti with affection, at other times she would ask, 'Are you Irving?' As her mind became more and more clouded, the word 'Irving' was more and more on her lips. She became silent for long periods; she ate little and her husband, although he also employed a nurse, was no longer able to care for her as she needed to be cared for. When she entered the Motion Picture Country Hospital her body had shrivelled to under 80lbs and she did not know who she was or where she was. Soon she suffered a mild stroke and there were signs of physical paralysis. She knew hardly anyone but when they were leaving she would grip their hands and wouldn't let go. Her hair was white and her face ravaged by anxiety and she was all but blind. After a year in this twilight zone Norma's mind became weaker still. She no longer cared about getting dressed, she wandered about the hospital, lost in herself and unreachable most of the time.

Early in 1983 Norma contracted bronchial pneumonia and, as in the case of her beloved first husband, it sapped her remaining strength until she lay, silent, fading and all but forgotten. On 12 June, at five o'clock in the afternoon, she died; almost imperceptibly, aged 80 years and nine months. She was buried as she had wished, beside Irving Thalberg, in the marble mausoleum in Forest Lawn and every day since her death fresh roses have been found placed in the urn beside the grave.

Alfred Hitchcock

-

Master of the Macabre

Whenever he was asked if he was ever really frightened about anything, Hitchcock invariably replied: 'Always.' And perhaps he was; he certainly never forgot the terrifying fear he experienced one night when he was only five or six years old. He found himself awake in the middle of the night (as he thought) in the house where he was born in Leytonstone, London, in 1899. He called out but his parents, family greengrocers, had slipped out for a walk, confident that young Alfred would sleep until they returned. When no one answered the boy got up. 'Nothing but night all around me,' he said years later as he relived the terror. 'Shaking with fright I wandered about the empty dark house ... so I have known fear since childhood.'

He attended the Catholic church of St Francis, Stratford, and it was always the ceremonies that interested him; once he bribed a 'master of ceremonies' to allow him to be an acolyte at High Mass but he was soon found out since he had not learned the responses. Later Hitch would indulge his desire to be part of the show without learning the lines when he performed his famous momentary walk-on parts in all his films. The story goes that there was a temporary shortage of extras when he was shooting *The Lodger* (1927) so Hitch appeared himself and apparently enjoyed the experience.

He married Alma Reville in 1926, five years after they had met. She was born a day after Hitch and was a freelance editor at Islington Studios, living at Twickenham. Thereafter her opinions and her attitude to his films were of great importance to Hitch and she helped to script or technically assist in many of them; they were married for more than fifty years. They had a daughter, Pat, in 1928 who married a New England businessman and the couple presented Hitch and Alma with three grandchildren. In the long and fruitful years that were to follow no one ever really doubted the devotion that Hitch and Alma had for each other.

Much of the appeal in a Hitchcock thriller is the basic characteristic an ordinary person is caught up in extraordinary events. Powerful suspense was an ingredient in practically all his films, and his imagination in producing unusual cinematic effects, a sly humour and dramatic settings all helped create the considerable appeal and success of his films. Who can forget *The Thirty-Nine Steps* − the renowned author John Buchan congratulated Hitch on improving on his novel; the humorous thriller *The Lady Vanishes* (1938) and the impeccable *Rebecca* (1940)?

Joel McCrea has recalled that at the age of 40 Hitch had a habit of drinking a pint of champagne at lunchtime. After lunch one day when McCrea was working on *Foreign Correspondent* (1940), there was a scene with just McCrea standing and talking.

> *When the scene was over I expected to hear 'Cut!' and I looked over and there was Hitchcock snoring with his lips sticking out. He had fallen fast asleep! So I said 'Cut!' and with that he woke up and said: 'Was it any good?' and I said 'the best in the picture!' and Hitch said, 'Print it!'*

Hitchcock went on to make the classic 'perfect crime' story, *Strangers on a Train* (1951) and the unique horror of attack from an unexpected source, *The Birds* (1963).

With hindsight it is possible to see below the surface of many of Hitchcock's films a simmering, angry, sexual element; cool, icy blondes tied up, handcuffed, humiliated; and towards the end of his life, in particular, a dark side of his nature surfaced, just possibly related to or aggravated by his painful arthritis, his heavy drinking, his worrying heart condition and the operation and strokes suffered by his wife, who became a semi-invalid.

In his later years he engaged a woman from the Universal

Studios typing pool but she left after a few weeks, pale and furious for she said Hitch had increasingly made ugly, intimate demands that led to hysterical scenes. He used to indulge in long and preposterous flirtatious sessions with any young secretary he could corner; he would wrinkle his nose and give little waves to the embarrassed girls; he would give them money on the sly and ask them to do outrageous things for him. He really thought some of his leading ladies were in love with him. He used to say 'Ingrid's been in love with me for thirty years; mad for me all her life.' Grace Kelly 'had indulged his fancies,' he said, 'and she would hardly have done that if she had not been in love.' Tippi Hedren, the blonde former fashion model who suffered horribly in *The Birds*, was another actress who, Hitch believed, was in love with him and half-way through *Marnie* (1964), his second film with her, he propositioned her in her trailer – threatening to ruin her if she would not comply. She refused and he never spoke to her again; instead he would instruct his assistant, 'Tell that girl to do so and so.' And there were other girls, usually blonde and always beautiful.

During the winter of 1978 Hitch was admitted to Cedars-Sinai Medical Center for alcoholic detoxification. During the spring of 1979 he became depressed again and seemed to go downhill very quickly. People, he would say, only came to his house to drink his wine, even relatives; no one ever really cared; he had been betrayed all his life, he always felt alone, alone and in the dark, and his thoughts would often turn to death ...

Then in October 1979 Alexander Walker, the London film critic and author, was instrumental in having Hitchcock named in the 1980 Queen's New Year's Honours List, a Knight Commander of the British Empire. A journey to London was impossible and the British Consul General agreed to make the presentation at Universal Studios but Hitch's office was by this time little used and in disarray so a makeshift office set was erected and Hitch sat at the desk, giving the impression of a normal working day. In fact he was given injections of cortisone for the arthritis which was causing him more and more pain and discomfort and his pacemaker had had to be monitored the previous afternoon. For many the luncheon afterwards would be their final goodbye to Hitch.

So for the few months left to him it was Sir Alfred Hitchcock but within a few weeks he suddenly told Universal he couldn't work there any more and his office was closed. The furniture was moved out and his personal files and books and equipment taken to his bungalow at 10957 Bellagio Road, the only house the Hitchcocks ever owned in Los Angeles, looking out to the fairway of the Bel Air Country Club. He stayed at home a few days and then he started going to the studio again, as if nothing had changed. He found a new secretary and talked of new projects and plans but they all came to nothing.

In May 1979 Hitch had been saddened by the death of a colleague, Victor Saville, whom he had known since 1923 when, with Michael Balcon and John Freeman, a production company had been formed and Hitch had been engaged; it was his first real break. Saville, a member of my London club, often talked to me over lunch of Hitchcock, his problems and his achievements.

For Hitch the arthritis was becoming daily more painful and he was subjected to generous injections of cortisone and his pacemaker was monitored regularly but otherwise those last weeks for the man who had reportedly lived in abject terror of accident or sudden death all his life were quiet and uninterrupted except for the continual attention by nurses and doctors. Hitch seemed as content as he had ever been and he refused to have 'any truck with any clergyman'; but as one rare visitor commented afterwards: 'there are so many resentments locked up inside him'.

During April the pain eased somewhat and Hitch enjoyed more deep sleep than he could remember for ages but then his liver failed and his kidney functions slowed and his enlarged heart did not respond as it should to the device he had worn for six years. During the night of 28 – 29 April 1980 the doctor was hurriedly summoned and by early morning the family were gathered at his bedside. During the morning of 29 April, without violence or drama, Alfred Hitchcock died, by a strange quirk of fate for a man who loved drama, quietly in his sleep.

He had the last laugh too, in a way. At his Catholic funeral his coffin was absent. He had arranged to be cremated.

Hitch left his estate to his wife, his daughter and to his grandchildren. After all his suffering, real and imagined, perhaps at the end, in his last quiet sleep, he glimpsed the cloudless horizon that was always his image of serenity.

Select Bibliography

Anderson, Christopher P., *A Star, Is a Star, Is a Star*, Robson, 1981.

Arce, Hector, *Gary Cooper*, William Morrow, New York, 1979.

Austin, John, *Hollywood's Unsolved Mysteries*, Shapolsky, New York, 1990.

Barbour, Alan G., *Humphrey Bogart*, W. H. Allen, 1974.

Bawden, Liz-Anne (ed.), *The Oxford Companion to Film*, Oxford University Press, 1976.

Brownlow, Kevin, *The Parade's Gone By*, Martin Secker & Warburg, 1968.

—— *Hollywood: The Pioneers*, Collins, 1979.

Callow, Simon, *Charles Laughton – A Difficult Actor*, Methuen, 1987.

Cary, Diana Serra, *Hollywood's Children*, Houghton Mifflin, Boston, 1979.

Chaplin, Charles, *My Autobiography*, Bodley Head, 1964.

Coffee, Lenore, *Storyline*, Cassell, 1973.

Considine, Shaun, *Bette and Joan – the Divine Feud*, Century-Hutchinson, 1989.

Crivello, Kirk, *Fallen Angels*, Macdonald, 1990.

Crosby, Bing, *Call Me Lucky*, Simon & Schuster, New York, 1953.

Cushing, Peter, *An Autobiography*, Weidenfeld & Nicolson, 1986.

Davies, Marion, *The Times We Had*, Angus & Robertson, 1976.

Davis Jr, Sammy, *Hollywood in a Suitcase*, Granada, 1980.

—— *Why Me?*, Michael Joseph, 1989.

Finler, Joel W., *The Movie Directors Story*, Octopus, 1985.

Fountain, Leatrice Gilbert, *Dark Star*, Sidgwick & Jackson, 1985.

French, Philip, *The Movie Moguls*, Weidenfeld & Nicolson, 1969.

Frewin, Leslie, *Blond Venus − A Life of Marlene Dietrich*, MacGibbon & Kee, 1955.

Gronowicz, Antoni, *Garbo − Her Story*, Viking, 1990.

Guiles, Fred Lawrence, *Stan*, Michael Joseph, 1980.

Guinness, Alec, *Blessings in Disguise*, Hamish Hamilton, 1985.

Halliwell, Leslie, *The Dead That Walk*, Grafton, 1986.

Hamblet, Charles, *The Hollywood Cage*, Nart Pub., New York, 1969.

Hardwicke, Sir Cedric, *A Victorian in Orbit*, Methuen, 1961.

Herndon, Booton, *Mary Pickford and Douglas Fairbanks*, W. H. Allen, 1978.

Higham, Charles, *Cecil B. De Mille*, Charles Scribner, New York, 1973.

——and Roy Moseley, *Cary Grant − The Lonely Heart*, New English Library, 1989.

Hyams, Joe, *Bogie*, W. H. Allen, 1971.

Jordan, Ted, *Norma Jean − A Hollywood Love Story*, Sidgwick & Jackson, 1989.

Korda, Michael, *Charmed Lives*, Random House, New York, 1979.

Lambert, Gavin, *Norma Shearer*, Hodder & Stoughton, 1990.

Lee, Gypsy Rose, *Gypsy*, Futura/Macdonald, 1988.

Lenning, Arthur, *The Count − The Life and Films of Bela 'Dracula' Lugosi*, Putnams, New York, 1974.

Lesley, Cole, *The Life of Noël Coward*, Jonathan Cape, 1976.

Lindsay, Cynthia, *Dear Boris*, Alfred A. Knopf, New York, 1975.

McCabe, John, *Mr Laurel and Mr Hardy*, Robson, 1976.
——*Bebe, The Life of Oliver Hardy*, Robson, 1989.

Marx, Arthur, *My Life with Groucho*, Robson, 1988.

Marx, Samuel, and Joyce Vanderveen, *Deadly Illusions*, Century, 1990.

Mason, James, *Before I Forget*, Hamish Hamilton, 1981.

Morella, Joe, and Edward Z. Epstein, *Jane Wyman*, Delacorte Press, New York, 1985.

Morley, Sheridan, *Gertrude Lawrence*, Pavilion/Michael Joseph, 1986.

Moseley, Roy, *Rex Harrison*, New English Library, 1987.

Munn, Michael, *The Hollywood Murder Casebook*, Robson, 1987.

Niven, David, *Bring on the Empty Horses*, Hamish Hamilton, 1975.

Noble, Peter, *Ivor Novello – Man of the Theatre*, Falcon Press, 1951.

Owst, Ken, *Laurel and Hardy in Hull*, Highgate Pub., 1990.

Phillips, Perrott (ed.), *Out of This World*, Phoebus, 1976.

Powdermaker, Hortense, *Hollywood the Dream Factory*, Secker & Warburg, 1951.

Preminger, Erik Lee, *Gypsy and Me*, André Deutsch, 1985.

Rotha, Paul, *The Film Till Now* (3rd rev. ed.) Hamlyn, 1967.

Sands, Frederick and Sven Broman, *The Divine Garbo*, Sidgwick & Jackson, 1979.

Schulberg, Budd, *Moving Pictures*, Souvenir Press, 1981.

Shulman, Irving, *Harlow*, Mayflower, 1964.

Sommer, Robin Langley, *Hollywood: The Glamour Years* (1919–41) Hamlyn, 1987.

Spoto, Donald, *The Dark Side of Genius*, Muller, 1983.

Strick, Philip, *Great Movie Actresses*, Orbis, 1984.

Summers, Anthony, *Goddess – The Secret Lives of Marilyn Monroe*, Victor Gollancz, 1985.

Swindell, Larry, *Charles Boyer*, Weidenfeld & Nicolson, 1983.

Tabori, Paul, *Alexander Korda*, Oldbourne, 1959.

Taylor, Deems, Marcelene Peterson and Bryant Hale, *A Pictorial History of the Movies*, Simon & Schuster, 1949.

Thompson, Verita, *Bogie and Me*, W. H. Allen, 1983.

Todd, Ann, *The Eighth Veil*, William Kimber, 1980.

Underwood, Peter, *Horror Man – the Life of Boris Karloff* (*Karloff* in USA) Frewin/Drake, New York, 1972.

——*Exorcism!*, Robert Hale, 1990.

Wallace, Edgar, *My Hollywood Diary*, Hutchinson, n.d.

Wannamaker, Marc (ed.), *The Hollywood Reporter Star Profiles*, Octopus, 1984.

Windeler, Robert, *Mary Pickford*, W. H. Allen, 1975.

Printed in Great
Britain
by Amazon